WHO WROTE SHAKESPEARE?

JOHN MICHELL

WHO WROTE SHAKESPEARE

?

with 116 illustrations

THAMES AND HUDSON

© 1996 Thames and Hudson Ltd, London

First published in the United States of America in 1996 by
Thames and Hudson Inc., 500 Fifth Avenue,
New York, New York 10110

Library of Congress Catalog Card Number 95-62460
ISBN 0-500-01700-X

Printed and bound in Slovenia

CONTENTS

ACKNOWLEDGMENTS

To Roger Nyle Parisius, who knows more about this and many other subjects than this or any other single author, and is ever-generous in sharing his knowledge; and once again to Thomas Neurath for encouraging this and previous writings for Thames and Hudson.

Also, in no particular order, to:

Delia Bacon, pioneer anti-Stratfordian, for questioning the Authorship at the cost of her sanity. David Garrick for founding the Shakspere cult. Francis Carr for trying to bust it. Ignatius Donnelly for deciphering Shakespeare, discovering Atlantis and opposing Orthodoxy in many fields; and for his chivalrous defence of Delia Bacon. J.O. Halliwell-Phillips for his Shakespearian bibliomania. Sir George Greenwood for his scholarly, articulate, long-sustained battle against the Stratfordians. Mark Twain for the funniest book on the Authorship. Charlotte Stopes for upsetting the Orthodox and the Baconians alike. Samuel Schoenbaum for his deep scholarship and fine Stratfordian wit. Orville Owen for his cipher-wheel and Baconian excavations. Sir Edwin Durning-Lawrence for simplifying the Bacon case. Sigmund Freud and Thomas Looney for combining their names in the cause of the Earl of Oxford. Abel Lefranc, most learned of heretics, for seeing through Shakspere and discovering the Earl of Derby. Georges Connes for seeing through the whole subject. Calvin Hoffman for P.R. services to Christopher Marlowe. Célestin Demblon for reading 5000 books while deciding that Shakespeare was the Earl of Rutland. William and Elizabeth Friedman for services to Bacon–Shakespeare cryptography; for their good humour. Dorothy and Charlton Ogburn for the longest heretical book, 1297 pages on behalf of the Earl of Oxford. Charlton Ogburn Jr for standing up for his parents. Elizabeth Wells Gallup for her refined channelling. Caroline Spurgeon for statistical proof that Shakespeare was Christ-like. Frances Yates for revealing the occult philosophy in Shakespeare. Leslie Hotson for discovering Shakspere in London's gangland. Graham Phillips and Martin Keatman for exposing Shakspere as a spy.

To the many dedicated writers who have published books at their own expense, and to all who have written sincerely on the Authorship question:

ALL HAPPINESS
AND THAT ETERNITY PROMISED TO
WHOEVER FIRST DISCOVERS THE TRUE AUTHOR
OF SHAKE-SPEARE'S SONNETS ETC.
WISHES THIS WELL-WISHING ADVENTURER
IN SETTING FORTH

I

APPROACHES TO HERESY

THE RIVAL CERTAINTIES

Some people do not approve of this subject. They say that it denigrates Shakespeare and his legend, that it confuses the public and gives needless trouble to specialists in English literature. There is no doubt, they say, no doubt at all, that Mr William Shakspere wrote the plays and poems attributed to Shakespeare, and that Stratford-upon-Avon is his proper shrine and reliquary.

These very certain, positive people are called, in the jargon of Authorship studies, Stratfordians or the Orthodox. Opposing them are other groups, equally certain and positive, with names such as Baconians, Oxfordians, Rutlanders, Derbyites, Marlovians and Groupists. These are the anti-Stratfordians or Heretics. They join together in attacking the Orthodox but, as is usual with free-thinkers, they divide and subdivide into numerous sects, each critical of the others.

You might think that the Who-Wrote-Shakespeare question is the most harmless of subjects, academically interesting of course, but unlikely to change people's lives or embitter them or to lead to the rupture of friendships. Yet from its earliest days the debate has been extraordinarily acrimonious. The Stratfordians in particular have been vitriolic towards their rivals, with learned professors denouncing others, equally qualified but heretical, as stupid, malicious and, quite often, outright lunatics. A favourite tactic, particularly effective in class-inhibited England, is to accuse supporters of high-born, well-educated candidates of being motivated by snobbery.

The effect of this is to draw attention to the subject and sharpen interest in it. Whenever one party in a debate resorts to abusing its opponents, it is a sure sign that it is uncertain of its ground. There is a great deal of bluster in this subject. The Stratfordians are not really as secure in their position as they would like to think; nor are their rivals, the Baconians, Marlovians and so on. They too are abusive, partly towards the Stratfordians but mostly to the man from Stratford himself, Will Shakspere, that ignorant clod, clown, boor, butcher, thief, usurer, as their extremists have called him, who could barely so much as write his own name, let alone compose the immortal Works.

A good reason why the Stratfordians become agitated at the mention of the Authorship question is that they, alone of all the parties in the debate, have something to lose by it. The Shakespeare cult is established world-wide, with Stratford-upon-Avon at the hub of a vast industry, employing scholars, students, educationalists, authors, publishers, curators, tourist guides and trinket-sellers, pleasantly and in large numbers. The Stratford Birthplace, the prime asset of England's tourist trade, is now further aggrandized as a monument of Euro-culture. Heretics who question the faith on which all this rests are not welcome and must expect rough treatment at the hands of the Stratfordians.

This does not imply that the Stratfordian scholars are motivated to any significant degree by self-interest. They are perfectly sincere in their views on the Authorship, and are genuinely puzzled that other people see the matter differently.

'William Shakespeare, his method of work.' Max Beerbohm's comment on Baconianism.

Most of the literary experts are confirmed Stratfordians. Eminent scholars among them have examined their opponents' evidence and found nothing substantial in it. There is, they report, no real Authorship problem.

Yet, as a matter of visible fact, there is a problem. Lives and careers have been devoted to it, and it exists materially in the enormous body of literature on the question of Shakespeare's authorship. It would need a great library to accommodate the thousands of books, let alone the countless pamphlets, journals and articles which the debate has generated. A legend in this subject is that the Belgian professor, Célestin Demblon, author of *Lord Rutland est Shakespeare*, read 5000 books while researching for it. That was in 1912, before the flood of Authorship writing had fully risen. It would now be impossible to read it all. Not that anyone would want to, since much of it is repetitive, dull and cranky. It is the sheer weight of it that is so impressive. The fact that so many serious writers, having delved deep into the life and times of Shakespeare, have reached sincere, passionately held convictions, quite different from the Orthodox as well as from each other, is proof enough that the Authorship problem exists.

It is not a simple problem and it cannot be resolved by proclamations. Many an author has claimed to have decided the matter once and for all by 'proving' the case for one or other candidate, but no one's 'proof' has ever destroyed anyone else's theory. A trick that everyone uses is to attack the other candidates to distract attention from the weak points of their own favourite. Much of the Authorship literature is negative, disproving the claims for Shakspere (no known education), Bacon (emotionally unqualified), Oxford (died too early), Rutland (born too late), Queen Elizabeth (ridiculous), and so on. It is easy enough to cast doubt on the others, but no theorist has both answered the objections to, and made a positive case for, any particular author of Shakespeare. Everything that can possibly be said by all sides has already been said, and still the mystery remains. Unless some new, dramatically conclusive piece of evidence turns up, the whole subject looks to be approaching a dead end.

One stage of the debate has definitely reached a dead end. The Age of Certainties is over. It lasted from the nineteenth century up to quite recently, and its style was combative. Everyone adopted a champion as contender for the Shakespeare title, and then arranged the evidence around that chosen figure. The books they produced were not fair enquiries into the Shakespeare mystery, but polemical on behalf of one theory or another. Their combined efforts brought some useful results. New light was shed upon the circumstances of Shakespeare's times, and it became clear that no one really knows who Shakespeare was.

Moving beyond the Age of Certainties, and looking back on it, it seems almost incredible that so many equally educated, equally sincere compatriots and contemporaries, all drawing from the same limited stock of evidence on Shakespeare's life and works, should have reached so many, totally different conclusions – always with complete certainty. How can this happen? Fortunately we have a firsthand account of the process from Mark Twain, whose book of 1909, *Is Shakespeare Dead?* is the most enjoyable item in the entire Authorship literature.

As a young man, Mark Twain was made apprentice to a Mississippi river pilot, whose way of passing time during the long voyages was to read Shakespeare. He had heard of the Bacon theory, which was then just beginning; it preyed on his mind and he kept on denouncing it. His assistant realized that he wanted an argument so, to oblige him, took up the heretical position. This is how Mark Twain became a confirmed Baconian:

> Study, practice, experience in handling my end of the matter presently
> enabled me to take my new position almost seriously; a little bit later,
> utterly seriously; finally: fiercely, rabidly, uncompromisingly. After that,
> I was wedded to my faith. I was theoretically ready to die for it, and I
> looked down with compassion not unmixed with scorn, upon everybody

else's faith that didn't tally with mine. That faith, imposed upon me by self-interest in that ancient day, remains my faith today, and in it I find comfort, solace, peace, and never-failing joy.

Seeing how easy it is to centre one's mind upon a theory so that it becomes an image of the truth, the existence of all the rival certainties about Shakespeare is no longer such a puzzle. It is only too easy to adopt a particular candidate for Shakespeare and uphold his claims against all opposition, but it reduces the subject to an interminable competition of opinions. Those who pretend to certainty over the question of who wrote Shakespeare miss or misrepresent the central point, that it is a complete mystery. The whole subject is based upon doubts. There are doubts about Bacon, doubts about Oxford and, despite the pretensions and protestations of the Stratfordians, there are equally serious doubts about their candidate, William Shakspere.

> Fair, kind, and true, is all my argument,
> Fair, kind, and true, varying to other words. (Sonnet 105)

There is no prejudice in this book. It is conceived agnostically without preconception about the identity of Shakespeare. It cannot, of course, be impartial, because partialities naturally arise with the various points of evidence that seem to favour or disqualify one or other candidate. They arise also in the selection of contents. One can only try to be 'fair, kind, and true', while inevitably 'varying to other words'; but it is hoped that anyone reading this, whether they are pre-inclined to Stratfordism, Baconism, Oxfordism or any other school of opinion, will find their case adequately represented and will not be too angry at seeing the objections and rivalries to it. For those new to the subject, this book presents its overall structure, its history, texts, documents, illustrations and main debating points. These are the principal items from which so many researchers have come to so many different conclusions. From this evidence readers can make up their own minds, either in support of a likely candidate or acknowledging that no one really has the answer to 'Who Wrote Shakespeare?'

A CURIOUS COINCIDENCE

An excellent appetizer to this subject is in the form of a coincidence. Either it is an amazing freak of chance, or it imputes great cunning and daring to someone of high position in the time of King James, someone who oversaw the compilation of the Authorized Version of the English Bible and was also aware of a mystery about the works of Shakespeare.

1 The confidence which the Church hath in God. 8 An exhortation to behold it.

||Or, of.

¶ To the chiefe Musician || for the sonnes of Korah, a song vpon Alamoth.

GOD is our refuge and strength: a very present helpe in trouble.

2 Therefore will not we feare, though the earth be remoued: and though the mountaines be caried into †the midst of the sea.

†Hebr. the heart of the seas.

3 Though the waters thereof roare, and be troubled, though the mountaines shake with the swelling thereof. Selah.

4 There is a riuer, the streames wherof shall make glad the citie of God: the holy place of the Tabernacles of the most High.

5 God is in the midst of her: she shall not be moued; God shall helpe her, †and that right early.

†Heb. when the morning appeareth.

6 The heathen raged, the kingdomes were mooued: he vttered his voyce, the earth melted.

7 The LORD of hosts is with vs; the God of Jacob is †our refuge. Selah.

†Heb. an high place for vs.

8 Come, behold the workes of the LORD, what desolations hee hath made in the earth.

9 He maketh warres to cease vnto the end of the earth: hee breaketh the bow, and cutteth the speare in sunder, he burneth the chariot in the fire.

10 Be stil, and know that I am God: I will bee exalted among the heathen, I will be exalted in the earth.

11 The LORD of hosts is with vs; the God of Jacob is our refuge. Selah.

Psalm 46 in the 1611 King James version of The Bible.

The coincidence was first made public in 1900 in *The Publishers' Circular* (LXXVI, p. 30). It was observed that, in Psalm 46, the 46th word from the beginning is 'shake' and the 46th word from the end is 'spear'. In the latter calculation the word 'Selah' is omitted because it is not part of the text but a Hebrew musical notation, placed at the end of many verses in the Psalms.

Moreover, the Authorized or King James version of the Bible took six years to complete, ending in 1610 when Shakspere was forty-six years old.

In previous translations of the Bible the words 'shake' and 'spear' were differently placed in relation to the beginning and ending of the Psalm, and 'shake' had earlier been written 'shoke'.

The Authorized Version, published in 1611, was drawn up as a revision of the previous Bishops' Bible by a committee of the most learned clerical scholars in the kingdom, chosen without regard for their religious inclinations. Their work was submitted for approval to the bishops and leading theologians, then to the Privy Council and finally to the King himself. Francis Bacon was not at that time a member of the Privy Council, but, as Solicitor General and adviser to King James on matters of law and state, he most probably had some part in this revision of the Bible. Baconians speculate that he was the behind-the-scenes editor-in-chief but there is no record of that.

If 'Shake-spear' was deliberately encoded in the 46th Psalm and Francis Bacon was behind it, his most likely collaborator was Lancelot Andrewes, Bishop of Winchester. He was a great friend of Bacon, who consulted him frequently about his philosophical works, and he was famous for the puns, word-play and 'verbal conceits' with which he enlivened his sermons. Andrewes was perfectly placed to doctor the Psalms if he had wanted to, for his name was placed at the head of the list of divines who drew up the Authorized Version. If there was an editor-in-chief, it was he rather than Bacon. By another coincidence, the committee consisted of 46 members.

Nothing is proved by this chain of coincidences, certainly not that the works of Shakespeare were written by Francis Bacon or any other man of mystery. It is simply a curiosity, one of the many promising clues that seem to be leading towards the centre of the Shakespeare Authorship mystery but never actually reach it.

SHAKESPEARE'S NAMES

There is a time-worn joke, repeated by generations of Stratfordians, that those who dispute the official Authorship believe that the works of Shakespeare were not written by him but by 'another gentleman of the same name'. The Baconians and their allies are infuriated by this witticism, partly because they have heard it many times before, but also because it confuses them. They have to explain that the man who is supposed to have written the plays was not the same as the man whose name appeared on their title-pages, but that the name of this second man, though similar to that of the first man, was actually a made-up pseudonym of a person unknown. It is not easy after that to carry on a serious discussion.

The Authorship controversy begins with the fact that on almost all the plays and poems the author's name is spelt Shakespeare or Shake-speare. The hyphen is unusual and has been the cause of much suspicion. It implies perhaps a pseudonym, conveying the idea of a martial hero, or Pallas Athena, the spear-carrying goddess of wisdom. The spelling is also unusual. In and around Stratford-upon-Avon, where families of such a name were quite numerous, those who could write spelt it as they heard it, something like Shaxper or Shagsper. From the list of recorded spellings (overleaf) it seems that the first syllable in the name was not generally heard as 'shake' but as 'shack'. Shaksper is no nearer to Shake-speare than Maxton is to Make-stone.

Shakespeare is a good, dignified name for theatrical purposes, but Shagspere was the name under which William of Stratford engaged to marry Anne Hathwey. A licence to marry Anne Whately had been granted the previous day to Wm. Shaxpere. In his native town his name was commonly written as William Shakspere. His baptism was registered under that surname, so were those of his three children, the burial of his son and the marriage of his younger daugher. His elder daughter married in the name of Susanna Shaxpere, and his mother was Mayry Shaxpere in the record of her burial. The name on the Stratford monument is Shakspeare, retaining the 'shack' sound. On the many Stratford documents recording the legal or business transactions of William and his father, John, their name is spelt in a great variety of ways, but never as a hyphenated Shake-speare.

It is easy to find 57 documented varieties of William's family name. Fifty-five examples, together with their sources, are given in George Russell French's *Shakspeareana Genealogica* of 1868 and, as he says, others can be found. The collection here is given in the spirit of old Ripley, who used to include different spellings of Shakespeare in his 'Believe it or Not' feature as a popular curiosity.

57 varieties of Shakespeare's family name

Chacsper	Shakespar	Shakspeyr
Sackesper	Shakespare	Shakspeyre
Sakesper	Shakespear	Shakspurre
Sakespere	Shakespeare	Shakysper
Saxspere	Shakespeere	Shakyspere
Schackspeare	Shakesper	Shaskespeare
Schakespeire	Shakespere	Shaxberd
Schakspere	Shakespeye	Shaxeper
Shachespeare	Shakespeyre	Shaxespere
Shackespere	Shakesphear	Shaxkespere
Shackspare	Shakesphere	Shaxkspere
Shackspear	Shakesspere	Shaxpeare
Shackspeer	Shakispere	Shaxpeer
Shackspeere	Shakspear	Shaxper
Shackspire	Shakspeare	Shaxpere
Shadspere	Shakspeer	Shaxsper
Shagspere	Shakspeere	Shaxspere
Shakaspeare	Shaksper	Sheakspeare
Shakeseper	Shakspere	Shexpere

G.R. French is just one in a host of writers who have argued over many years and pages about Shakespeare's name, how it should be spelt and pronounced, its origin and its meaning. Following the debate in J.L. Haney's *The Name of William Shakespeare*, one learns that Camden thought people were named from what they carried: thus Palmer (a pilgrim bearing a palm), Wagstaffe, Shot-bolt, Shakestaffe and Shakespear. Against this was brought the authority of Hunter who found it difficult to see how 'the circumstance that he *shook a spear* can have given a name to any person'.

The only official contemporary record of Shakespeare as a playwright rather than an actor is in the 1604–5 accounts book of Edmund Tylney, Master of the Revels, showing performances of Measure for Measure, The Comedy of Errors *and other plays by 'Shaxberd'.*

Dr Charnock derived Shakespeare from Sigisbert (renowned for victory); a rival scholar took it from the Old German name, Sigispero, to which Charnock responded with a new guess, that it came from Shachsburh, a Saxon form of Isaacsbury, implying a Jewish origin.

Dr Mackay stated that it was neither Jewish nor Saxon but Celtic, from Schacspeir meaning Dryshanks. It has also been derived, just as plausibly, from Sheikh Zubair, the Great Chief. For those who enjoy theories about Shakespeare there is always plenty of choice.

The early Shakespearian scholars spelt the name as they felt inclined, but the need arose for a standardized version, equally applicable to the playwright, the actor and the native of Stratford. Assuming that these were the same person, the deciding factor was how he spelt his own name. There again there was plenty of choice, for the five Shakespeare signatures then known (there are now supposed to be six) seemed in every case to be spelt differently, and experts were unable to agree on the exact letters contained by any one. The field was finally narrowed down to four contenders, each with powerful scholarly backing. These were SHAKESPEAR, SHAKSPERE, SHAKSPEARE and SHAKESPEARE. In the course of time the last and longest of these has generally prevailed.

In Authorship writing, however, it is crucial to keep a distinction between the poet-playwright and the Stratford candidate. The Stratfordians call them both Shakespeare, because they believe they are one and the same. Whether or not they are right, two different names are needed when it comes to debating the matter. The convention has therefore arisen that the Stratford man is referred to by the usual form of his name, Shakspere, while the great author, as everyone agrees, is Shakespeare.

This rule is followed here throughout – as far as possible. But it is not ideal, because the name of the London actor was spelt Shakespeare, the same as the playwright, yet he was really Shakspere from Stratford. Or perhaps he was not; there is a theory that the author, the actor and the Stratfordian were three different people, each spelling his name differently. So there is bound to be confusion, and the reader's good will is requested and presumed on this daring venture into the field of Shakespeare authorship. We shall be abused and laughed at for our interest, for even thinking that there is any doubt about who wrote Shakespeare. They will tell the 'other gentleman of the same name' joke against us. All that we can say in return is that we enjoy the subject, find mystery in it and are introduced by it to the finest literature and some of the greatest, as well as the crankiest minds of our age and culture. It is a harmless, stimulating and instructive subject to dwell upon, which is more than can be said for many other types of obsession.

II

THE MIND BEHIND THE WORKS

THE WRITER WHO KNEW EVERYGTHING

As a complete, all-inclusive account of nature and humanity, Shakespeare's works have been compared to the Bible. Their author, it is said, was a Universal Man, certainly the greatest mind of his time, not just an inspired poet but a master of all knowledge. Professionals in many fields have written monographs, showing from detailed references in the plays and poems that Shakespeare was a master of their own particular craft, infallible in its jargon and technical language. The arts and sciences were all within his grasp; he wrote about them fluently and gracefully; his learning was governed by the highest philosophy and, above all else, he was a constitutional expert with profound knowledge of the law.

The Flower portrait in the Shakespeare Memorial Gallery at Stratford is thought to have been copied from the engraving in the Shakespeare Folio of 1623.

Those who regard Shakespeare in that awesome light are, for the most part, Heretics, the most reverent being the Baconian and Group theorists. The case against Orthodoxy rests on the apparent discrepancy between the life and character of Will Shakspere and the noble, refined, educated mind behind the Works. This is greatly emphasized by the Heretics, while the Stratfordians concentrate on bringing Shakespeare down to earth. One side tries to widen the gap between the man and the writings, while the other tries to span it by suggesting that Shakspere was better educated and informed than is generally supposed, and denying that there is any special knowledge in Shakespeare beyond the range of a lively-minded genius with access to books and learned company.

The following list includes most of the subjects in which specialists have claimed that Shakespeare must have been initiated. Most of the claims have been challenged and reaffirmed, with much bickering among rival experts, leaving outsiders with very little to go on in deciding between them.

Shakespeare's specialities

The law and legal terms, contemporary and historical

The manners of the royal court, the aristocratic mind, ways and language

Sports of the nobility, hunting and falconry

Philosophy, classical and esoteric

Statecraft and statesmanship

Biblical scholarship

English and European history

Classical literature and languages

French, Italian and Spanish languages

Italian geography and travel

France and the court of Navarre

Danish terms and customs

Horticulture and the designing of gardens

Wales and the Welsh

Music and musical terms

Painting and sculpture

Mathematics

Astronomy and astrology

Natural history

Angling

Medicine and psychology

Military life

Heraldry

Exploration and the New World

Navigation and seamanship

Printing

Folklore, fairy mythology, the supernatural

Theatrical management and the habits of players

Cambridge University jargon

Freemasonry

Cryptography and the Secret Service

The writings of every author are bound to some extent to reflect his own personal tastes and cast of mind, and thus it is normal for literary critics to discuss the relationship between texts and writers. In the case of Shakespeare, however, where authorship is the question at issue, there is no way of corroborating anyone's picture of the man derived from his works. A scientific attempt at delineating Shakespeare was Caroline Spurgeon's *Shakespeare's Imagery*, in which she extracted and analysed all the themes she could identify in his writings. These were further analysed by Pierre Porohovshikov, a Russian lawyer who later became an American professor of history. In *Shakespeare Unmasked* he classified Shakespearian allusions and listed them in order of frequency.

Themes	*Allusions*
Classics and mythology	260
Sports and games	196
War and weapons	192
The sea and ships	172
The law	124
The drama	74

Not surprisingly, since he was a committed Rutlander, Porohovshikov's interpretation pointed to an author not dissimilar from Roger Manners, fifth Earl of Rutland. Caroline Spurgeon's analysis led her to see her own candidate, the man from Stratford, in an ideal light. His main attributes, she concluded, were courage, sensitivity, balance, humour and wholesomeness. He was 'gentle, kindly, honest, brave and true', and his overall character was 'Christ-like'.

One can select from this list of alleged Shakespearian talents to picture the man as Christ, or an inspired country genius, or a brilliant aristocrat or, if one accepts all the claims, a person of complete, universal learning. Any imaginative artist who attempts an honest portrait of Shakespeare, derived from his writings, has to decide on the contents of his mind. The following components of the Shakespearian mentality are most widely claimed and most vigorously debated.

His vocabulary

An admitted problem for Stratfordians is the extent of Shakespeare's vocabulary, which is said to be far greater than that of any other English writer. This was first observed by Max Müller in the nineteenth century. Greenwood in *Is There a Shakespeare Problem?* (pages 471–72) quotes the relevant passage from Müller's *Lectures on the Science of Language*:

> We are told on good authority by a country clergyman that some of the labourers in his parish had not 300 words in their vocabulary . . . a well-educated person in England who had been at a public school, and at the university, who reads his Bible, his Shakespeare, *The Times*, and all the books of Mudie's Library, seldom uses more than about 3000 or 4000 words in actual conversation. Accurate thinkers and close reasoners, who avoid vague and general expressions, and wait till they find the word that exactly fits their meaning, employ a larger stock, and eloquent speakers

may rise to a command of 10,000. The Hebrew Testament says all that
it has to say with 5642 words; Milton's works are built up with 8000,
and Shakespeare, who probably displayed a greater variety of expression
than any writer in any language, produced all his plays with about
15,000 words.

According to Greenwood, 'Other estimates have put the Shakespeare
vocabulary even higher. Thus Chalk estimates it as 21,000 words, without
counting inflectional forms, while he estimated the vocabulary of Milton at
but 7000.' In Clark's *Elements of the English Language* he found: 'The vocabulary of Shakespeare becomes more than double that of any other writer in
the English language. . . . English speech, as well as literature, owes more
to him than to any other man.'

The problem of Shakespeare's vocabulary, and whether it really is twice
as rich as any other author's, does not seem to have been confronted by
the Stratfordians. Like Bacon, Shakespeare introduced many new words
into the English language. This seems to be a point in favour of the
Baconians, and it is also favourable to the Groupists, who discern several
different hands, minds and vocabularies in the works of Shakespeare.

His law

That he was a great legal expert is the most firmly stated and disputed of
all Shakespeare's alleged attainments. The Authorship question hangs
largely on this point because, if Shakespeare was a dyed-in-the-wool
lawyer, so too was Francis Bacon, and many of the other candidates were
also legally educated. On the other hand, it is most unlikely that William
Shakspere had any formal training in law. It is agreed by all that
Shakespeare's works are permeated with legal terms and references. The
question from this is whether young Mr Shakspere could have acquired his
lawyers' talk from text books and personal experience (he and his father
being notably litigious), or whether Shakespeare's legalisms were altogether
beyond his range.

Rightly and inevitably, this debate has been conducted mostly between
lawyers. The Authorship question has always attracted them, and many
distinguished judges and advocates have weighed in on one side or another.
The greatest among them have inclined towards Baconism, including
Judge Lord Penzance (James Wilde), Judge Holmes of the US Supreme
Court, Judge Webb of Dublin, Judge Stotsenburg of Indiana and other
bigwigs. Many more, Stratfordians or agnostics, have been deeply
impressed and puzzled by Shakespeare's legal mind. 'Legal phrases flow
from his pen as part of his vocabulary and parcel of his thought,' wrote the

Among the many legal bigwigs whose studies of Shakespeare's legal terminology convinced them that he was an expert lawyer (probably Francis Bacon), were the English judge, Lord Penzance (left), and Nathaniel Holmes of the US Supreme Court.

lawyer-Shakespearian, Richard Grant White. The great Victorian Lord Chancellor, Lord Campbell, stated in *Shakespeare's Legal Acquirements Considered* that Shakespeare's law was inherent and infallible. 'There is nothing so dangerous as for one not of our craft to tamper with our freemasonry,' he warned. Yet Shakespeare 'uniformly lays down good law. While novelists and dramatists are constantly making mistakes as to the law of marriage, of wills and inheritance, to Shakespeare's law, lavishly as he propounds it, there can be neither demurrer, bill of exception, or writ of error.'

The business of lawyers being to argue any side, the Stratfordian case has gained plenty of advocates. Literary lawyers have found that, far from being infallible, Shakespeare made endless mistakes in his legal conceptions and that his knowledge of law was nothing special, no greater than that of other contemporary playwrights.

The lawyers' argument about Shakespeare's law dragged on into the twentieth century. In 1908 Sir George Greenwood MP, a London barrister, summarized the evidence for 'Shakespeare as a Lawyer' in *The Shakespeare Problem Restated*. As the leading anti-Stratfordian writer of his time, Greenwood was courted by the Baconians, but he held aloof from them, attributing the Authorship to a mysterious Great Unknown. His friend and fellow MP, J.M. Robertson, took issue with him in *The Baconian Heresy: A Confutation*, a large section of which he devoted to a criticism of Shakespeare's legal knowledge. A battery of Shakespearian lawyers supported Robertson's contention that the author of the plays knew no more law than other writers of his age and constantly made errors in his terminology. It was pointed out that in Shakespeare's time the law and litigation were of great interest to ordinary people, played a large part in their lives

The most formidable anti-Stratfordian writer in the early years of the twentieth century was Sir George Greenwood, MP.

and were widely discussed. Shakspere, like everyone else, would have known and used many legal phrases.

Greenwood replied, bitterly and at length, in a further book, *Is There a Shakespeare Problem?*, and fired his last shot in 1920 with *Shakespeare's Law*. Shakspere, he insisted, could not have acquired the legal expertise displayed in the Works. Lord Chancellor Francis Bacon was a tempting candidate, but Greenwood maintained his advocacy of the Great Unknown. His experience at law had taught him that it was easier to pursue the negative, anti-Stratfordian case than to defend any positive claim to the Authorship.

If lawyers cannot decide the matter among themselves, it is impossible for a layman to do so. It is significant, though, that the Shakespeare-as-Lawyer theory was not invented by Heretics but arose long before the Baconian movement started up. The great eighteenth-century Shakespearian, Edmond Malone, was a practising lawyer and in Shakespeare he recognized one of his own kind. His conclusion was that Shakespeare in his youth must have worked in a lawyer's office. The image of Will Shakspere as a law clerk, perhaps in some small town near Stratford, became popular with later biographers. A century after Malone, another Shakespearian barrister, Dr E.J. Furnivall, declared: 'That he was [an attorney's clerk] at one time in his life I, as a lawyer, have no doubt.' This theory has not really stood the test of time. As Lord Campbell pointed out, if Shakspere had worked in a lawyer's office, he would have had to sign and witness many documents, but in the exhaustive search of records conducted by Shakespeare scholars his name has never turned up.

The idea of a legally trained Shakespeare has recently been revived by Eric Sams in his book of 1995, *The Real Shakespeare*. A maverick among Stratfordians, he takes the Malone-Campbell-Greenwood side in the debate over Shakespeare's legal knowledge. 'Not only the plays but the Sonnets are crammed with legal references and allusions, far more so than any comparable oeuvre in any period or language.' One of his examples is the Gravedigger scene in *Hamlet*, which 'shows detailed technical knowledge of the unpublished arguments recorded in the case of *Hales v. Pettit* 1550.'

Sams sees the problem in a Shakspere without legal training: that it casts doubt on his authorship and plays into the hands of the Baconians. His answer is to accuse his fellow Shakespearians of snobbery (the same deadly charge which they themselves bring against Oxfordians and other Heretics), because they have been looking for a full-time lawyer-Shakspere. He was, says Sams, a 'legal penman' or part-time law clerk, helping his illiterate father in his constant litigation and executing private commissions.

There seems here to be a genuine mystery. Not only Heretics but leading orthodox Shakespearians have been impressed by the quality of Shakespeare's legal language. This is naturally emphasized by the Baconians and supporters of other lawyer-candidates. To Stratfordians it is a puzzle, not fatal to their case because nothing is known about Shakspere's education, legal or otherwise, but it has always been one of their weak spots.

His classical learning

It is now generally agreed that Shakespeare was a Latin scholar, widely read in classical literature, including works which were not at the time available in English. His writings are permeated with classical phrases and allusions, and the freedom with which he misquoted or paraphrased his sources, while boldly adapting them to his own purpose, indicates that he wrote largely from memory without constant reference to books. Shakespeare did not flaunt his learning, but it was at the centre of his mind and culture so he could not avoid displaying it in his writing.

This image of the Bard, as a man of high education, was not recognized by the Romantics of the eighteenth century. The Shakespeare that they perceived was a simple country genius, a prodigy of nature, who (as Milton put it) 'warbled his native wood-notes wild', untainted by book learning. It was impossible to ignore the classical references in the plays, but this difficulty was dealt with by Richard Farmer, Master of Emmanuel College, Cambridge, and a friend of Dr Johnson. Shakespeare's genius, he claimed, was peculiarly English and entirely a work of Nature. Apart from the 'small Latin, and less Greek' which Ben Jonson allowed him, he knew no foreign language and needed none to become master of his own. In his *Essay on the Learning of Shakespeare* (1767), Dr Farmer used his own formidable learning to show that all Shakespeare's knowledge of classical literature could have been drawn from existing translations. He owed nothing to ancient or foreign writers and everything to the spirit of his native culture.

Farmer's romantic nationalism suited the mood of his times, but many Shakespearians found chapter and verse to refute his opinions. The most impressive statement on Shakespeare's classical scholarship is an essay in J. Churton Collins's *Studies in Shakespeare*, where themes and passages in the plays are traced to their original sources among the Greeks and Romans. Shakespeare could have read Terence, Virgil and parts of Seneca and Ovid in translations, but many of the works he referred to were only to be found in Latin. *The Rape of Lucrece*, for example, was based on Ovid's *Fasti* which had not been translated in Shakespeare's time, so he must have read it in the original. Other authors well known to Shakespeare, whose works he could only have read in Latin, included Plautus, Horace, Juvenal, Lucretius, Cicero and St Augustine.

Many Greek writers and dramatists were identified by Collins among Shakespeare's sources. He was certainly familiar with Plato, Aeschylus, Sophocles, Euripides and the verses and epigrams of the Greek Anthology. All these he could have known through Latin translations, but Shakespeare's mind was so attuned to the spirit of Greek drama that Collins believed he had read the original texts.

He also read French and Italian. Montaigne was one of his favourite sources, and he doubtless referred to Florio's translation published in 1603. In other cases, however, he could only have known the French or Italian originals. Schoenbaum in *Shakespeare's Lives* names several books which Shakespeare certainly referred to – Belleforest's *Histoires tragiques*, Ser Giovanni's *Il Pecorone*, Cinthio's *Epitia* and *Hecatommithi* – where he had no access to translations.

All Shakespearians are impressed by the breadth and quality of Shakespeare's reading. Even Farmer, who wanted to play down his scholarship and deny him Latin, was forced to admit that he had read a great many ancient and modern books in English. With the evidence that he also knew the literature, and to some degree the languages, of Greece, Rome, France, Italy and Spain, the picture emerges of a dedicated scholar, educated from childhood in an atmosphere of high culture.

This leads right to the central question of the Authorship debate. How could William Shakspere, the son of illiterate parents, brought up in a 'bookless neighbourhood' (J.O. Halliwell's memorable but questionable description of old Stratford) and known there only for his business deal-ings, how could this man have acquired all the knowledge attributed to Shakespeare?

To this question there are two main answers. First, that he was a genius. To some people this explains everything, to others very little. The notion of a genius, as someone who can speak in tongues and 'channel' the writings of ancient authors without having studied them, is romantically appealing, but there is no record of any such person. Shakespeare was certainly a genius, but his art was that of an educated genius, not just a spirit medium.

The other answer is that Shakspere of Stratford wrote learned plays and poems because he was himself learned. The problem then is to suggest how and where he could have gained his fine education. He did not go to a university, and there is no evidence that he even attended the local grammar school. If the orthodox theory is correct, he must have done so, and it is therefore generally assumed that he did. In that case he might have been sufficiently grounded in Latin to read the classical authors; but it is still a mystery how he acquired the temperament and leisure for these studies, and where he found the necessary libraries.

A schoolroom in Shakespeare's time according to a sixteenth-century woodcut.

Between the classical, universal learning of Shakespeare and the limited educational opportunities of William Shakspere, the Stratfordians have an obvious gap to bridge; but the task has not daunted them, and Shakspere's education is said to have been quite compatible with the playwright's scholarship. Nothing is known directly about the curriculum at the old Stratford school, but the early biographers saw it as a primitive establishment with a harassed master beating some Latin grammar into the town boys. Later, however, it acquired a grander image, and in modern Lives of Shakespeare it is depicted as a model academy, teaching Latin and classical literature to a high standard and well qualified to have produced the author of *Hamlet*.

The Baconians, of course, say that Shakespeare's scholarship is explained very simply by attributing his works to the learned Bacon. They emphasize the classical tone of the plays, and J. Churton Collins is their leading witness to it. Collins himself felt threatened by their unwelcome support, and the final essay in his *Studies in Shakespeare* was on 'The Bacon–Shakespeare Mania'. It was the most blistering attack on the Bacon heresy that anyone has ever written. 'This monstrous movement', he raged, 'This ridiculous epidemic', comparing it to the dancing mania of the Middle Ages. As to its followers, they were dishonest, deluded, ignorant, impudent and fit only for the madhouse. 'This Bacon craze is a subject in which the student of morbid psychology is far more intimately concerned than the literary critic.'

So angry was Collins, so intemperately abusive, that he must have felt uneasy about something; and the reason for that is clear enough. In the course of his essays he had admired Shakespeare's legal expertise, his classical scholarship, his familiarity with French, Italian and old English writers. The Shakespeare he presented was so awesomely learned that he was in danger of losing contact with the man of Stratford. Collins saw the gap, was appalled by it, and he was furious with the Baconians for pointing it out.

Aristocracy and the court

Tolstoy's famous criticism of Shakespeare was that he did not identify with the common people and showed no sympathy for them. The grievances of the lower orders were not his concern: Jack Cade, the peasant leader in *2 Henry VI*, is depicted as a mere upstart rebel. Shakespeare's predilections, as far as they can be judged from his plays, were conservative and monarchical – for traditional, lawful authority and the principles of hierarchy.

Shakespeare's noble birth and mentality have been discerned by many writers and emphasized by the Oxfordians and Derbyites, both of whose candidates belonged to the most ancient and high-ranking of noble families. They are supported in this view by most of the Heretic theorists, and even, up to a point, by orthodox Stratfordians. The following is a dispassionate judgment quoted from *English Literature* by the distinguished critics, Richard Garnett and Edmund Gosse, who had no particular interest in the Authorship question.

> Nothing is more remarkable in his [Shakespeare's] earliest productions than their perfect polish and urbanity. The principal characters in *Love's Labour Lost* are princes and nobles, true to the models which he might have found in contemporary society. The young patricians in *The Two Gentlemen of Verona* have in every respect the ideas and manners of their class. The creator of such personages must have been in better company and enjoyed a wider outlook upon society than can easily be believed attainable by an actor or a resident in a single city.

From there it is but a short step to saying that Shakespeare himself must have been an aristocrat. That step has been taken, unhesitatingly, by the supporters of high-born candidates. J. Thomas Looney, founder of the Oxfordian theory, wrote:

> Kings and queens, earls and countesses, knights and ladies move on and off his stage 'as to the manner born'. They are no mere tinselled models representing mechanically the class to which they belong, but living men and women. It is rather his ordinary 'citizens' that are the automata walking woodenly on to the stage to speak for their class. . . . It is, therefore,

not merely his power of representing royalty and the nobility in vital, passionate characters, but his failure to do the same in respect to other classes that marks Shakespeare as a member of the higher aristocracy.

Looney's opinion, that Shakespeare was not only a born aristocrat but deeply involved in court life and affairs of state, is echoed by Derbyite and Group theorists. A typical expression occurs in A.W. Titherley's Derby-promoting book, *Shakespeare's Identity*.

No author ever moved so easily among Kings, Princes, Dukes and Noblemen, especially in France and Italy, as Shakespeare; they and their women counterparts are not only well and truly drawn but the whole atmosphere of the Court is so charged with realism in minor details that it would seem impossible for anyone who had not lived the life to portray it all with such unerring truth.

Everyone agrees that Shakespeare had a noble mind, but, as the Stratfordians point out, this does not prove that he was of noble birth. R.C. Churchill in *Shakespeare and his Betters* launched a strong counter-attack on the Heretics over this point, beginning with Titherley. What qualifications, he asked, had Dr Titherley, a lecturer in Organic Chemistry, to pronounce on Shakespeare's familiarity with the details of Elizabethan court life? Very little was known about the subject, not even by Miss St Clare Burne, the leading expert on the sociology of the period. She, however, knew enough to criticize many items in Shakespeare's representations of court etiquette and ceremonial, as when his characters enter a royal presence without being announced by gentlemen-ushers. In matters of Organic Chemistry, said Churchill, he would accept Dr Titherley's authority, but in this case he would prefer to rely on Miss St Clare Burne. Her observation was that Shakespeare's references to the aristocracy increase and improve throughout his later plays, implying that the Stratford author was moving up the social ladder.

The Stratfordian argument was further developed in H.N. Gibson's *The Shakespeare Claimants*. He took up Authorship studies with an open mind, but the inadequacies he found in all the rival theories confirmed him in the Orthodox faith. He saw no need for Shakespeare to have been a noble courtier. All the playwrights of his time wrote about kings, queens and courts for dramatic reasons. The ways of the aristocracy were of great interest to the common people, many of whom had the opportunity of observing them at first hand. Shakspere had that opportunity since he played before the court and probably in noblemen's houses. Nor did the playwright confine himself to themes and characters from high life.

The author of the Shakespeare plays . . . did write of persons and scenes of lower stations in the social scale. The amateur dramatic society of the hard-handed workers of Athens in *Midsummer Night's Dream* is one case, the sheep-shearing festivities in *Winter's Tale* is another, and there are several others, including the London tavern scenes in *Henry IV*. It is also to be remarked that Shakespeare often drew on 'low life' for his imagery. There are, for instance, seventeen references to the butcher's trade in his plays.

As for Shakespeare's conservative, traditional cast of mind, Gibson found it typical of Shakspere's bourgeois class and in keeping with the importance he attached to acquiring a coat of arms. Shakspere, he hinted, was a bit of a snob.

The question here is whether Shakespeare's aristocratic tone and knowledge prove that his works were written by a nobleman with access to the royal court, or whether an observant young provincial could have produced the effect by the genius of his art. For all that is known about his early life, Shakspere may have had an intimate noble patron, or lover. He may have entered service in some great house. In such a case, he could have learnt to imitate the speech and manners of aristocratic associates who, perhaps, initiated him into affairs of state. Much has been speculated along these lines, but no plausible theory has emerged, leaving the Stratfordian case at this point somewhat strained. Against it is the impressive weight of testimony on the quality of Shakespeare's mind, which points away from Stratford towards the nobleman-courtier type of candidate.

A ship from John Dee's navigational manual of 1577.

Seamanship

Strong evidence that Shakespeare was an experienced seaman was provided by Master Mariner W.B. Whall in 1910. He was a veteran from the old days of sail, who had made a special study of archaic sea terms. In *Shakespeare's Sea Terms Explained* he quoted many phrases and passages in the plays which, he stated, could only have been written by one who had served aboard ships. Shakespeare's nautical references were not mere similes, but technical terms the meanings of which had sometimes eluded Shakespearian scholars.

'Whoever wrote or edited the plays had an intimate professional knowledge of seamanship. Words and phrases of an extremely technical nature
are scattered throughout them, and a mistake in their use is never made.
Could a mere "land-lubber" have steered clear of error in the use of such
terms?' No! answered Whall to his own question. 'It is . . . small wonder
that a playwright in such times should make use of sea words, but the wonder is that without professional acquaintance he should always use these
terms correctly. No modern writer is able to do this. An author who writes
in that direction invariably "gives himself away" unless he is a sailor
author: this the writer of the plays never does.'

Typically nautical, for example, are three lines spoken by Pistol in *The
Merry Wives of Windsor* (ii. 2). The sea terms are those in italics.

> This punk is one of Cupid's carriers:
> Clap on more sails: pursue: up with your *fights*;
> *Give fire*: she is my *prize*, or ocean *whelm* them all!

This, said Whall, is Elizabethan sailor-talk pure and simple. *Fights* were
canvas screens hung round the sides of a ship to conceal the men from the
enemy; *give fire* is the proper sea order, and so on. As the examples accu-
mulate, it does indeed appear that Shakespeare was nautical-minded.
Whall's suggestion was that the young man from Stratford was pressed into
Queen Elizabeth's navy and, perhaps, took part in the defeat of the
Armada in 1588.

A later writer, Lieutenant-Commander A.F. Falconer, went over the
same ground and reached similar conclusions. In *Shakespeare and the Sea*
(1964) he discussed the nautical passages in the plays and found that from
the very beginning the author's use of sea language was invariably correct
and appropriate. It is quite certain, he said, that during the six years up to
1590 Shakespeare served in the Royal Navy.

None of the mariner-Shakespearians has found it necessary to doubt the
traditional authorship, but half-way through the book Whall dropped a
bombshell, declaring that Francis Bacon's writings contained just as much
faultless sea terminology as Shakespeare's. That was an unexpected bonus
for the Baconians, but Bacon was no professional seaman. Nor were
Oxford, Derby and Rutland, though all of them had experience of seafaring, and Oxfordians point out that Oxford contributed a vessel to the
fleet that defeated the Armada. Their founder, however, was not impressed
by Oxford's seamanship. 'The Earl was not a seafaring man, nor is there
anything in the record of his life that suggests a special enthusiasm for the
sea,' admitted J.T. Looney.

The name of Sir Francis Drake has been put forward as one of a group that may have written Shakespeare, and in a book of 1947 (*The Real Shakespeare*) a canoeing expert, William Bliss, fantasized that Shakespeare's early voyages included a circumnavigation of the globe in Drake's *Golden Hind*. Yet Drake was a sea-captain, not a poet. By far the most obvious seaman-Shakespeare among all the candidates is Sir Walter Ralegh. Claims to the Authorship on his behalf go back to the middle of the nineteenth century and are largely based on the nautical language in the plays. At least two authors have attributed all Shakespeare to him, but he figures more commonly in Group theories, many theorists placing him within the 'magic circle' whose writings were published under the pseudonym of Shake-speare.

Military matters

Military men who have read Shakespeare while on active service have often been impressed by the language and attitudes of the soldier characters in his historical plays. His Elizabethan men-at-arms, they observe, are absolutely true to life, and are just like the English soldiers of today. Shakespeare was clearly very interested in military affairs and knew a great deal about them, seemingly from first-hand experience. It has often been suggested, therefore, that Shakespeare as a young man served in the army.

In the trenches during the First World War, Alfred Duff Cooper, the future diplomat, was impelled to that same conclusion. The ordinary soldiers alongside him spoke and behaved in exactly the same way as their Shakespearian predecessors. He wrote a short book about it, *Sergeant Shakespeare*, in the form of a letter to his wife, formerly Lady Diana Manners, who had shown interest in the Authorship claims of her forebear, Roger Manners, Earl of Rutland. Duff Cooper dissuaded her from that notion. Quoting widely from the plays, especially *1 King Henry VI*, he demonstrated Shakespeare's proficiency in soldiers' talk and the ways and customs of the army. His own belief was that, at the age of 21, the man from Stratford had joined the Earl of Leicester's expedition to the Low Countries and had served under him for a few months, probably as a non-commissioned officer, before returning to London.

John Fortescue's *History of the British Army* supports the idea of a soldier-Shakespeare. 'Shakespeare', he wrote, 'is as truly the painter of the English Army in his own day as was Marryat of the Navy in later years. Falstaff the fraudulent captain, Pistol the swaggering ensign, Bardolph the rascally corporal, Nym the impostor who affects military brevity . . . all these had their counterpart in every shire of England.' Modestly deferring to Shakespeare's authority in his own special subject, Fortescue concluded: 'Not in these poor pages, but in Shakespeare must the military student read the history of the Elizabethan soldier.'

Duff Cooper's theory was by no means original. Ninety years earlier, in 1859, the antiquary William J. Thoms published *Was Shakespeare Ever a Soldier?*, giving a positive answer to the question and backing it up with certain hints of evidence. In September 1585, he noted, the Earl of Leicester was made commander of the army in the Netherlands, and began by recruiting a retinue of 500 men to accompany him there. His headquarters was at Kenilworth, only fifteen miles from Stratford-upon-Avon. Men from Stratford were among his followers, and Will Shakspere, whose twins Hamnet and Judith had been christened earlier that year, could easily have been one of them. A late legend of Shakspere was that Leicester protected him when he was in trouble for poaching deer, and in 1589 he appeared in London as one of Leicester's company of players.

From a fellow Shakespearian, John Bruce, Thoms learnt of a strange letter, written from Utrecht in March 1586, by Sir Philip Sidney, Leicester's nephew and companion on his expedition. Addressed to his father-in-law, Secretary Walsingham, it contained the following significant remarks. 'I wrote to yow a Letter by Will, my Lord of Lester's jesting plaier, enclosed in a letter to my wife, and I never had answer thereof. . . . I since find that the knave deliver'd the letters to my ladi of Lester, but whether she sent them yow or no I know not.'

John Bruce could not believe that anyone would refer to Shakspere as a 'knave' and a 'jesting player', and he suggested that some other entertainer, Will Johnson, Will Sly or Will Kempe, was the bearer of Sidney's letters. Thoms, however, was not so squeamish about the epithets, showing by literary parallels that they implied no disrespect on the part of Sidney and properly described a young man of inferior rank. That man, he believed, was Will Shakspere.

As his final proof Thoms cited that, in 1605, among the names of trained soldiers in the hundred of Barlichway was that of William Shakespeare of Rowington. The hundred of Barlichway includes Stratford-upon-Avon, and the Stratford Shakspere is known to have owned property in Rowington. With all these connections, Thoms felt able to conclude his book with the triumphant assertion, SHAKESPEARE WAS A SOLDIER. Later Shakespearians have been grudging, and the prevailing view is that the trained soldier of Rowington was not the famous William but someone else of the same name.

Apart from these slight hints and possibilities, there is nothing in the record of Shakspere's life to show that he ever was a soldier. Yet the author of Shakespeare certainly was, or so say the military experts.

Psychology and medicine

Shakespeare, as revealed in his writings, was well versed in medicine and medical terms, with a doctor's knowledge of the functions and diseases of the body and with special understanding of morbid psychology and types of madness. The first book on this was in 1860 by a psychiatrist, Sir John Bucknill. His *Medical Knowledge of Shakespeare* did not claim that Shakespeare was a professional doctor, but showed that he was no less experienced in medicine than in legal matters. Other doctors have been more eager to enlist Shakespeare in their profession. G.R. French recorded in *Shakspeareana Genealogica* statements by several doctor friends that only one of their kind could properly appreciate Shakespeare's subtle descriptions of insanity.

In support of Bucknill, bringing his medical terms and interpretations up to date, was R.R. Simpson's *Shakespeare and Medicine*, published in 1959. More recently Dr Aubrey Kail of Australia has contributed *The Medical Mind of Shakespeare*, stating that, 'Shakespeare's plays bear witness to a profound knowledge of contemporary physiology and psychology, and employed medical terms in a manner which would have been beyond the powers of any ordinary playwright or physician.'

Shakespeare introduced medical characters into seven of his plays. Two of them were historical figures, Sir William Butts, royal physician in *King Henry VIII*, and Dr John Caius, founder of Caius College, Cambridge. Generally, apart from the ridiculous Caius in *The Merry Wives of Windsor*, the doctors were favourably depicted.

Dr Kail says that Shakespeare mentions practically all the diseases and drugs that were known in his time. One such list (with Kail's explanations) is quoted from *Troilus and Cressida* (v. 1).

> Now, the rotten diseases of the south [regarded as an unhealthy region],
> the guts-griping, ruptures, catarrhs, loads o' gravel i' the back, lethargies,
> cold palsies, raw eyes, dirt-rotten livers, wheezing lungs, bladders full of
> imposthume [abscess], sciaticas, limekilns i' th' palm [arthritis], incurable
> bone-ache, and the rivelled fee-simple [permanent ownership] of the
> tetter [eruption].

Medicine in Shakespeare's time was bound up with the traditional or Pythagorean philosophy which held that the physical world derived from various mixtures of the four elements, earth, air, fire and water. In the human body earth corresponded to 'black bile' and the melancholic humour, cold and dry. Air was blood and the sanguine humour, hot and moist; fire was 'choler' and the choleric humour, hot and dry; water was 'phlegm' and the phlegmatic humour, cold and moist. With these types of humour were many other correspondences – to minerals, herbs and astrological signs. In a healthy body the four elements were harmoniously balanced, and illnesses were treated by bringing them into a proper relationship.

Shakespeare evidently understood the intricacies of this system, for he refers correctly to the elements, the humours and the herbs and drugs which remedied their imbalances. This was a learned subject, but not beyond the range of a highly educated man, steeped in philosophy and the classics. Robert Burton, author in 1621 of *The Anatomy of Melancholy*, had the appropriate knowledge of mental illnesses, but the most popular candidate as a scientific philosopher has been Francis Bacon. His claim to the Authorship, on the grounds of his medical learning, were first put forward by an Australian doctor, originally from Scotland, William Thomson, in one of his seven Baconian pamphlets, *On Renascence Drama* (1880).

In Shakespeare's time, however, there was much more common knowledge about herbs, drugs, poisons and potions than there is today. Shakespeare's contemporaries, Marlowe, Jonson, Webster, Ford, Beaumont and Fletcher, often alluded to medicine. Experts have found their references far less detailed and authentic than Shakespeare's, but this is just one more case in which he is their superior.

Country sports and pastimes

The very same claims that are made by experts in law, seamanship, medicine and many other subjects – that Shakespeare was an initiated member of their fraternity – are repeated by specialist writers on hunting, hawking and country sports generally. Again we are told that Shakespeare never put a foot wrong in his use of technical language, and that clearly he was a man who knew at first hand the subjects he wrote about.

'Whatever else this man may have been, he was beyond doubt a sportsman, with rare skill in the mysteries of woodcraft, loving to recall the very names of the hounds with which he was wont to hunt; a practical falconer . . . a horseman and horsekeeper.' That was the weighty opinion of the Right Hon. D.H. Madden, Vice-Chancellor of Dublin University, a staunch upholder of Orthodoxy in opposition to Baconism. His Shakespeare scholarship was deep rooted, and he also found time for hunting.

Putting the two together, he compiled a long book, *The Diary of Master William Silence*, on the sporting terms in Shakespeare, together with his theory on how the author could have acquired such intimate knowledge of all country pursuits.

The pastimes with which, according to Madden and other writers, Shakespeare was highly familiar include deer and fox hunting, hare coursing and beagling, falconry, angling, wildfowling and archery. The last of these was the subject of a book by one of the Shakespearian lawyers, William L. Rushton, whose *Shakespeare an Archer* explained the poet's many informed references to toxophily by supposing that he was both well read and personally practised in the subject.

There is a rare attraction in this Shakespeare-as-sportsman perception. No one is made angry by it and hardly any of the parties in the Authorship debate has challenged it, for it suits almost all of the major candidates. The Orthodox, and the romantic public in general, like the image of a sporting Shakespeare, the Warwickshire lad whose genius was nurtured by the traditional culture of old England. The supporters of aristocratic candidates say that only a man of noble breeding would have been familiar with such recondite sporting terms. Most reticent at this point are the Baconians, because Francis Bacon, though of a country family, was a Londoner and not known for his sporting activities.

Madden's fixed belief in Shakespeare's knowledge of field sports did not square easily with his Stratfordianism. The author of the plays, he concluded 'was not a town-bred youth', but a true countryman. Allusions to hunting and horses 'well up spontaneously as from the poet's inmost soul'. Moreover, the topographical references in Shakespeare's sporting scenes are not so much to Warwickshire as to Gloucestershire. His favourite river was not the Avon but the Severn. In Dursley, south-west of the Cotswolds, Madden discovered a local legend that Shakespeare had lived there. Around Dursley, he suggested, Shakespeare had enjoyed all manner of field sports and became initiated into the jargon of hunters. No other dramatic writer was so initiated. You can tell, said Madden, whether any disputed text is genuinely Shakespearian by the number and quality of its sporting allusions.

The most controversial claim is that Shakespeare was an expert in falconry. This once popular sport was discouraged by Puritanism and new farming methods; in Shakespeare's time it was practised only by aristocrats and a few traditional countrymen. Its peculiar language, full of archaic terms, was dying out; few people could speak it without fault. Yet Shakespeare knew it well. Madden listed over eighty specialized falconry terms that occur in his plays. Therefore, claim the Oxfordians, the Derbyites and others, he must have been a great nobleman.

He could, on the other hand, have been a Stratford tradesman's son who spent much of his youth in aristocratic company, or with an old-fashioned family in Gloucestershire. Alternatively, a good knowledge of falconry terms could have been acquired through books. Ben Jonson wrote that 'to speak the hawking language' was an affectation of upstarts, imitating the language of the old gentry.

A woodcut of 1575 shows Queen Elizabeth and her courtiers hunting with hawks.

Yet the prevailing testimony of those who have gone into the matter is that Shakespeare's practical and historical knowledge of hunting, hawking, fishing and the other old country sports was greater than that of any other writer in his time, and was not merely from book-learning. There is a chart in Caroline Spurgeon's *Shakespeare's Imagery* showing the 'daily-life' allusions in Shakespeare's plays compared with those of Marlowe, Jonson, Chapman, Dekker and Massinger. In Shakespeare's case and no other, images from country sports are the most frequent, especially riding, bird-snaring and falconry. Her impression was that in these pursuits, and also in archery, Shakespeare wrote from personal experience.

If Shakespeare reveals himself at all in his writings, then he seems to have been a genuine countryman, one of a dying breed that still maintained the sporting traditions of medieval England.

Plant lore, folklore, mythology

Soldier, sailor, doctor, lawyer, clergyman, scholar, sportsman, man of the court, man of the people . . . Shakespeare, according to those qualified to judge, was all these characters and more besides. Like an actor he played many parts, 'as if to the manner born'.

It is quite a relief to come across a subject in which Shakespeare, though as usual highly proficient, has not been claimed as a professional. He was a keen gardener, an observant plant-lover and well versed in the lore of flowers and herbs, but he was not a professional gardener, nor was he a scientific botanist. That was the considered opinion of Rev. Henry

Ellacombe, whose *Plant-Lore and Garden-Craft of Shakespeare* is one of many books that have been written on Shakespeare's flowers, trees, birds and natural history in general. Shakespeare, he said (with his eyes firmly on the Warwickshire lad), was a countryman born and bred, steeped in the traditional lore and culture of his native pastures. He knew his plants by their popular and sometimes their Latin names, and he knew their legends, symbolism and applications in folk medicine. He was also interested in the design of gardens, from cottage plots to the environs of manors and palaces.

This pleasant image of Shakespeare, the studious, sharp-eyed country-man, is bolstered by an army of books on his knowledge of folk and fairy lore, of witches, spells and the mystical side of nature. Some writers dwell upon Shakespeare's Puck or Robin Goodfellow, and the spooks and spirits that still in his day haunted the dark corners of the English countryside. Others look deeper, into the old German, French and classical myth-ologies that Shakespeare apparently drew upon for many of his scenes and characters.

This again leaves a two-sided impression of Shakespeare the author. On one side appears the image of a poetic youth, simple-hearted, high-spirited, the exemplary product of old England's rural culture. The other shows a courtly scholar, whose natural history and country lore come from Pliny, Paracelsus and the foresters on his ancestral estates. You can choose either of these characters, identify him as Shakespeare and dispute angrily with those who have chosen the other; but that diminishes Shakespeare, reduces him by half. If he had been a man of normal limits, conforming to one recognizable type of personality and cast of mind, he would be easily identified and there would be no Authorship problem. But he was not average and limited. Many of the claims made about his breadth and depth of learning and professional skills have doubtless been exaggerated, but even when watered down they paint an awesome picture of a man who went everywhere and knew everything. It is not easy to find the individual who could have accommodated the mind of Shakespeare, nor, if you do find him, entirely to believe in him.

A clue that may prove useful in sorting out the Authorship candidates is provided by Mr Ellacombe while discussing the plants that are not mentioned by Shakespeare. Strangely enough for a country lad, he makes no reference to such common flowers as the snowdrop, the forget-me-not, the foxglove and the lily-of-the-valley. Nor does he once speak of tobacco. Evidently Shakespeare was a non-smoker. That seems to rule out Sir Walter Ralegh.

Well favoured by the botanical evidence is Sir Francis Bacon. His supporters have found that in his essay, 'On Gardens', Bacon named thirty-two of the thirty-five flowers mentioned by Shakespeare.

THE CANDIDATES FOR SHAKESPEARE

What author could have had all the learning, talents and experience attributed to Shakespeare, or could give the impression that he had them? Many candidates have been proposed, beginning, of course, with William Shakspere. If only his personal connection with the works of Shakespeare could be established, there would be no Authorship problem and no dispute in the matter. There is, however, dispute, first over the claim on behalf of Shakspere, then Bacon, then Oxford, Derby, Rutland, Marlowe and a procession of others. They are listed below in approximate order of popularity, judged by the number of books and articles which have been published in support of their claims. First come the individual candidates, those to whom all or most of Shakespeare's works have been ascribed, followed by those who have been included with others as theoretical group-authors of Shakespeare.

Sole or principal authors

William Shakspere
Francis Bacon, Lord Verulam
Edward de Vere, Earl of Oxford
William Stanley, Earl of Derby
Roger Manners, Earl of Rutland
Sir Walter Ralegh
Christopher Marlowe
Anthony Bacon
Michael Angelo Florio
Robert Devereux, 2nd Earl of Essex
William Butts
Sir Anthony Shirley
Henry Wriothesley, Earl of Southampton

Cardinal Wolsey
Robert Cecil, Earl of Salisbury
Robert Burton
Sir John Barnard
Sir Edward Dyer
Charles Blunt, Lord Mountjoy, Earl of Devon
Queen Elizabeth
Sir William Alexander, Earl of Stirling
John Richardson of Temple Grafton
Anne Whateley
John Williams, Archbishop of York

Contributors to a group authorship

Barnabe Barnes
Richard Barnfield
Richard Burbage
Henry Chettle
Samuel Daniel
Thomas Dekker
John Donne, Dean of
  St Paul's
Thomas Sackville, Lord
  Buckhurst, Earl of
  Dorset
Sir Francis Drake
Michael Drayton
Walter Devereux,
  1st Earl of Essex
Henry Ferrers

John Fletcher
John Florio
Robert Greene
Bartholomew Griffin
Thomas Heywood
King James I
Ben Jonson
Thomas Kyd
Thomas Lodge
John Lyly
Thomas Middleton
Anthony Munday
Thomas Nashe
Henry, Lord
  Paget
George Peele

Mary Sidney,
  Countess of Pembroke
William Herbert, Earl
  of Pembroke
Henry Porter
Elizabeth Sidney,
  Countess of Rutland
Sir Philip Sidney
Wentworth Smythe
Edmund Spenser
Richard Vaughan,
  Bishop of London
William Warner
Thomas Watson
John Webster
Robert Wilson

The Rosicrucians, the Jesuits and the Freemasons have also been claimed as group-authors of Shakespeare. In that case there is almost no limit to the names that can be added to the list. The evidence for many of these seems slight and is often based on an unusual, idiosyncratic view of Shakespeare and his writings. Only a few candidates stand in the mainstream of the debate. Their lives, characters and qualifications for the title of Shakespeare are examined in the following chapters, beginning with the long-reigning title-holder, William Shakspere of Stratford-upon-Avon.

III

WILLIAM SHAKSPERE
THE LIFE AND THE LEGENDS

MARK TWAIN'S ANTI-BIOGRAPHY

The finest writer among all those who have contributed to the Authorship debate is undoubtedly Mark Twain. *Is Shakespeare Dead?*, which he published in 1909, is the only good book on the subject which is also short and very funny. Even confirmed Stratfordians are disarmed by its humour. In his Chapter 3 he sums up the known facts on William Shakspere's life. Almost every anti-Stratfordian writer does the same thing, the purpose being to contrast the image revealed by the documents, of a provincial tradesman and play-actor, with that of the noble Shakespeare. Mark Twain's brief Life of Shakspere is certainly not the most fair or accurate account, but, as an expression of the heretical viewpoint, it is by far the most entertaining. It was written under the heading, *Facts.*

He was born on the 23d of April, 1564.
Of good farmer-class parents who could not read, could not write,
could not sign their names.
At Stratford, a small back settlement which in that day was shabby and
unclean, and densely illiterate. Of the nineteen important men charged
with the government of the town, thirteen had to 'make their mark' in
attesting important documents, because they could not write their names.
Of the first eighteen years of his life *nothing* is known. They are a blank.
On the 27th of November (1582) William Shakespeare took out a
license to marry Anne Whateley.
Next day William Shakespeare took out a license to marry Anne
Hathaway. She was eight years his senior.
William Shakespeare married Anne Hathaway. In a hurry. By grace
of a reluctantly granted dispensation there was but one publication
of the banns.
Within six months the first child was born.
About two (blank) years followed, during which period *nothing at all
happened to Shakespeare,* so far as anybody knows.
Then came twins – 1585. February.
Two blank years follow.

39

Then – 1587 – he makes a ten-year visit to London, leaving the family behind.

Five blank years follow. During this period *nothing happened to him*, as far as anybody actually knows.

Then – 1592 – there is mention of him as an actor.

Next year – 1593 – his name appears in the official list of players.

Next year – 1594 – he played before the queen. A detail of no consequence: other obscurities did it every year of the forty-five of her reign. And remained obscure.

Three pretty full years follow. Full of play-acting.

Then – in 1597 – he bought New Place, Stratford.

Thirteen or fourteen busy years follow; years in which he accumulated money, and also reputation as actor and manager.

Meantime his name, liberally and variously spelt, had become associated with a number of great plays and poems, as (ostensibly) author of the same.

Some of these, in these years and later, were pirated, but he made no protest.

Then – 1610–11 – he returned to Stratford and settled down for good and all, and busied himself in lending money, trading in tithes, trading in land and houses; shirking a debt of forty-one shillings, borrowed by his wife during his long desertion of his family; suing debtors for shillings and coppers; being sued himself for shillings and coppers; and acting as confederate to a neighbor who tried to rob the town of its rights in a certain common, and did not succeed.

He lived five or six years – till 1616 – in the joy of these elevated pursuits. Then he made a will, and signed each of its three pages with his name. A thoroughgoing business man's will. It named in minute detail every item of property he owned in the world – houses, lands, sword, silver-gilt bowl, and so on – all the way down to his 'second-best bed' and its furniture.

It carefully and calculatingly distributed his riches among the members of his family, overlooking no individual of it. Not even his wife: the wife he had been enabled to marry in a hurry by urgent grace of a special dispensation before he was nineteen; the wife whom he had left husbandless so many years; the wife who had had to borrow forty-one shillings in her need, and which the lender was never able to collect of the prosperous husband, but died at last with the money still lacking. No, even this wife was remembered in Shakespeare's will.

He left her that 'second-best bed'.

And *not another thing*, not even a penny to bless her lucky widowhood with.
It was eminently and conspicuously a business man's will, not a poet's.
It mentioned *not a single book*.
Books were much more precious than swords and silver-gilt bowls and
second-best beds in those days, and when a departing person owned one
he gave it a high place in his will.
The will mentioned *not a play, not a poem, not an unfinished literary work,
not a scrap of manuscript of any kind*.
Many poets have died poor, but this is the only one in history that has
died *this* poor; the others all left literary remains behind. Also a book.
Maybe two.
If Shakespeare had owned a dog – but we need not go into that:
we know he would have mentioned it in his will. If a good dog,
Susanna would have got it; if an inferior one his wife would have
got a dower interest in it. I wish he had had a dog, just so we could see
how painstakingly he would have divided that dog among the family,
in his careful business way.
He signed the will in three places.
In earlier years he signed two other official documents.
These five signatures still exist.
There are *no other specimens of his penmanship in existence*. Not a line.
Was he prejudiced against the art? His granddaughter, whom he loved,
was eight years old when he died, yet she had had no teaching, he left no
provision for her education although he was rich, and in her mature
womanhood she couldn't write and couldn't tell her husband's manuscript
from anybody else's – she thought it was Shakespeare's.
When Shakespeare died in Stratford *it was not an event*. It made no more
stir in England than the death of any other forgotten theatre-actor would
have made. Nobody came down from London; there were no lamenting
poems, no eulogies, no national tears – there was merely silence, and
nothing more. A striking contrast with what happened when Ben Jonson,
and Francis Bacon, and Spenser, and Raleigh and the other distinguished
literary folk of Shakespeare's time passed from life! No praiseful voice
was lifted for the lost Bard of Avon; even Ben Jonson waited seven years
before he lifted his.
So far as anybody actually knows and can prove, Shakespeare of
Stratford-on-Avon never wrote a play in his life.
So far as anybody knows and can prove, he never wrote a letter
to anybody in his life.
So far as any one knows, he received only one letter during his life.

So far as any one *knows and can prove*, Shakespeare of Stratford
wrote only one poem during his life. This one is authentic.
He did write that one – a fact which stands undisputed; he wrote
the whole of it; he wrote the whole of it out of his own head.
He commanded that this work of art be engraved upon his tomb,
and he was obeyed. There it abides to this day. This is it:

> Good friend for Iesus sake forbeare
> To digg the dust enclosed heare:
> Blest be ye man yt spares thes stones
> And curst be he yet moves my bones.

In the list as above set down, will be found *every positively known* fact of
Shakespeare's life, lean and meagre as the invoice is. Beyond these details
we know *not a thing* about him. All the rest of his vast history, as furnished
by the biographers, is built up, course upon course, of guesses, inferences,
theories, conjectures – an Eiffel Tower of artificialities rising sky-high
from a very flat and very thin foundation of inconsequential facts.

Mark Twain's little history of Shakspere is neither complete nor correct,
and he did not labour to make it so. It was a satire upon Shakspere's monumental biographers, contrasting their long-windedness with the sparsity
and paucity of known facts on their subject's life. His particular target, and
the chief bugbear of all anti-Stratfordian writers in the early part of the
twentieth century, was the distinguished biographer, Sir Sidney Launcelot
(formerly Solomon Lazarus) Lee. Among his mighty works, which included
editing and writing many entries for *The Dictionary of National Biography*, and
an early Life of Queen Victoria, Lee in 1898 produced the latest, driest,
most authoritative *Life of William Shakespeare*.

The known facts about Shakspere's life, as the Heretics constantly
exclaim, can be written down on one side of a sheet of notepaper. Yet his
innumerable biographers have managed to spin out versions of his life-
story through ponderous works, sometimes in several volumes. One could
build up a small library of books about Shakspere's youth, including for
example the 256-page *Shakespeare the Boy* by William J. Rolfe, Litt. D. – a
period of his life on which not one single fact is known. Sir Sidney Lee's
Life expanded through several editions, the last of which ran to 720 closely
printed pages.

How could this possibly have been done? Critics of Lee's biography said
that his method was to write knowledgeably and at length about the social,
historical and theatrical background to Shakspere's life and times, and then

The boy genius, romantically displayed in Westall's Dreams of the Youthful Shakespeare, *1827.*

to bring Shakspere himself into the picture by saying that he 'doubtless' knew this and 'doubtless' did that. In the Authorship controversy this is known as Lee's catch-word.

In his parody Mark Twain imagined himself back sixty years to the time when, as a Sunday School pupil, he took it into his head to write a Life of Satan. The only reliable source of facts about this being, he was told, is the Bible, but it contains no more than five facts on Satan. Everything else is rumour and legend. Following the methods of Sir Sidney Lee, this is how Mark Twain described the biographical process.

> We set down the five known facts by themselves, on a piece of paper, and numbered it 'page 1'; then on fifteen hundred other pieces of paper we set down the 'conjectures', and 'suppositions', and 'maybes', and 'perhaps', and 'doubtlesses', and 'rumors', and 'guesses', and 'probabilities', and 'likelihoods', and 'we are permitted to thinks', and 'we are warranted in believings', and 'might have beens', and 'could have beens', and 'must have beens', and 'unquestionablys', and 'without a shadow of doubts' – and behold!
> *Materials?* Why, we have enough to build a biography of Shakespeare!

Lee was not amused. In the enlarged 1915 edition of his book he referred to Mark Twain as 'the American humourist' and observed ponderously that 'his idiosyncrasies unfitted him for treating seriously matters of literary history or criticism'.

The Stratfordians' attitude to Shakspere's meagre biography is that it is perfectly normal and unexceptional. Dr A.L. Rowse goes on the offensive and declares that there are more records of his activities than of any other contemporary dramatist – Ben Jonson excepted. This is perhaps a hyperbole. Charlton Ogburn in *The Mysterious William Shakespeare* points to several literary figures of Shakespeare's time, whose lives are well documented by records, their own letters and the writings of others. Two examples are John Lyly and Edmund Spenser.

Professor Hugh Trevor-Roper made a telling point in the November 1962 issue of *Réalités*:

> Since his [Shakspere's] death, and particularly in the last century, he has been subjected to the greatest battery of organized research that has ever been directed upon a single person. Armies of scholars, formidably equipped, have examined all the documents which could possibly contain at least a mention of his name. One hundredth part of this labour applied to one of his insignificant contemporaries would be sufficient to produce a substantial biography.

One of the attractions of writing a Shakspere biography is that the known facts can be learnt quickly, and imagination can then be given full rein. The imaginations of Stratfordians, particularly those connected with the tourist business, maintain the popular image of an ideally lovable Shakspere, a simple English countryman, deeply imbued with his native culture, who drew from the well of inspiration and rose far above his educated contemporaries to set a literary standard which has never since been equalled.

This is a formidable cult-figure, and it is jealously defended. Many innocent writers have thought it a harmless exercise to point out its flaws and renew the question of Shakespearian authorship. Many of them have been surprised by the violence of the reaction. Charlton Ogburn gives the example of his parents, Dorothy and Charlton Ogburn, who wrote a long, earnest Oxfordian book, *This Star of England*. They were stunned by the 'malevolence of the abuse' they received for it. Critics attacked them personally as snobs, lunatics and rascals. Even Mark Twain's light-hearted Shakespeare book has been held against him, and editors have omitted it from his list of works.

Behind all the myths, theories and arguments, and giving rise to them all, is the same small set of biographical facts.

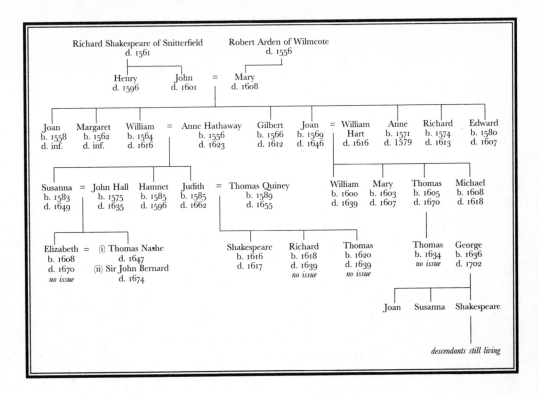

Richard Shakespeare of Snitterfield
d. 1561

Robert Arden of Wilmcote
d. 1556

| Henry | John | = | Mary |
| d. 1596 | d. 1601 | | d. 1608 |

Joan
b. 1558
d. inf.

Margaret
b. 1562
d. inf.

William = Anne Hathaway
b. 1564   b. 1556
d. 1616   d. 1623

Gilbert
b. 1566
d. 1612

Joan = William
b. 1569   Hart
d. 1646   d. 1616

Anne
b. 1571
d. 1579

Richard
b. 1574
d. 1613

Edward
b. 1580
d. 1607

Susanna = John Hall
b. 1583   b. 1575
d. 1649   d. 1635

Hamnet
b. 1585
d. 1596

Judith = Thomas Quiney
b. 1585   b. 1589
d. 1662   d. 1655

William
b. 1600
d. 1639

Mary
b. 1603
d. 1607

Thomas
b. 1605
d. 1670

Michael
b. 1608
d. 1618

Elizabeth = (i) Thomas Nashe
b. 1608   d. 1647
d. 1670   (ii) Sir John Bernard
no issue   d. 1674

Shakespeare
b. 1616
d. 1617

Richard
b. 1618
d. 1639
no issue

Thomas
b. 1620
d. 1639
no issue

Thomas
b. 1634
no issue

George
b. 1636
d. 1702

Joan   Susanna   Shakespeare

descendants still living

JOHN AND MARY, THE PARENTS

John Shakspere was a farmer from a village near Stratford who moved into the town around 1551, took a house in Henley Street and was fined a shilling for making a dungheap, a pile of refuse and night soil, on the road in front of it. He set up as a whittawer (dresser of hides and skins) and a general dealer in corn, malt and wool. Legends say that he was a butcher; certainly he was a glover, and he was also an illegal money-lender. In the course of his businesses he was constantly engaged in small-time litigation.

Prospering in business, he entered municipal life and by 1568 he had risen to become Stratford's bailiff or mayor. Ten years later his fortunes took a downward turn and he lost or mortgaged much of the property he had acquired.

He was twice charged with illegal wool dealing, and in 1570 he was accused in the Exchequer court of usury, lending money at rates of 20 and 25 per cent.

The wife of John Shakspere was Mary Arden, a farmer's daughter from an old-established local family. She bore him eight children in all, five of whom, four boys and a girl, lived to maturity. William was the eldest of the survivors.

Both John and Mary were illiterate. Shakespearians like to suggest that John could write his name, but as one commentator put it, 'If he possessed that skill he did not care to demonstrate it.' On all documents he signed with a cross or mark.

There is good evidence that John Shakspere was a recusant Roman Catholic. He died intestate in September 1601. There was no memorial and his place of burial is unknown.

Only one person claimed, or was said to have claimed, that he saw John Shakspere. In the middle of the seventeenth century, Archdeacon Thomas Plume of Rochester wrote down some legends about Shakspere, including the following: 'He was a glover's son. Sir John Mennes saw once his old father in his shop – a merry cheekt old man, that said, "Will was a good honest fellow, but he *darent* have crackt a jesst with him att any time." '

The word in italics is disputed, because the original is 'durst', but Plume must have meant 'durst not' or 'daren't', or the remark would not properly make sense. The meaning intended is evidently that William was a serious lad and did not care for his father's jokes.

It is likely enough that John Shakspere was merry, but unfortunately this account gives no firm ground for believing so. Sir John Mennes was only two-and-a-half when John died; his parents lived in Kent, therefore it is improbable that he was taken to Stratford as an infant and remembered the words of an old shopkeeper there.

EARLY LIFE

1564 26 April. In the baptismal register of Stratford parish church: '*Gulielmus filius Johannis Shakspere*'.

1582 27 November. In the Bishop of Worcester's register: Wm. Shaxpere was granted a licence to marry Anne Whateley of Temple Grafton.
28 November. In the same register: marriage bond issued to William Shagspere and Anne Hathwey of Stratford.

1583 26 May. Baptism of Susanna Shakspere (daughter) in Stratford parish church.

1585 2 February. Twins, Hamnet and Judith, baptized in Stratford church.

1589 William Shakspere was named together with his parents in a legal action against neighbour John Lambert over some land at Wilmcote.

These bare records tell all that is known about Shakspere's life up to the age of twenty-one. Nor is there any further mention of him during the 'lost years' that followed. The date and place of his birth are uncertain, and there is nothing about his schooling. The mystery which surrounds his whole life begins at the very start with the Whateley-Hathwey puzzle. Perhaps they were the same woman, or perhaps Mr Shaxpere and Mr Shagspere were different men, or perhaps William was confused in his love affairs. One theory is that Anne Whateley was a widow, born Hathwey. There was a Whateley family in Stratford at the time; George Whateley of Henley Street was the town Bailiff when William Shakspere was born. Shakspere was eighteen-and-a-half when he married, and according to her gravestone Anne Hathwey was eight years older than her husband. She was three months pregnant at her marriage. It is not certain who she was, but she is conventionally identified with Agnes Hathaway, the eldest daughter of a farmer in Shottery, a mile west of Stratford. One of the surviving yeoman's farmhouses in that village has been exhibited for many years as 'Anne Hathaway's Cottage'.

MIDDLE YEARS

1595 15 March. Shakespeare, William Kempe and Richard Burbage were listed in the accounts of the Treasurer of the Royal Chamber as receiving payment for 'two comedies or interludes' played by the Lord Chamberlain's Men before the queen the previous December.

1596 11 August. Hamnet Shakspere, aged eleven, buried at Stratford.
October. Shakspere assessed for 5s tax on property worth £5 in St Helen's parish, Bishopsgate. In November the following year posted as tax defaulter for that sum, having either left the parish or avoided the tax collectors.
29 November. William Wayte, stepson of a Surrey gangster, William Gardiner, petitioned for sureties of the peace against William Shakspere, Francis Langley and their two women associates 'for fear of death' (discovered 1931).

1597 4 May. Shakspere bought a mansion with gardens, New Place, the second largest house in Stratford, for £60.

1598 In the Folio of Ben Johnson's plays published in 1616, Shakespeare's name heads the list of principal actors in the 1598 production of Jonson's *Every Man in his Humour*.

4 February. A Stratford inventory listed William Shakspere as owning ten quarters of malt.

1 October. Shakspere assessed for 13*s* 4*d* tax. Listed as a defaulter with a marginal note, 'Surrey', implying that he had moved south of the Thames.

25 October. Stratford citizen Richard Quiney wrote to his 'Loving good friend and countryman, Mr. Wm. Shackespere', requesting a loan of £30. The letter was apparently never sent as it was found in the Stratford archives. Correspondence about this transaction between Quiney, his father Adrian and their friend, Abraham Sturley, indicates that Shakspere would have expected security and interest on the loan.

1599 16 May. An inventory of the property of Sir Thomas Brend recorded that the newly built Globe Theatre was in the occupation of William Shakespeare and others. Two years later 'Richard Burbage and William Shackespeare, Gent.' were mentioned as tenants of the Globe. Shakspere held varying proportions of the theatre's lease up to at least 1611.

6 October. Shakspere again listed as a tax defaulter, owing 13*s* 4*d*.

1600 March. 'William Shackspere' obtained judgment against John Clayton, yeoman, of Wellington, Bedfordshire, for £7 with £1 costs, on account of a debt. It is not known for certain if this was Shakspere of Stratford.

6 October. Shakspere's tax debt still being unsettled, the case was referred to the Court of the Bishop of Winchester, whose jurisdiction included the Clink in Southwark, south of the river, where Shakspere was presumably then living.

The Shakspere family at home. Father John studies his books in the chimney corner while the Bard instructs the children. Artistic imagination ignores the fact that neither John nor his granddaughter, Judith, could write even their own names.

1601 March. Thomas Whittington, shepherd to Hathaway of Shottery, died and left a will recording that William and Anne Shakspere owed him 40 shillings.

1601 1 May. Shakspere paid £320 in cash for 107 acres of arable land with grazing rights on the common pasture near Stratford. Bought a cottage with a garden opposite New Place.

1603 19 May. A Royal Patent was issued to nine named actors and their associates, including William Shakespeare, authorizing them to stage plays at the Globe Theatre. Shakespeare's name headed the list of the principal comedians who played in Jonson's *Sejanus his Fall.*

1604 In this year and perhaps earlier Shakspere was lodging at the house of Christopher Mountjoy, a French Huguenot 'tire-maker' (maker of ladies' headdresses), on the corner of Silver Street and Muggle Street in the Cripplegate ward of London, near St Paul's. This is recorded in the documents of the *Belott v. Mountjoy* lawsuit of 1612.

15 March. In the accounts of the Great Wardrobe is a list of nine players, headed by Shakespeare, who each received 4¹/₂ yards of red cloth to make liveries for participating, as grooms of the King's Chamber, in King James's coronation procession.

LAST YEARS

1604 Summer. Retirement to Stratford? The production of Shakespeare's plays was at its height in 1604 and continued for some years, so biographers generally date Shakspere's retirement to Stratford to 1610–11. The record of his life, however, suggests that after 1604 Shakspere was chiefly engaged in Stratford business, though retaining interests in London.

July. Shakspere sued the Stratford apothecary, Philip Rogers, for £1 19*s* 10*d*, the price of some malt he had sold him. Rogers borrowed a further 2*s*, repaid 6*s*, and later in the year Shakspere sued him again for the £1 15*s* 10*d* outstanding.

1605 24 July: Shakspere invested £440 in a share of the lease of the Stratford parish tithes. They yielded £60 a year net.

Augustine Phillips, an actor, left 30*s* in gold to his 'fellow William Shakespeare'.

1608 Shakspere began proceedings in the Stratford Court of Record against John Addenbroke to recover a debt of £6. The following year he obtained

judgment plus 25*s* costs, but Addenbroke absconded, so Shakspere
proceeded against his surety, a local blacksmith and alehouse keeper.
William Shakespeare took a seventh-part share in the Blackfriars Theatre.
19 October. Shakspere stood godfather to William, the son of Henry
Walker, mercer, bailiff of Stratford.

1610 Shakspere brought 20 acres of land near Stratford from William
and John Combe.

1612 11 May. Shakspere in London testified and signed an affidavit in the
Court of Requests in connection with a lawsuit, *Belott v. Mountjoy*. In 1604
he had acted as go-between in the marriage arrangements of his
landlord's daughter, Mary Mountjoy, and apprentice Stephen Belott.
Belott later sued Mountjoy to establish his right to inherit from him,
and Shakspere was called upon to state what had been agreed.

1613 March. Shakspere purchased the old Blackfriars gatehouse in London
for £140, taking from the vendor a temporary £60 loan on mortgage,
unpaid at his death. He subsequently let the house, and complications
led to a lawsuit. His alleged signature is on both the purchase and the
mortgage deed.
31 March. In the Belvoir Castle accounts book of Francis Manners, sixth
Earl of Rutland is a record of 44*s* paid to 'Mr. Shakspeare in gold about
my Lord's *impresa*'. Another 44*s* was paid to 'Richard Burbadge [Burbage
the actor] for painting and making it'. The *impresa* was a design on a
shield to be carried in a tournament. Charlotte Stopes believed that the
artificer here was not William but a certain John Shakespeare, the royal
bit-maker.

1614 12 July. John Combe died in Stratford and left £5 to Mr William
Shakespeare.
Shakspere was involved with the Combe family in an attempt to enclose
the Stratford borough common lands, extinguishing ancient popular
rights. The Stratford Corporation opposed the project, and after
Shakspere's death it was abandoned.
An unnamed visiting preacher was entertained at New Place, and
Stratford Corporation contributed 20 pence for one quart of sack
and one quart of claret.

1616 25 January. First draft of Shakspere's will presented to him. It was
signed in three places after revision on 25 March. Most of Shakspere's
estate went to his elder daughter, Susanna Hall, while his wife Anne

received the most famous legacy in history, his second-best bed.

23 April. Shakspere died and was buried two days later in Stratford church as 'Will Shakspere gent.' No name was put on the stone over his grave.

THE SHAKSPERE OF RECORD

From the bare facts alone, Shakspere's career can be summed up as follows. He was born in Stratford and married a local woman who conceived their last children, twins, in 1584 when Shakspere was twenty years old. Then followed the 'lost years', and nothing further was heard about him until at the age of thirty he was listed in a company of London actors who played before the Queen. This was not his first appearance on the London stage, for two years earlier, in 1592, Robert Greene the dramatist referred to 'an upstart crow, beautified with our feathers', who was almost certainly the actor from Stratford. Greene's remarks imply that Shakspere was by then well known in the theatre world, so the conventional guess is that he came to London when he was about twenty-six.

The record of Shakspere's stage career is disappointingly thin. Twice, in 1598 and 1603, he was in the cast of a play by Ben Jonson, but there is no mention of what parts he took in these or any other performances. All the theatre companies of his time made regular, extensive tours of the provinces, and generations of scholars have searched through municipal archives, from Edinburgh to Plymouth, looking for Shakspere's name on lists of players, but never finding it. The most dedicated researcher of the early twentieth century, Charlotte Stopes, spent years among the public records in London, discovering a great deal about plays and players in Shakspere's time, but nothing about him as an actor.

By the age of thirty-three Shakspere had acquired such wealth that he could buy a fine house in Stratford, and the following year a fellow-townsman asked him for a £30 loan. Yet in London at about the same period he was dodging taxes, shifting his lodgings and quarrelling with a man who complained against him in fear of his life. He took shares in theatrical enterprises and, in 1602, made further investments in Stratford property. Two years later he was lodging in Cripplegate, his only known London address. After that he is mainly heard of in Stratford, where he engaged in property deals and sued for small business debts.

Without taking into account Shakespeare the poet and dramatist, and without making any biographical assumptions on the basis of his works, the documented life of William Shakspere is a poor thing. Like his father, a

Venus and Adonis in 1593 was dedicated by 'William Shakespeare' to the young Earl of Southampton.

tradesman, money-lender and municipal dignitary, he was always a man of Stratford, and his recorded activities were much the same as John Shakspere's, but rather more successful. By the time of his death, aged fifty-two, he had acquired a substantial landholding in and around Stratford and an investment property in London. His main object in life, as far as the evidence goes, was to make himself wealthy and respected in his native town.

That, of course, is only half the story. For about fourteen years (estimates differ) until he was about forty (again there is no certainty) he lived mainly in London, acted in plays and was involved in theatre business. In 1593 a long, passionate, classically refined poem, *Venus and Adonis*, was dedicated in the name of William Shakespeare to the nineteen-year-old Earl of Southampton. The following year a second poem, *The Rape of Lucrece*, was similarly dedicated. Southampton made no acknowledgments and, despite ardent scholarly researches, there is no hint of evidence that he ever had any connection with William Shakspere.

In 1598 the name Shakespeare or Shake-speare began appearing on the title-pages of plays, many of which had previously been published anonymously. These works were famous and highly praised, yet their nominal author remained obscure. No literary people – with the exception of Ben Jonson – ever claimed to have known him. His only known associates were his Stratford neighbours and, in London, crooked businessmen and theatre folk. His main activities are unknown.

Apart from a name similar to his on title-pages, there is no contemporary proof of Shakspere's connection with the Shakespeare plays. They were published without Shakspere's initiative or authority, often during his lifetime in pirated editions. Yet he did nothing about it, even though he was a sharp businessman, zealous in asserting his rights down to the last halfpenny. Nor did he complain when other, unknown writers published inferior works under the name of Shakespeare. While he was still alive and active, plays such as the *Life of Sir John Old-castle, The London Prodigall* and *A Yorkshire Tragedy* were published as by William or W. Shakespeare, but experts have constantly denied the attribution. There is no indication that Shakspere himself either claimed or rejected authorship of any of the Shakespearian writings.

The author of Shakespeare was a genius, and so perhaps was William Shakspere. Behind the mask of an ordinary, unpretentious, unacclaimed Stratford property-owner was another Shakspere, poetic and learned, courtly and philosophical, a high-flown stylist with a vocabulary more extensive than that of any other English writer. That person has left no trace of himself in the biography of William Shakspere, but to be orthodox we have to believe that he and Shakespeare were one and the same man. It is not an easy faith, and many learned people

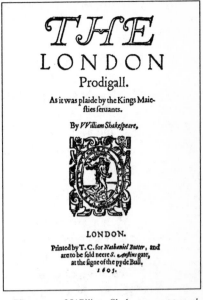

The name of William Shakespeare appeared on the title-pages of several plays whose real authors are unknown.

have been unable to accept it; but it is upheld universally, by all the established authorities, so it cannot lightly be rejected. It is not quite rejected in this book, and it never can be as long as there are honest scholars who sincerely believe in it. Yet so much evidence has been brought against it – and not always adequately refuted – that it seems reasonable to suppose that there really is a Shakespeare Authorship problem.

SHAKSPERE NOTICED IN HIS LIFETIME

Shakspere's biographers work under the severe handicap that he never wrote a single word about himself. Strictly speaking, there is one exception, that in the preliminaries to his will he declared himself 'in perfect health and memorie god be praysed' – a legal formality. No one who met him made a record during his lifetime of what he was like or what he said or did. In *Shakespeare's Centurie of Prayse* (1879) Dr C.M. Ingleby collected a great many references to Shakespeare or his works, written between 1591 and 1693. Mostly they are brief allusions to a Shakespeare work, most commonly to the poems, *Venus and Adonis* and *The Rape of Lucrece*, saying nothing about the author.

In an age when people gossiped, kept diaries, wrote letters and published remarks and satires on their contemporaries, only one person recorded an anecdote about Shakspere himself. In his *Diary* under 13 March 1601 a young law student, John Manningham, wrote:

> Upon a time when Burbidge played Richard III there was a citizen grew
> so far in liking him that, before she went from the play, she appointed
> him to come that night unto her by the name of Richard the Third.
> Shakespeare, overhearing their conclusion, went before, was entertained
> and at his game ere Burbidge came. Then, message being brought that
> Richard the Third was at the door, Shakespeare caused return to be
> made that William the Conqueror was before Richard the Third.
> Shakespeare's name William.

This story embarrassed the Victorian biographers, and they were probably right not to take it too literally. Manningham heard it from a fellow-student, who probably heard it from someone else. Its main significance is that it gives a hint at how Shakspere was regarded in his time. Evidently his name was not well known, or Manningham would not have had to explain the joke.

Apart from this, literary references to Shakspere in his own time were always to the author of poems and dramas, never directly to the man. The earliest was in 1594, the year when Shakespeare's poem, *The Rape of Lucrece*, was published. In verses prefixed to a poem by Henry Willobie, *Willobie his Avisa*, is the line, 'And *Shake-speare* paints poor *Lucrece* rape'. A certain W.S. in this poem, who has cured himself of infatuation with the lovely Avisa, is taken by some as meant for William Shakspere. Much has been written about this, from all kinds of viewpoints, but with no general agreement.

In 1598 an obscure clergyman, Francis Meres, published a book of sayings, anecdotes and quotations under the title *Palladis Tamia: Wits Treasury*, in one section of which he listed the great writers of Greece, Rome and Italy together with the names of Englishmen who he thought were comparable. Shakespeare was mentioned among thirteen English dramatists in the list of those judged 'best for Tragedie', and with sixteen others, beginning with the Earl of Oxford, as 'the best for Comedie amongst us'. Many of the names are little known, and Shakespeare was not especially distinguished among them. Meres had more to say about others, such as Michael Drayton. His most interesting paragraphs on Shakespeare were:

> As the soul of Euphorbus was thought to live in Pythagoras, so the sweet
> witty soul of Ovid lives in mellifluous and honey-tongued Shakespeare,
> witness his 'Venus and Adonis', his 'Lucrece', his sugared sonnets among
> his private friends, etc.

As Plautus and Seneca are accounted the best for Comedy and Tragedy among the Latins, so Shakespeare among the English is the most excellent in both kinds for the stage; for Comedy, witness his 'Gentlemen of Verona', his 'Errors', his 'Love's Labour's Lost', his 'Love's Labour's Wonne', his 'Midsummer Night's Dream', and his 'Merchant of Venice'; for Tragedy, his 'Richard the 2', 'Richard the 3', 'Henry the 4', 'King John', 'Titus Andronicus', and his 'Romeo and Juliet'.

As Epius Stolo said that the Muses would speak with Plautus' tongue, if they would speak Latin; so I say that the Muses would speak with Shakespeare's fine filed phrase, if they would speak English.

In the same year appeared these lines by the poet Richard Barnfield:

> And Shakespeare thou, whose honey-flowing Vein
> (Pleasing the World), thy Praises doth obtain.
> Whose *Venus*, and whose *Lucrece* (sweet, and chaste)
> Thy Name in Fame's immortal Book have placed.
> Live ever you, at least in Fame live ever:
> Well may the Body die, but Fame dies never.

John Weever in 1599 wrote some stilted lines to 'Honey-tongued Shakespeare', comparing his verses to Apollo's. Then, in 1610, came John Davies's tribute, *To our English Terence, Mr Will. Shake-speare*:

> Some say good *Will* (which I in sport do sing)
>   Had'st thou not plaid some Kingly parts in sport,
> Thou had'st bin a companion for a *King*;
>   And beene a King among the meaner sort.
> Some others raile but raile as they thinke fit,
> Thou hast no rayling, but a raigning Wit:
>   *And* honesty *thou sow'st which they do reape*;
>   *So, to increase their* Stocke *which they do keepe*.

No one knows quite what to make of these lines. Shakespeare, says Davies, played some kingly parts, presumably in historical dramas, but he gives no clue as to which they were. Nor does he explain why Shakespeare might have consorted with a king, nor what is meant by a 'king among the meaner sort'. And why did others rail? These mysterious lines are popular among the heretical theorists. Advocates of the Earl of Derby quote them in his favour, because Derby was hereditary king of the Isle of Man, and his brother, the previous earl, Ferdinando, was looked to by the Catholic party as the future king of England, after they had deposed Elizabeth.

The title, 'our English Terence', which Davies bestowed on Shakespeare, has also attracted suspicion, because Terence was an impoverished Roman writer who, it was rumoured, published under his own name works which noblemen had written but did not care to acknowledge.

The record of tributes to Shakespeare up to 1623 contains two further poems. In 1614 Thomas Freeman's *To Master W. Shakespeare* began, 'Shakespeare, that nimble Mercury thy brain . . .', proclaimed that all the virtues and vices were to be found in his poetry and mentioned the 'borrowing' habits of Terence.

> Besides in plays thy wit winds like Meander:
> Whence needy new-composers borrow more
> Than Terence does from Plautus or Menander.

In 1622, after Shakspere's death, William Basse wrote lines beginning,

> Renowned Spenser lie a thought more nigh
> To learned Beaumont, and rare Beaumont lie
> A little nearer Chaucer, to make room
> For Shakespeare in your threefold, fourfold tomb.

In his poem to the Author at the beginning of the 1623 Folio edition of Shakespeare's plays, Ben Jonson rejected Basse's idea that the three poets should move up to make room for Shakespeare, saying that he was 'a monument, without a tomb'.

Basse's poem seems to have been a plea for Shakespeare to be commemorated in Westminster Abbey, along with the other poets. If so, he was the only writer among his contemporaries to raise that proposal. It was not until 1740 that the elegant statue of Shakespeare, pointing to a Latin scroll, was erected by public subscription among the literary monuments in the Abbey.

MYTHMAKERS AND THE FIRST SCEPTICS

For almost fifty years after Shakspere's death nothing personal was written about him. No one appeared in Stratford, notebook in hand, to find out what the locals knew and thought about the great man commemorated in their parish church. Shakspere's sister, Joan Hart, outlived him by thirty years, his younger

The Shakespeare memorial in Westminster Abbey, erected 1740.

daughter, Judith, by forty-six years, and his last descendant, granddaughter Elizabeth, lived on to 1670. Yet no writer interviewed them, and no one from Stratford who had known William Shakspere recorded any statement about him.

The remembrance of Shakspere in his native town did not survive the Civil War and the ensuing reign of Puritanism. Even after the restoration of the monarchy in 1660, when the theatres were reopened and secular literature was made respectable, scholars were slow to investigate Shakspere's life in Stratford. Posterity was thus deprived of any direct information and has had to make do with the legends, rumours and inventions by which, from the very beginning, Shakspere's biographers have padded out the few certain facts of his career.

An early legend is that Shakspere wrote some 'witty and facetious verses' for the tomb of his neighbour, the money-lender John Combe. This was noted by Lieutenant Hammond while looking round Stratford church in 1634. He did not quote the verses, but they had previously, in 1618, been printed in Richard Brathwaite's *Remains after Death*, with no mention of who wrote them. They refer to Mr Combe's habit of lending at 10 per cent.

> Ten in the hundred must lie in his grave,
> But a hundred to ten whether God will him have.
> Who then must be interr'd in this tomb?
> 'Oh,' quoth the devil, 'my John a Combe.'

Similar verses to satirize usurers were current even earlier, so the inscription on Combe's tomb was not original. His heirs, it was said, had it erased. Several different versions of it were given by Shakspere's early biographers.

Other epitaphs and witty verses attributed to Shakspere include the lines carved on the slabstone over his own tomb.

GOOD FREND FOR IESVS SAKE FORBEARE,
TO DIGG THE DVST ENCLOASED HEARE:
BLESE BE Y MAN Y SPARES THES STONES,
AND CVRST BE HE Y MOVES MY BONES.

This rhyme was seen by a Mr Dowdall who visited Stratford in 1693. The elderly parish clerk who showed him round the church said that the inscription had prevented Shakspere's widow and daughters from being buried with him. He went on to say that Shakspere in his youth had been apprenticed to a local butcher, but escaped to London where he took service in a playhouse.

The following year another visitor, William Hall, quoted the verses on Shakspere's tombstone in a letter to a friend and added that Shakspere himself had written them. He had an ingenious explanation for their crudity. 'The little learning these verses contain would be a very strong argument for the want of it in the author, did they not carry something in them which stands in need of a comment.' Hall's comment was that, in composing the verses, Shakspere had brilliantly adapted his style to his audience – to parish clerks and sextons, 'for the most part a very ignorant set of people', who might otherwise be tempted to disturb his burial.

The only inhabitant of Stratford who wrote anything at all about Shakspere in the hundred years after his burial was not a local person but an Oxford graduate, the Rev. John Ward. In 1662, aged thirty-three, he went to Stratford to practise medicine and was appointed vicar of the parish. At that time he knew nothing about the great Stratfordian, but he must have heard talk about him, for he wrote down in his notebook, 'Remember to peruse Shakespeare's plays, and be versed in them, that I be not ignorant in that matter.'

Ward made a few notes on stories he had heard about Shakspere, but said nothing about his informants. Shakspere's younger daughter died early in the year of his arrival, but though other relatives were still living in his time, there is nothing to show that he ever questioned them. All he recorded were the following items of hearsay:

> I have heard that Mr Shakespeare was a natural wit, without any art at all; he frequented the plays all his younger time, but in his elder days lived at Stratford and supplied the stage with two plays every year, and for that had an allowance so large, that he spent at the rate of a thousand a year, as I have heard.
>
> Shakespeare, Drayton, and Ben Jonson had a merry meeting, and it seems drunk too hard, for Shakespeare died of a fever there contracted.

This sketch of about 1594, showing actors playing in Titus Andronicus, *is the only contemporary illustration of a Shakespearian performance.*

One of the earliest theatrical anecdotes about Shakspere is given in Sir Sidney Lee's biography. The violent tragedy, *Titus Andronicus*, is fully accredited as a Shakespeare play, being listed among his works by Meres in 1598 and appearing in the First Folio. Yet in 1678 the dramatist, Edward Ravenscroft, who revised it for a new staging, told a different story about its authorship. 'I have been told by some anciently coversant with the stage that it was not originally his but brought by a private author to be acted, and he only gave some master-touches to one or two of the principal parts or characters.'

This story, said Lee, deserves acceptance. The 'repulsive plot' of *Titus Andronicus* was probably the work of Kyd with Greene or Peele. 'Shakespeare's hand is only visible in detached embellishments.' This view of Shakspere, as a writer who adapted other people's work for the stage, fits well with Greene's and Jonson's allusions to him, and it also appeals to the moderate anti-Stratfordians who are willing to allow that Shakspere played some minor part in the writing of plays published under his name.

In 1680 John Aubrey included some anecdotes about Shakspere in his *Brief Lives*. This was more than a hundred years after Shakspere's boyhood, but the Stratford people could still think up some stories to tell about him from that time.

> His father was a Butcher, and I have been told heretofore by some of the neighbours, that when he was a boy he exercised his father's Trade, but when he kill'd a Calfe he would doe it in a high style, and make a Speech. There was at this time another Butcher's son in this Towne that was held not at all inferior to him for a naturall witt, his acquaintance and coetanean, byt dyed young.
>
> He was a handsome, well-shap't man: very good company, and of a very readie and pleasant smoothe Witt.
>
> He was wont to goe to his native Countrey once a yeare. I thinke I have been told that he left 2 or 300 pounds per annum there and thereabouts to a sister.
>
> He understood Latine pretty well: for he had been in his younger yeares a schoolmaster in the countrey.

Aubrey quoted a version of Shakspere's epitaph on John Combe and said he wrote it at the local tavern. Shakspere and Jonson, he continued, were always on the look-out for characters to put in their plays. A certain constable of Grendon in Buckinghamshire, who was still alive when Aubrey first went to Oxford, was the original of the Constable in *A Midsummer*

Night's Dream. On his annual journeys to Warwickshire, Shakspere used to stay with a friend at Oxford, John Davenant, a vintner, whose son, the Poet Laureate Sir William Davenant, would later imply while drinking with close friends that Shakspere was his real father.

Sir Thomas Lucy's badge of three white luces is in the top left-hand corner of a family coat-of-arms.

Aubrey used to write down whatever story anyone told him, so it is impossible to say what degree of truth there may be in any of his Shakspere anecdotes. He missed out one of the more plausible legends of Shakspere's youth, that he was a convicted poacher.

The story that Shakspere used to poach deer and other game on the estate of Sir Thomas Lucy of Charlecote Park, was caught and punished and thereafter left Stratford for the London theatre, was told independently by several early writers, beginning with the Rev. Richard Davies in 1688. Davies found it among the papers of another clergyman, William Fulman, who had collected a few notes on the life of Shakspere. Shakspere, according to the story, had his revenge on Lucy by lampooning him in the character of Justice Shallow in *The Merry Wives of Windsor*, whose coat of arms bore 'a dozen white luces' or pike. The arms of Lucy of Charlecote displayed three luces, but on the Lucy tomb the shield is depicted four times, making the twelve white luces.

Nicholas Rowe in 1709 gave an expanded account of Shakspere's poaching exploits, and in the course of the eighteenth century other versions appeared. Most biographers have dismissed the whole story as folklore, believing it to have arisen from, rather than prompting, the reference in *The Merry Wives*. There was no licensed deer park at Charlecote in Shakspere's youth; but a tapestry map of that period shows that there was an enclosed park which probably contained deer, and Peter Razzell, who has gone thoroughly into the matter in his *Anatomy of an Enigma*, finds that the weight of evidence supports the legend that Shakspere was a deer-poacher on Sir Thomas Lucy's land.

Rowe was the first to mention Shakspere's schooling. He was said to have attended a free school 'where 'tis probable he acquir'd that little *Latin* he was Master of'. His father was too poor to keep him there, and he needed his help in business, so William was forced to leave early. He worked in the family wool business until the Lucy incident drove him away to London.

Also in Rowe are the stories that Shakspere received £1000 from the Earl of Southampton; that he helped Ben Jonson to stage his first play; that he played the Ghost in his own *Hamlet*; that Queen Elizabeth wanted him to write a play about Falstaff in love; that Susanna was his favourite daughter, and that he spent an easy retirement in conversation with his friends.

Later legends of the eighteenth century tell of Shakspere beginning his London career by holding horses for theatre-goers, planting a mulberry tree at New Place, and spending a night under a crab-apple tree. These are enjoyable stories, giving an attractive picture of Shakspere's high-spirited youth and his convivial, contented retirement. All they lack is anyone's account of Shakspere writing, studying or identifying himself as the author of Shakespeare.

As the supply of legends finally dried up, a discordant tone began to be heard in the chorus of praise for Shakspere. Two eighteenth-century writers each published a strange kind of humorous fable, presenting the Stratford hero in a disconcertingly new light. In 1769 *The Life and Adventures of Common Sense: An Historical Allegory* by a medical man, Herbert Lawrence, spun an odd story about a group of allegorical figures, including Wisdom, Genius and Humour, who travelled through time and eventually arrived in England and the year 1588. There they encountered a shifty theatrical character, a reputed deer-stealer and incorrigible thief, who was ready to deal in whatever goods came to hand. He latched on to Wisdom and the others and stole from them various talismanic objects, a book, a mask and an eyeglass, which equipped him to set up as a playwright. The name of this thief, it turned out, was Shakspeare.

The Story of the Learned Pig (1786) by an unknown 'Officer of the Royal Navy' is a fantastic tale of a soul passing through a succession of bodies, including Romulus, Brutus, a cat and a fly, and ending as a performing pig in a London theatre. In the Elizabethan age it was incarnated as a rascally Londoner, Pimping Billy, who looked after horses for playgoers and was an agent for prostitutes. He made friends with Shakspere who, it appeared, was exiled from Stratford, not because he stole the local magistrate's deer but for being caught in dalliance with his wife. The plays attributed to Shakespeare were written by Pimping Billy himself. Shakspere merely posed as the author; but when everyone from the queen downwards hailed him as a dramatic genius, Billy was cut out of the profits and died in a fit of jealous rage.

The allegorical framework of these stories hides, perhaps deliberately, their authors' personal views on the Shakespeare question and whether they really believed Shakspere to have been a thief and a plagiarist. At about the same time, James Wilmot was privately expressing doubts on Shakspere's authorship and developing the Bacon theory. If there was any link between Wilmot, Lawrence and the Naval Officer it has not been discovered, but it is imaginable that towards the end of the eighteenth century a few people were beginning to have certain suspicions about Shakspere and his literary pretensions.

THE STRATFORD MONUMENTS

Stratford-upon-Avon in the summer, with swans on the river and streets of ancient-looking houses and hostelries, is a lovely place. Visitors are rarely disappointed by it. The villages and countryside around are steeped in the tranquil atmosphere of old England, and in the town itself are the impressive relics of our National Bard, the place of his nativity and the scenes of his early inspiration.

Over a million tourists a year pay a total of several million pounds to view the properties of the Shakespeare Birthplace Trust and purchase the souvenir goods displayed in them. It is a pleasant experience, even for those who realize that everything they are shown is entirely spurious.

The headquarters of the Birthplace Trust is a large, modern, concrete building, overshadowing the quaint little Birthplace house beside it. It is one of the most lucrative tourist businesses in England. Yet, according to the Stratford magistrates, it is not a business at all.

In 1969 Francis Carr, a writer and campaigner for the Baconian cause, took out a summons against the Shakespeare Birthplace Trust under the Trade Descriptions Act, which forbids false statements and claims in advertising. His case was that, having paid to be shown the house where Shakespeare was born, he had been defrauded. What he saw was not Shakespeare's birthplace but a fictitious reconstruction of a house in Henley Street which had no demonstrable connection at all with the birth in 1564 of William Shakspere.

The facts of the matter are that neither the day nor the place of Shakspere's birth are recorded. In 1552 his father-to-be, John Shakspere, then aged about twenty-two, was presumably lodging or carrying on business somewhere in Henley Street, for that was where he made his famous muckheap. Four years later he purchased two houses in Stratford. One of them, somewhere in Henley Street, had a garden, and the other, nearby in Greenhill Street, came with a garden and a croft or paddock. This was the year before his wedding, and it seems likely that the more pleasantly sited house with grounds in Greenhill Street was where he chose to raise his family.

He sold it in 1590 when the children were mostly grown up, leaving him with only two Stratford properties, both somewhere in Henley Street. Two adjoining houses in that street, now replaced by a nineteenth-century replica of an earlier building on the site, are identified as those of John Shakspere. One of them is firmly linked with his family, because up to 1806 it belonged to descendants of William's sister, Joan Hart, several of whom used it as a butcher's shop. The other was for about two hundred years an inn, The Maidenhead, later The Swan and Maidenhead. The western house of the two is exhibited today as the true Birthplace; guides can even show in it the room where William was born. In actual fact, as Francis Carr pointed out to the Stratford magistrates, there is nothing to prove that he was born anywhere in Henley Street.

Mr Carr's case put the court in an awkward situation. In popular guide-books, still issued by the Birthplace Trust, it is stated categorically that 'William Shakespeare was born in the house preserved as his Birthplace in Henley Street'. This surely falls foul of the spirit if not the letter of the Trade Descriptions Act. The magistrates held council and declared that in this case the Act did not apply. The Shakespeare tourist trade in Stratford, they ruled, was not a business but something quite different, namely, a Birthplace Trust.

Other old houses in Stratford have been claimed as the Birthplace. In April 1808 *The Gentleman's Magazine* printed an engraving by John Jordan, the early, myth-making Stratford antiquarian, showing a 'View of the Brook House, in which it is generally admitted that Shakspeare was really born'. This and other possible rivals to Henley Street were later demolished, removing the competition.

Brook House, Stratford-upon-Avon, one of Shakspere's legendary birthplaces.

Even before 1768, when David Garrick's Grand Shakespeare Jubilee gave it impetus, the Shakespeare cult was already alive in Stratford. Its most popular relic was the mulberry tree which, according to legend, Shakspere had planted with his own hands in the garden at New Place. The house itself had been demolished in the reign of Queen Anne, and Shakspere's timber-framed residence was replaced by a fine brick mansion. This in 1751 was bought by the Rev.

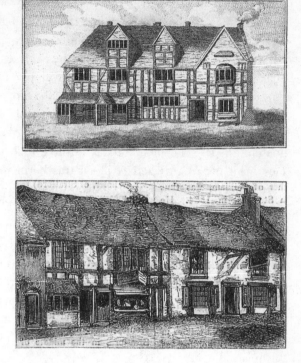

An engraving of Shakspere's alleged birthplace in the eighteenth century provided the model for its later reconstruction.

Before the Stratford cult developed, the Birthplace site was occupied by an inn and a butcher's shop.

A goblet carved from the legendary mulberry tree.

Francis Gastrell as his place of retirement. To his great annoyance, Shakespearian tourists kept disturbing him with their enquiries. Some of them wanted twigs from the mulberry tree, while others broke into his garden and took away whole branches. After three years of this, he ordered the mulberry tree to be cut down and sold to a local carpenter, who thereafter made a living by selling busts, boxes and other objects carved from its timbers. Gastrell, however, was still persecuted by visitors, until in 1759 he pulled down the entire house, sold off its materials and made a new start to his retirement in another part of the country.

The Shakespeare cult thereafter became centred upon the Henley Street 'Birthplace'. For many years it was humble and primitive. An early American visitor, Washington Irving, in 1815 found a small mean-looking edifice of wood and plaster and was shown round it by a talkative old woman with a fantastic collection of relics. In its 'squalid chambers', with walls covered by scrawled graffiti, Irving inspected the Poet's old gun, sword and tobacco-box and was invited to sit in his favourite chair – a replacement of a former Shakspere's chair, which had been sold to another visitor some years earlier. In Stratford church Irving met the old sexton, who quietly hinted that not only the Shakspere relics but the alleged Birthplace itself, were of dubious authenticity. Scepticism about the Birthplace is still a tradition among the local people of Stratford.

Soon after Washington Irving's visit, the same custodian of the Birthplace showed a lady pilgrim a new stock of Shakspere relics, including her own children, who, she said, were direct descendants through herself of William Shakspere.

The trafficking in bogus relics brought discredit to the Birthplace. The first Stratford guidebook, published in 1806, had a picture of the house but made no mention of it in the text. In the years that followed it sank further into dilapidation, and in 1847 it was put up for sale. Largely through the efforts of James Orchard Halliwell, the great biographer, collector and Shakespearian enthusiast, a Shakespeare Birthplace Committee was formed; £3000 were raised for the purchase and further sums for the rebuilding of the property. A new set of Shakspere relics was brought in to furnish it, old houses adjoining it were pulled down, and the reformed Birthplace was set in respectable isolation, as it is today.

James Orchard Halliwell (later Halliwell-Phillipps), 1820–89, biographer of Shakspere and promoter of his cult at Stratford.

Even now, under the scholarly management of the Trust, guides at the Birthplace cannot always resist the old legends. Visitors in 1994 were still shown the traditional wooden chair from the Falcon Inn at Bidford, where Shakspere sat on the evening when he and his companions, the Stratford Swillers, were drunk under the table by the local reserve team, the Bidford Sippers. According to the eighteenth-century legend, he spent the night beneath a local crab-apple tree. John Jordan improved the story by adding a rhyme which, he said, Shakspere made up on the occasion: that he had drunk with: Piping Pebworth, Dancing Marston,

> Haunted Hillborough, Hungrey Grafton,
> Dadgeing Exhall, Papist Wicksford,
> Beggarly Broom and Drunken Bidford.

Souvenir-hunters descended on the tree which Jordan identified as Shakspere's shelter, and by 1824 it had been reduced to a dead stump. The chair was carried off to the Birthplace where it is now exhibited. Experts say it was made no earlier than the mid-seventeenth century, but its legend and Shakspere's rhyme are still rehearsed for the amusement of tourists.

Anne Hathaway's cottage was not known by that name until the end of the eighteenth century when this aquatint was made after Samuel Ireland's picturesque drawing.

Visitors to the Birthplace can buy a ticket which admits them to four other Trust properties: the room in the Grammar School where Shakspere would have been taught if he had been educated there; Hall's Croft, a modern name for an old house, rebuilt and furnished to show how Shakspere's son-in-law, Dr John Hall, might have lived; a farmhouse at Wilmcote of the sort that Shakspere's maternal grandparents, the Ardens, might well have inhabited, and the charming Cottage of Anne Hathaway, a shrine to the female aspect of the cult. A short walk across fields from Stratford leads to the old village of Shottery where – perhaps even in that very cottage itself – lived Richard Hathaway, a husbandman, whose daughter Agnes, so it is speculated, married William Shakspere under the name Anne Hathwey. In the Cottage is shown an old wooden settle on which it can be imagined that she was courted by her young lover.

This whole display is most kindly described as a pious fraud. Pilgrims generally prefer atmosphere to strict veracity, and the Birthplace Trust skilfully satisfies the natural yearning for a sanctuary where the genius of Shakespeare can be venerated in an appropriate, old-world setting. Even Delia Bacon, the pioneer Baconian who went to Stratford in 1856 for the purpose of digging up Shakspere's bones, acknowledged the charm of the place. One cannot resist teasing the Birthplace Trust, even as Francis Carr did with his provocative summons, but one is drawn to admire their revival of the pilgrimage spirit and the cult of relics, extinguished elsewhere in England by the Protestant Reformation. The cult they administer is harmless and edifying. It has nothing really to do with the Authorship question, but it demonstrates the power and resources of orthodox Stratfordianism and the futility of insisting that the works of Shakespeare were written by anyone other than the established cult-hero.

IV

DOUBTS AND QUESTIONS

SHAKSPERE CHARGED WITH PLAGIARISM

According to this woodcut of 1598, Robert Greene wrote his last work dressed in a shroud.

There are probable allusions to Shakspere, though not by name, in the works of several contemporary writers. The most notorious of these was Robert Greene, a dramatist and pamphleteer who died in 1592. He was a Cambridge graduate, a classical scholar whose life had gone downhill through vice, drink and debauchery to end in penury and squalor. In his bitter last days he reviewed the failure of his career which he blamed upon other people. Scheming rivals had robbed him of his works and fame, and the most ruthless of these was a certain young upstart in the world of theatre.

The product of his deathbed was a pamphlet entitled *Greene's Groats-worth of Wit, Bought with a Million of Repentance: Describing the Folly of Youth, the Falsehood of Makeshift Flatterers, the Misery of the Negligent, and Mischiefs of Deceiving Courtesans.* It was a fable about Greene's own downfall in the character of Roberto, a young scholar who had disgraced himself and finally been cheated by a whore. In despair and solitude he bewailed his woes in Latin verses. His elegant lamentations were overheard by a richly clad stranger, who approached him with a proposition. He was a successful actor who could turn his hand to writing, and he needed an assistant to write plays for his theatre company. Roberto fell for the temptation and into an abyss of vice. In the riotous company of players and theatrical adventurers he became utterly depraved and beyond redemption.

The story was Greene's dramatized, self-pitying account of what had happened to his own life. At the end of his pamphlet he turned to plain, direct speaking, and from his final remarks it is reasonable to suppose that the evil exploiter in his fable, the man of theatre who preyed upon literary men, was meant to represent Shakspere. It was certainly Shakspere to whom Greene alluded in the personal letter that concluded his *Groats-worth.* Addressed to three of Greene's fellow-scholars, identified as Marlowe, Nashe and Peele, he warned them as dramatists about certain stage people,

67

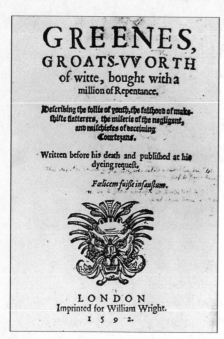

GREENES,
GROATS-VVORTH
of witte, bought with a
million of Repentance.

Deſcribing the follie of youth, the falſhood of make-
ſhifte flatterers, the miſerie of the negligent,
and miſchiefes of deceiuing
Courtezans.

Written before his death and publiſhed at his
dyeing requeſt.

Fælicem fuiſſe infauſtum.

LONDON
Imprinted for William Wright.
1 5 9 2.

*The earliest allusion to Shakspere in the
theatre was as the 'upstart crow' in Greene's
Groats-worth, 1592.*

one in particular, who could corrupt and
destroy them as they had destroyed Greene.
This is an extract from his letter:

> Yes, trust them not: for there is an
> upstart crow, beautified with our
> feathers, that with his *tiger's heart
> wrapped in a player's hide* supposes he is
> as well able to bombast out a blank
> verse as the best of you; and, being an
> absolute *Johannes Factotum*, is in his own
> conceit the only Shake-scene in a
> country. O, that I might entreat your
> rare wits to be employed in more
> profitable courses, and let those apes
> imitate your past excellence, and
> never more acquaint them with your
> past inventions.

The bombastic actor, Shake-scene, the theatrical man-of-all-trades (Johannes Factotum), who
steals other people's work and thinks himself
better than them; this man is William Shakspere. His identity is proclaimed
by the 'tiger's heart wrapped in a player's hide' which is adapted from a
line in Shakespeare's third part of *King Henry VI* (i. 4), 'O, tiger's heart
wrapt in a woman's hide!' – part of York's outburst against his triumphant
captor, Queen Margaret.

Greene's outburst against Shakspere, uttered at a time when he had
nothing to lose by plain speaking, is one of the most important texts in the
Authorship debate. He died at the age of thirty-two and was four years
older than Shakspere. In abusing his younger rival as an 'upstart crow' he
specifically charged him with plagiarism; in classical fables the crow was a
thievish bird, stealing the finer plumes of others, and in Renaissance literature it was the recognized symbol of a plagiarist.

The reference to the line in *Henry VI* has further significance. According
to Sir Sidney Lee, whose *Life of William Shakespeare* has been the standard
biography for most of the twentieth century, the three parts of *Henry VI*
were not originally by Shakespeare. He merely 'revised and expanded
other men's works'. The first part of the trilogy was not published until
1623, in the Shakespeare First Folio, but prototypes of the second and
third parts were in circulation before the death of Greene, and were first

published anonymously. Lee's explanation for Greene's bitterness was that he, together with George Peele, produced the original draft of the three parts of *Henry VI*, which Shakespeare and Marlowe helped to recast. That, he wrote, 'can alone account for Greene's indignant denunciation of Shakespeare as "an upstart crow, beautified with the feathers" of himself and his fellow-dramatists'.

Greene's audacity in exposing Shakspere as a plagiarist scandalized certain authorities. There is no knowing exactly what happened, because it all took place behind the scenes, but those involved in the publication of the *Groats-worth* pamphlet were frightened into disowning it. It was suspected at the time, and it is believed by some experts today, that Greene's name was used, as soon as he had conveniently died, as a cover for someone else. Thomas Nashe, who was rumoured to be the real author, published an immediate denial, angrily dissociating himself from the pamphlet. The publisher, William Wright, who entered it in the Stationers' Register, did so 'upon the peril of Henrye Chettle', meaning that it was not he but Chettle who took responsibility for it. Chettle, a printer and hack writer, found himself in a tight corner and got out of it by issuing an elaborate apology. He had copied out and edited Greene's work, removing, he claimed, some of the more offensive remarks in it. Nevertheless, he admitted, offence had been given to several playwrights, two of whom had complained. Chettle knew neither of them personally, and in the case of one, probably Marlowe, he saw no need to apologize, but the second case was quite different. In apparent reference to Shakspere, Chettle wrote, ingratiatingly:

> I am as sorry, as if the original fault had been my fault, because myself
> have seen his demeanour no less civil than he excellent in the quality he
> professes: besides, divers of worship have reported, his uprightness of
> dealing, which argues his honesty, and his facetious grace in writing, that
> approves his art.

Chettle's praise of Shakspere was for his grace and honesty, the two qualities that Greene had accused him of lacking. His high opinion of him was derived from 'divers of worship'; these, according to the meaning of the phrase, were men of high rank, whose word on Shakspere could not be gainsaid. It seems that, even at that early stage of his career, Shakspere had powerful defenders.

Two years after this affair, Greene's complaint, that he had been robbed of his literary works, was repeated in a small book of poems, *Greene's Funerals*, by R.B. Gent (supposedly Richard Barnfield). After praising Greene with punning references to his name, the poet added two lines,

Nay more, the men that so eclipsed his fame,
Purloined his plumes: can they deny the same?

In 1598 this same Barnfield wrote verses in honour of Shakespeare, promising him immortality for his poems, *Venus and Adonis* and *The Rape of Lucrece*, but saying nothing about him as a dramatist.

Ben Jonson (c.1573–1637), the only contemporary of Shakspere who remarked on him personally and by name.

In the Authorship controversy Greene is quoted by Stratfordians to show that Shakspere was reputed among his contemporaries as a writer of plays. Yet Greene implied that he was a plagiarist. He may also have caricatured him as the rich, corrupt actor-writer who lured poor Roberto to his downfall. If so, Robert Greene let a large cat out of the bag, and the panicky, apologetic behaviour of his associates (Greene himself being safely dead) indicates that certain authorities took a serious view of the matter.

Another of Shakspere's contemporaries, Ben Jonson, may have hinted that he stole other people's work. In 1616, the year of Shakspere's death, Jonson published a collection of his 'epigrams', short, witty verses on his literary friends and other well-known people of the time. Shakspere was not named in them but, according to all Shakespearians, he was possibly, probably or even certainly the subject of the epigram called 'On Poet-Ape'.

Poor Poet-Ape, that would be thought our chief,
    Whose works are e'en the frippery of wit,
From brokage is become so bold a thief
    As we, the robb'd, leave rage, and pity it.
At first he made low shifts, would pick and glean,
    Buy the reversion of old plays, now grown
To a little wealth, and credit on the scene,
    He takes up all, makes each man's wit his own,
And told of this, he slights it. Tut, such crimes
    The sluggish, gaping auditor devours;
He marks not whose 'twas first, and aftertimes
    May judge it to be his, as well as ours.
Fool! as if half-eyes will not know a fleece
From locks of wool, or shreds from the whole piece.

Jonson's meaning is fairly plain. There is a plagiarizing poet whose works are the 'frippery' or cast-off items of other writers' wit. He began as a broker of plays, buying and selling them, and now he behaves as if he owns them, taking parts out of them to make up other plays which he passes off as his own. When the writers he has robbed complain about this, the Poet-Ape makes light of his crimes, saying that the average 'gaping auditor' or slow-witted playgoer does not care who wrote any particular play and it may later be attributed to the Poet-Ape as readily as to the original writer. What a fool this man is! Anyone with their eyes half shut can tell an original play from one made up of bits and pieces of other people's writings.

The straightforward, orthodox view is that Jonson was merely saying what Shakespearians have always admitted, that Shakespeare borrowed freely from contemporary as well as ancient authors, and that certain parts of his plays were probably contributed by other dramatists. This does not satisfy the heretics. In his anti-Stratfordian classic, *Is There a Shakespeare Problem?*, Sir George Greenwood argued that, if the Poet-Ape was meant to be Shakspere, the plain inference was that, in Jonson's opinion, Shakspere was 'an egregious and audacious plagiarist . . . one who puts forth the work of others as his own'.

This opens the way to the full-blown heretical contention, that Shakspere did not write Shakespeare's plays, and his contemporaries knew it.

BEN JONSON AND THE SWAN OF AVON

Of all Shakspere's contemporaries the most likely to have written about him was Ben Jonson. About nine years younger than Shakspere, with no advantages of birth or wealth, Jonson was educated by a patron at Westminster School and took degrees at both universities. One of his early jobs was as a bricklayer. After a spell of military service in Flanders, where he distinguished himself against the Spaniards, he returned to London and, before the age of twenty, became a successful actor and dramatist. Jonson was a man of great learning, a classical scholar and lively wit. He was popular in the royal court and knew all the notable and interesting people of his time, from rulers and noblemen to writers, actors and bohemians in the London taverns. In the course of his rumbustious career he was often in trouble, once for killing a fellow-actor, and later, more seriously, when a play that he, Chapman and Marston had written together gave offence to the authorities and the authors were arrested. In each case Jonson was rescued by powerful friends.

Jonson loved good company and was a great gossip. Throughout his writings are many references, though mostly guarded without naming names, to his famous contemporaries. He certainly knew William Shakspere, both as an actor and a playwright, and praised him as the author of immortal works. That should have settled the Authorship question once and for all, and it would have done so if only Jonson had been less equivocal. The trouble is that he said and wrote quite different things at different times about his senior colleague. Officially, in his commendatory verses introducing the First Folio of Shakespeare's plays in 1623, he lauded him to the skies. Elsewhere, in a reported conversation of 1619 and in a later note, he spoke critically about him, and it is widely believed that certain ridiculous, depraved characters in his satirical plays were at least partly modelled on Shakspere.

Jonson's rancorous epigram about Shakspere, lightly disguised as the 'Poet-Ape', is thought to have been written in about 1602, a year after his play, *The Poetaster*. In that play there are several poet-apes and pretentious theatrical characters. One of them is named Pantalabus, meaning a writer who, like the Poet-Ape, 'takes up all'. He is a pompous, ranting 'parcel-poet' who claims to be a 'gent'man'. Then there is Crispinus, another 'parcel-poet', who boasts absurdly about his 'arms', meaning his coat of arms, the warrant of his gentility. His name, he declared, is 'Crispinus, or "Cri-spinas" indeed', which may have been Jonson's way of poking fun at the hyphenated Shake-speare.

Always on the look-out for other people's weaknesses, Jonson must have observed Shakspere's efforts to obtain a coat of arms. In 1596 the Garter King of Arms at the Heralds' Office drafted the Shakspere coat of arms, with a punning crest, a falcon supporting a spear. The motto was *Non sanz Droict* meaning 'Not without Right'. The justification for this grant was a genealogical fiction about the antiquity of Shakspere's lineage. It is unlikely that Jonson would have missed this opportunity of mocking his rival's pretentiousness, and it is generally supposed that he did so in his play, *Every Man out of his Humour*, registered in 1600. One of the characters in it is Sogliardo, a rustic boor who is ludicrously proud of his newly acquired coat of arms. In Act iii, Scene 1, he boasts about it in conversation with Sir Puntarvolo and Carlo the jester.

Sogliardo. Nay, I will have them, I am resolute for that. By this parchment, gentlemen, I have been so toiled among the harrots [heralds] yonder, you will not believe; they do speak i' the strangest language and give a man the hardest terms for his money, that ever you knew.
Carlo. But ha' you arms? ha' you arms?
Sog. I' faith, I thank God. *I can write myself a gentleman now*; here's my

patent, it cost me thirty pounds, by this breath.

Puntarvolo. A very fair coat, well charged and full of armory.

Sog. Nay, it has as much variety of colours in it, as you have seen a coat have; how like you the crest, sir?

Punt. I understand it not well, what is't?

Sog. Marry, sir, it is your boar without a head, rampant.

After more jokes and badinage about this ridiculous coat of arms, Sogliardo reads from a paper where it is described in heraldic language:

Sog. On a chief argent, a boar's head proper, between two ann'lets sables.

Car. (to Puntarvolo). 'Slud, it's a hog's cheek and puddings, in a pewter field, this.

Sog. How like you 'hem, signior?

Punt. Let the word be, '*Not without mustard*': Your crest is very rare, sir.

Shakspere's ambition, to acquire a coat-of-arms and the rank of a gentleman incurred the mockery of Ben Jonson. The draft of the grant of arms is headed, Non sans Droict *('Not without Right'), of which Jonson's 'Not without mustard' is an evident parody.*

Sogliardo, described as 'an essential clown, brother to Sordido, yet so enamoured of the name of gentleman that he will have it, though he buys it', is more a caricature than a portrayal of an actual person, but Jonson probably had Shakspere in mind when he created his ridiculous character. Shakspere may well have been 'toiled among the heralds' to obtain his dubious coat of arms, exposing himself to Jonson's malicious fantasy of a rustic dish, 'a hog's cheek and puddings on a pewter field' as his appropriate emblem. This is typical of the jibes which metropolitan writers make against provincial newcomers. Sogliardo is most clearly identified with Shakspere by the motto, *Not without Mustard*, a parody of Shakspere's *Non sanz Droict*. The allusion to mustard is possibly elucidated by a phrase in *2 Henry IV* (ii. 4), 'His wit's as thick as Tewksbury mustard'.

During the lifetime of Shakspere Ben Jonson did not once mention his name in writing. The first remark he is known to have made about him was in 1619, in Scotland. Having walked from London to Edinburgh, Jonson stayed for two or three weeks with a fellow-poet, William Drummond, laird of Hawthornden. Over the whisky, Jonson talked freely about the other writers he knew, often with disparaging anecdotes, and Drummond carefully noted down what he said. One of his comments was: 'That Shakspeer wanted arte . . . Shakspeer, in a play, brought in a number of men saying they had suffered shipwrack in Bohemia, where there is no sea neer by some 100 miles.'

Critics have pointed out that Bohemia did at one time have a sea coast, but it is a trifling matter because *The Winter's Tale* with its reference to a Bohemian shipwreck was based on a novel by Robert Greene. The main interest in Jonson's remark is that he accused Shakspere of lacking art. Yet four years later, in his verses for the First Folio, Jonson was effusive about Shakespeare's art and emphasized it above all his qualities.

Jonson's opinion of Shakspere is highly relevant to the Authorship question. Everything, in fact, depends upon it, because Jonson's eulogy of Shakespeare in the Folio, plainly identifying him as the man of Stratford, is the strongest bastion of the orthodox, Stratfordian case. Every heretical writer has had to confront it. It has been the most hotly debated text in the entire controversy. Stratfordians regard it as the clinching evidence in favour of their own candidate, while their rivals ingeniously pick holes in it, claiming either that Ben Jonson was insincere in his flattery of Shakespeare or that he was secretly praising another man, the real author, whose identity he knew.

Jonson's famous poem (opposite) is addressed in straightforward manner 'To the memory of my beloved, the Author, Mr William Shakespeare: and

To the memory of my beloved,
The AVTHOR
Mr. VVilliam Shakespeare
And
what he hath left us.

TO draw no envy (Shakespeare) on thy name,
Am I thus ample to thy Booke, and Fame:
While I confesse thy writings to be such,
As neither Man, nor Muse, can praise too much;
Tis true, and all mens suffrage. But these wayes
Were not the paths I meant unto thy praise:
For seeliest Ignorance on these may light,
Which, when it sounds at best, but eccho's right;
Or blinde Affection, which doth ne're advance
The truth, but gropes, and urgeth all by chance;
Or crafty Malice, might pretend this praise,
And thinke to ruine, where it seem'd to raise.
These are, as some infamous Baud, or whore,
Should praise a Matron. What could hurt her more?
But thou art proofe against them, and indeed
Above th' ill fortune of them, or the need.
I therefore will begin. Soule of the Age!
The applause! delight! the wonder of our Stage!
My Shakespeare rise; I will not lodge thee by
Chaucer, or Spenser, or bid Beaumont lye
A little further, to make thee a roome:
Thou art a Monument, without a tombe,
And art alive still, while thy Booke doth live,
And we have wits to read, and praise to give.
That I not mixe thee so, my braine excuses;
I meane with great, but disproportion'd Muses:
For, if I thought my judgement were of yeeres,
I should commit thee surely with thy peeres,
And tell, how farre thou didst our Lily out-shine,
Or sporting Kid, or Marlowes mighty line.
And though thou hadst small Latine and lesse Greeke,
From thence to honour thee, I would not seeke
For names; but call forth thund'ring Aeschilus,
Euripides, and Sophocles to us,
Paccuvius, Accius, him of Cordova dead,
To live againe, to heare thy Buskin tread,
And shake a Stage: Or, when thy Sockes were on,
Leave thee alone for the comparison

Of all, that insolent Greece, or haughty Rome
sent forth, or since did from their ashes come.
Triumph, my Britaine, thou hast one to showe,
To whom all Scenes of Europe homage owe.
He was not of an age, but for all time!
And all the Muses still were in their prime,
When like Apollo he came forth to warme
Our eares, or like a Mercury to charme!
Nature her selfe was proud of his designes,
And joy'd to weare the dressing of his lines!
Which were so richly spun, and woven so fit,
As, since, she will vouchsafe no other Wit.
The merry Greeke, tart Aristophanes,
Neat Terence, witty Plautus, now not please;
But antiquated, and deserted lye
As they were not of Natures family.
Yet must I not give Nature all: Thy Art,
My gentle Shakespeare, must enjoy a part.
For though the Poets matter, Nature be,
His art doth give the fashion. And, that he,
Who casts to write a living line, must sweat,
(such as thine are) and strike the second heat
Vpon the Muses anvile: turne the same,
(And himselfe with it) that he thinkes to frame;
Or for the lawrell, he may gaine a scorne,
For a good Poet's made, as well as borne.
And such wert thou. Looke how the fathers face
Lives in his issue, even so, the race
Of Shakespeares minde, and manners brightly shines
In his well torned, and true filed lines:
In each of which, he seemes to shake a Lance,
As brandish't at the eyes of Ignorance.
Sweet Swan of Avon! what a sight it were
To see thee in our water yet appeare,
And make those flights upon the bankes of Thames,
That so did take Eliza, and our James!
But stay, I see thee in the Hemisphere
Advanc'd, and made a Constellation there!
Shine forth thou Starre of Poets, and with rage,
Or influence, chide, or cheere the drooping Stage;
Which, since thy flight from hence, hath mourn'd like night,
And despaires day, but for thy Volumes light.

of
BEN. IONSON.

what he hath left us.' That, together with the epithet, 'Sweet Swan of Avon', leave no apparent doubt that the dramatist from Stratford-upon-Avon was the author referred to. Yet critics have persistently nibbled away at this certainty, discovering ambiguities and inconsistencies in Jonson's verses. His emphasis on Shakespeare's 'art', for example, contradicts his previous remark, to Drummond of Hawthornden, that Shakespeare 'wanted [lacked] art'. Also puzzling are the lines that attribute to Shakespeare 'small Latin, and less Greek', while comparing him favourably with the greatest of classical authors. Jonson's opinion of Shakespeare's scholarship is left uncertain. Perhaps he was judging it by his own high standards of classical learning, or perhaps he meant to indicate that the Stratford man had no education worth speaking of.

Grammarians have pointed out that Jonson's lines,

> And though thou hadst small Latin, and less Greek,
> From thence to honour thee, I would not seek
> For names...

do not really impute any classical knowledge to Shakspere. The words, 'hadst' and 'would' form a conditional construction. 'Though' is used in the sense, 'even if', so Jonson is actually saying that, even if Shakspere had had a smattering of Latin and Greek, that would not be his reason for praising him; he would still compare him with the best of the ancients.

Theorists have examined closely every line in Jonson's verses to Shakespeare, looking for double meanings in them. Some find significance in the line, 'Thou art a monument, without a tomb', which, if taken literally, implies that the author was still alive in 1623 – as were Bacon, Derby and other prominent candidates. Shakspere by that time had been entombed for seven years at Stratford-upon-Avon.

Groupists are intrigued by the fifth line from the end of Jonson's poem, where Shakespeare is compared to a 'constellation'. This term, they point out, is more appropriate to a number of poets than to just one. Yet the next line addresses Shakespeare as 'thou Starre of Poets'. Poet is a word of Greek origin, and the Greek for a star is *aster*. Putting the two together makes 'Poetaster'. That is the title of the Jonson play in which, according to some critics, Shakspere was caricatured as the vain poetaster and 'parcel-poet', Crispinus. If such a pun was intentional, then Jonson was up to his old tricks, concealing in grandiloquent language his real opinion of Shakspere as a mere 'poet-ape'.

Baconians assert that Ben Jonson worked for Francis Bacon as a secretary and literary assistant; that he edited and oversaw the publication of the

First Folio, while recognizing Bacon's authorship of the 'Shakespeare' plays; and that his verses to 'my beloved, the Author' were cryptically addressed to Bacon. A point in their argument is that Jonson praised Shakespeare's plays above 'all that insolent Greece or haughty Rome sent forth . . .' and referred to his 'true-filed lines'. Later, in his *Discoveries*, Jonson eulogized Francis Bacon in almost the same terms, as 'he who hath *filled up all numbers*, and performed that in our tongue which may be compared or preferred either to *insolent Greece or haughty Rome*'.

Swans in the lace collar of Mary, Countess of Pembroke, as portrayed in 1618, contribute to the theory that she was the true 'Swan of Avon'. She lived opposite the village of Stratford on the Wiltshire Avon.

Even Jonson's allusion to Shakespeare as 'Sweet Swan of Avon' has been found enigmatic. The Oxfordians make the rather feeble point that the Earl of Oxford had an estate, Bilton, bordering the river Avon at Rugby; but he had sold it by 1580, when he was thirty. Far more interesting is the case of Mary Herbert. She was the sister of Sir Philip Sidney, married the Earl of Pembroke and gave birth to 'the most Noble and Incomparable Paire of Brethren, William Earle of Pembroke . . . and Philip, Earl of Montgomery', to whom the First Folio was dedicated. In Gilbert Slater's *Seven Shakespeares* Mary Herbert, Countess of Pembroke, is proposed as one of the most likely candidates for the Authorship. There is, said Slater, clear evidence of a woman's hand in Shakespeare. Lady Pembroke was intimate with many of the young philosophers and poets of the time, and was herself a poet, much praised by her contemporaries. She lived at Wilton House, situated upon the banks of the Wiltshire River Avon. A further coincidence, which Slater missed, is that the village across the Avon from Wilton is called Stratford-sub-Castle. She could therefore have been described, equally as well as Will Shakspere, as a resident of Stratford-on-Avon. Slater posed the question: 'Does the title "Sweet Swan" better fit the money-lending maltster of Stratford or the "peerless Ladie bright," of Wilton? Which of the two would Jonson most naturally think of as "My Beloved"?' Slater naturally preferred the claims of Mary Herbert.

Ben Jonson was a crafty professional writer, versed in all the literary techniques of wordplay and subtle allusion by which, in an age of ruthless censorship, secret ideas and information were communicated among the initiated. The Stratfordians naturally insist that his lines to Mr William Shakespeare, Swan of Avon, should be taken at face value as clearly intended for William Shakspere of Stratford. But they are not necessarily right. Their opponents emphasize the complete difference in tone between Jonson's unstinting praise of Shakespeare in the First Folio and the scornful allusions he made to him elsewhere, both before and after Shakspere's death.

There are many mysteries about the First Folio, how and by whom it was edited, the circumstances of its publication and so on. It is widely agreed among experts on all sides that Jonson played a larger part in the enterprise than was publicly disclosed. He may well have had a commercial interest in the success of the Folio, thus explaining his enthusiastic 'blurb' on behalf of its named author. That theory was upheld by the mighty anti-Stratfordian writer, Sir George Greenwood. In hundreds of closely argued pages throughout his numerous books he examined the Jonson–Shakespeare relationship, concluding that Jonson commended the author of the Folio simply in order to give the publication 'a good send-off'.

MYSTERIES OF THE FIRST FOLIO

When William Shakspere died in 1616, no one beyond Stratford paid any attention or wrote in tribute to his memory. The date of his death is known only from the anonymous inscription on his Stratford monument. Shakespeare's plays were famous and popular, yet no one seemed interested in the man who was associated with them by name.

The silence which met the death of Shakspere contrasted strangely with the public lamentations in 1637, when Jonson died. The literary world was vociferous in his praise. Within six months a volume of collected poems celebrating him in English and Latin was published, and he was buried with great ceremony in Westminster Abbey. Francis Beaumont, who died in the same year as Shakspere, was also buried in the Abbey with poetic tributes, and it was the same with Drayton and Spenser. Fletcher, Chapman, Massinger and other, lesser writers were honoured by many verses at their deaths. Thirty-six poets contributed praises to Beaumont and Fletcher's folio of plays in 1647. In an age when literary men wrote profusely to and about each other, it seems incongruous that the reputed author of Shakespeare so thoroughly escaped their attention.

In 1623, thirty-six plays by William Shakespeare were published in a Folio edition of some five hundred copies, priced at £1 each. About 238 copies exist today, of which seventy-nine are in the Folger Library in Washington. The editors, Shakspere's old theatrical associates, John Heminges and Henry Condell, signed the Dedication, which was largely a paraphrase of Pliny's dedication to Vespasian of his *Natural History*, and they also signed a Preface *To the great Variety of Readers*. This was followed by Ben Jonson's verses to Shakespeare and by three shorter poems, two by obscure versifiers, Hugh Holland and Leonard Digges, and the third by an unidentified 'I.M.' The main point of interest in these formal poems is Digges's reference to Shakespeare's Stratford Monument. Evidently he accepted the Stratford man as the author of the Folio. Holland and I.M. both made it plain that Shakespeare was then dead, so they could hardly have had Bacon in mind.

To the Reader.

This Figure, that thou here seeſt put,
  It vvas for gentle Shakeſpeare cut;
Wherein the Grauer had a ſtrife
  with Nature, to out-doo the life :
O, could he but haue dravvne his vvit
  As vvell in braſſe, as he hath hit
His face ; the Print vvould then ſurpaſſe
  All, that vvas euer vvrit in braſſe.
But, ſince he cannot, Reader, looke
  Not on his Picture, but his Booke.

B. I.

Jonson's verse as printed in the First Folio opposite the engraving of Shakespeare.

Featured on the title-page of the First Folio was a crude likeness of Shakespeare, the famous Droeshout engraving, and on the flyleaf adjoining it was printed a ten-line poem (illustrated above), signed with the initials of Ben Jonson, to commend this portrait.

All these items have been viewed suspiciously by the anti-Stratfordians, and their doubts on some points are shared by many orthodox scholars. Generations of experts have agreed that the Preface and the Dedication, both signed by Heminges and Condell, was actually written by Ben Jonson, who was the real editor of the Folio. It is also agreed that certain statements in the Preface were patently untrue and purposely misleading. The most glaring examples occur in the second paragraph.

It had bene a thing, we confesse, worthie to have been wished, that the author himselfe had lived to have set forth, and overseen his owne writings; But since it hath bin ordain'd otherwise, and he by death departed from that right, we pray you do not envie his Friends, the office of their care and paine, to have collected and publish'd them; and so to have publish'd them, as where (before) you were abus'd with divers stolne, and surreptitious copies, maimed and deformed by the frauds and stealths of injurious imposters, that expos'd them: even those are now offer'd to your view cur'd, and perfect of their limbes; and all the rest, absolute in their numbers, as he conceived them: Who, as he was a happie imitator of nature, was a most gentle expresser of it. His mind and hand went together: And what he thought, he uttered with that easinesse, that wee have scarce received from him a blot in his papers.

This claim, that the plays in the Folio were printed from perfect, almost unblotted manuscript copies (that is, without erasures or insertions), has been rejected by all the authorities. Several of the plays were demonstrably reproduced from earlier Quarto editions with printer's errors left uncorrected.

79

Others seem to have been copied, with additional inaccuracies, from already defective manuscripts. The reference to perfect, original, unblotted copies of Shakespeare's plays was an editorial fiction.

Eighteen of the plays included in the First Folio had never before been printed, and their sources are quite unknown. Others, previously issued under Shakespeare's name or initials, were excluded. There is nothing to indicate the dates of the plays or the order in which they were written, and none of them is prefaced by any personal remarks from the author. Other dramatists of the period embroidered their works with dedications, addresses to friends, prologues and epilogues, in which they displayed their own thoughts and characters. Shakespeare alone remained totally aloof.

This lack of connection between the Shakespeare plays and their supposed author is a constant theme in anti-Stratfordian writings, and even the Orthodox admit to being puzzled by it. The editors of the First Folio hinted by two or three phrases that the author was the man buried at Stratford-upon-Avon, but they never openly stated it. There were no biographical notes on the great dramatist, nor any indications of where and when the plays were written. On the question of how they acquired authentic copies and the rights to plays previously unpublished, the editors were secretive and mendacious. The originals from which they worked have never been seen since. Plays in manuscript by the other leading dramatists of the age – such as Marlowe, Jonson, Fletcher, Beaumont, Greene, Heywood, Dekker and Middleton – are still in existence, but there is no record of a Shakespeare manuscript.

Adding to the mystery is a note written by Ben Jonson, probably in the 1630s, which was found among his papers after his death in 1637. It was published four years later in a collection of Jonson's writings under the title, *Timber, or Discoveries, Made upon Men and Matter . . .* The note on Shakespeare was headed, *de Shakespeare nostrati* (about our fellow-country-man Shakespeare).

I remember the players have often mentioned it as an honour to Shakespeare, that in his writing (whatsoever he penned) he never blotted out a line. My answer hath been, 'Would he had blotted a thousand,' which they thought a malevolent speech. I had not told posterity this but for their ignorance who choose that circumstance to commend their friend by which he most faulted; and to justify mine own candour, for I loved the man, and do honour his memory on this side idolatry as much as any. He was, indeed, honest, and of an open and free nature; had an excellent phantasy, brave notions and gentle expressions, wherein he flowed with that faculty that sometimes it was necessary he should be stopped. *Sufflaminandus erat*, as Augustus said of Haterius. His wit was in his own power; would the rule of it had been so too! Many times he fell into those things could not escape laughter, as when he said in the person of Caesar, one speaking to him, 'Caesar, thou dost me wrong.' He replied, 'Caesar never did wrong but with just cause'; and such like, which were ridiculous. But he redeemed his vices with his virtues. There was ever more in him to be praised than to be pardoned.

This is another example of Jonson's evasiveness. He referred specifically to Shakspere's penmanship and how the players used to admire it, while saying nothing at all about him as an author. Jonson's earliest allusions to Shakspere, as in his lines on the Poet-Ape, were to a man who made up plays by copying out and putting together passages of other people's work. Here again he is seen as a copyist, and as one who put too much inferior writing into circulation. Jonson wished that he had blotted much of it out. But that, he implied, was typical of the man. He wrote too much just as he talked too much. As Augustus said of a certain Roman chatterbox, it was sometimes necessary to stop him. The Shakspere that Jonson knew was a witty fellow, who made people laugh, sometimes without meaning to, as on the occasions when he comically fluffed his lines on stage.

This was certainly not the Shakespeare whom Jonson had earlier praised so rapturously as,

> Soul of the age!
> The applause! delight! the wonder of our stage!

No doubt remembering those lines, and to defend himself from the charge of malevolence, Jonson protested that he did indeed love Shakspere; yet Jonson had the irony of a born Londoner. Having described Shakspere as an uninhibited, hearty character, he mentioned the 'gentle' or gentlemanly expressions that flowed out of him so readily. Those who understand the Cockney way of speaking will infer from this that Shakspere's expressions were rough and humorous and anything but genteel.

It is quite possible that Jonson arranged the publication of the First Folio at the behest of Bacon, knowing that he or some other great man was its actual author. In that case, Jonson had two Shakespeares in his life. One was the great dramatist to whom he addressed the commendatory verses, praising his genius in all sincerity and without reservation. The other Shakespeare was a down-to-earth character with his full share of human faults. 'But he redeemed his vices with his virtues.' Jonson enjoyed his company, his free and easy manner, his amusing anecdotes and the quaint expressions he used in conversation. Sometimes he went on too much and became a bore. He was then told to shut up.

It sounds as if Jonson was writing about an old drinking companion, whom he patronized as an inferior but remembered with affection. 'There was ever more in him to be praised than to be pardoned.' This second Shakespeare was William of Stratford-upon-Avon. He was also the Shakespeare remembered by Cuthbert Burbage, brother of Richard the actor. In 1635 Cuthbert and other family members petitioned the Earl of Pembroke, one of the 'paire of brethren' to whom the Folio was dedicated, for support in the affairs of the Globe Theatre. To strengthen their case, the Burbages mentioned the associations of the playhouse with their family and 'those deserving men, Shakspere, Heminge, Condall, Phillips, and others, partners in the profits'. They also referred to the Blackfriars Theatre which they occupied from 1608, where they 'placed men players, which were Heminge, Condall, Shakespeare, etc.'

The Globe Theatre in an early seventeenth-century drawing of London in the time of Shakespeare.

This Shakespeare or Shakspere was evidently not the first Shakespeare, the immortal poet, the Soul of the Age whom the Burbages would have surely linked to their cause, rather than the deserving actor, especially in appealing to Pembroke.

It was clearly Jonson's intention in the Folio to let it be assumed that the two Shakespeares were one and the same man. That was all right as far as the incurious public was concerned, and Shakspere's fellow actors knew better than to challenge the official fiction. Yet they were not deceived, and neither of course was Pembroke. In writing to the Earl, the Burbages naturally dropped the pretence that William Shakspere was the author of Shakespeare's plays, and referred to him as the man they all knew, the former actor and businessman from Stratford.

There are two main theories about the secret involvement of Francis Bacon in the First Folio. Either he wrote the plays himself or, as the Oxford groupists have it, he was the archivist of a Shakespeare-writing committee and commissioned Jonson to see the volume of collected works through the press. To these, however, there is one rather serious objection. The texts in the Folio are notoriously muddled, full of errors and misprints and sometimes more defective than the quarto editions preceding them. The last thing that any author wants is to be published in this way. If he is a lawyer he is likely to be even more insistent on accuracy. It is barely conceivable that, after years of plotting and secrecy, Bacon would have handed the plays to his agent or printer in such an imperfect state.

MARTIN DROESHOUT'S BRAZEN PORTRAIT

Everyone who has looked sceptically into the authorship claims on behalf of William Shakspere has been impressed by his persistent anonymity. His documented life tells only of his money-lending, property-dealing and theatrical activities, and the few personal remarks about him, those of Ben Jonson, are thoroughly enigmatic. His contemporaries praised Shakespeare's poems but said next to nothing about the man, and there is no evidence that anyone ever painted his portrait from the life.

No comparable figure in history has ever been so anonymous. In all Shakespeare's writings there is nothing but his bare name to identify the author. He presents himself as a mask rather than an actual person. It is not even known what he looked like. Only two likenesses of Shakspere, or possibly of a mask, have claims to being authentic; both were made after his death, and they are both highly controversial.

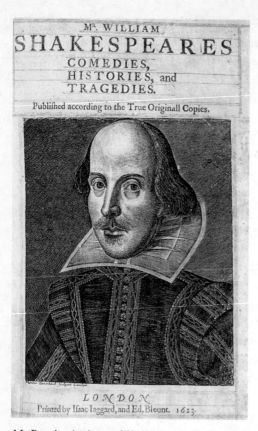

Mʳ. WILLIAM
SHAKESPEARES
COMEDIES,
HISTORIES, and
TRAGEDIES.

Publiſhed according to the True Originall Copies.

LONDON
Printed by Iſaac Iaggard, and Ed. Blount. 1623.

M. Droeshout's picture of Shakespeare in the First Folio was twice altered as the edition was being printed. In earlier copies the figure was paler, less shadowed than in the final version, above.

The first image of Shakspere was the memorial bust in Stratford parish church. Then, in 1623, on the title-page of the First Folio, appeared a copper-engraved portrait, inscribed '*Martin Droeshout: sculpsit. London*'. Verses by Ben Jonson on the opposite page identified it as a portrait of Shakespeare.

Martin Droeshout, born in London into an immigrant Flemish family of engravers, was only fifteen years old when Shakspere died, so it is most improbable that he ever saw him. Either he was working from someone's instructions or from someone's drawing. The result in either case was lamentable. If Droeshout intended a life-like portrayal of an actual individual, his effort was a complete failure. He succeeded greatly, however, in fanning the flames of the Authorship Controversy.

Shakespearians ever since have cursed and derided young Martin Droeshout for missing his opportunity of making a worthy portrait of Shakespeare. Ludicrous, grotesque, monstrous, inane, are among the terms applied to his engraving. Schoenbaum in *Shakespeare's Lives* lists some of its deficiencies.

> In the Shakespeare engraving a huge head, placed against a starched ruff, surmounts an absurdly small tunic with oversized shoulder-wings ... The mouth is too far to the right, the hair on the two sides fails to balance. Light comes from several directions simultaneously: it falls on the bulbous protuberance of forehead – that 'horrible hydrocephalous development', as it has been called – creates an odd crescent under the right eye, and (in the second state) illuminates the edge of the hair on the right side.

Even the printers of the First Folio had little respect for their title-page engraving, for they altered it twice as their edition went through the press, adding a shadow on the ruff below the shapeless ear. For the Fourth Folio of 1685 the plate was re-engraved to make the features less wooden. Shakespeare's face was darkened and acquired highlights, giving it a greasy look, while the moustache was enlarged and further stubble was dotted round the chin. In its various stages the Droeshout picture expresses all the most wretched qualities which anti-Stratfordian writers have attributed to Shakspere, from stupidity to villainy.

In the most rumbustious of Baconian books, *Bacon is Shake-speare*, Sir Edwin Durning-Lawrence triumphantly laid bare the secret of the Droeshout portrait. According to his assertion, 'There *is* no question – there *can be* no possible question – that in fact it is a cunningly drawn cryptographic picture, shewing two left arms and a mask.' His suspicions were aroused by Droeshout's clumsy treatment of Shake-speare's right arm. 'Every tailor will admit that it is not and cannot be the front of the right arm, but is, without possibility of doubt, the back of the left arm.' Professional reviewers in *The Tailor and Cutter* (9 March 1911) and *The Gentleman's Tailor* (April 1911) duly admitted the fact.

The printers of the Fourth Folio edition of Shakespeare's plays in 1685 had so little confidence in the Droeshout portrait that they had it re-engraved. The figure was given a more rounded, more life-like appearance by the addition of shadows and highlights.

Shakespeare's expressionless face, continued Durning-Lawrence, is definitely an actor's mask. The ear is part of it, and the edge of the mask can be seen in the thick line downwards from the earlobe.

Baconians have found great significance in these observations, but there is no obvious message in the alleged depiction of two left arms, and the dark line from the ear could merely be bad drawings. It does seem strange, however, that such a stiff, incompetent work by an obscure apprentice should have been chosen to represent the Author in the First Folio. The publishers of that volume were either giving poor value to their subscribers by hiring the cheapest engraver they could find, or else they were unable to display the true features of their author and so put in his place a lifeless effigy, perhaps a mask.

Jonson's lines to the Droeshout portrait are headed, 'To the Reader':

> This Figure, that thou here seest put,
>   It was for gentle Shakespeare cut;
> Wherein the Graver had a strife
>   With Nature, to out-doo the life:
> O, could he but have drawne his wit
>   As well in brasse, as he hath hit
> His face; the Print would then surpasse
>   All, that was ever writ in brasse.
> But, since he cannot, reader, looke
>   Not on his Picture, but his Booke.
>
>   B.I.

These lines seem lightly apposite, but there is a playful, almost flippant tone to them which even Stratfordian critics have noticed. Greenwood believed that Jonson was writing tongue-in-cheek, outwardly commending the portrait while, by subtle ambiguities of phrase, quietly mocking it. Some of Jonson's key words have alternate meanings which completely alter the sense of his poem. 'For gentle Shakespeare' could mean 'instead of gentle Shakespeare'; 'out-doo' could mean 'erase'; 'hit' was sometimes used to mean 'hid'. The word 'brasse', curiously repeated, prompts the idea of something brazen, suggesting bare-faced trickery. Droeshout's engraving was not in brass but in copper. Jonson in these verses does just enough to arouse suspicions, but without giving anything away. The most that can be said is, as the Baconian Walter Begley said in his book, *Is it Shakespeare?*, 'There is more here than meets the eye.'

Once suspicions are aroused there is plenty for them to feed on. After Droeshout's effort, the second picture of Shakespeare to be published was seventeen years later in a pirated edition of his poems. As shown opposite, it is a remarkable travesty. The lines below the picture are a pastiche of Jonson's commendatory poem in the Folio, and the man who published and sold the edition was called John Benson, an inversion of Ben Jonson. His introduction 'To The Reader' was signed I.B., a reversal of Jonson's B.I. below his verse 'To the Reader' in the Folio. Also inverted is the picture of Shakespeare, adapted from the Droeshout but turned the other way round. Most disturbing of all are the question marks in the verse beneath it. As printed, the first two lines read:

> This Shadowe is renowned Shakespear's? Soule of th'age
> The applause? delight? the wonder of the Stage.

This Shadowe is renowned Shakespear's? Soule of th'age
The applause? delight? the wonder of the Stage.
Nature her selfe, was proud of his designes
And joy'd to weare the dressing of his lines;
The learned will Confess, his works are such,
As neither man, nor Muse, can prayse to much.
For ever live thy fame, the world to tell;
Thy like, no age, shall ever paralell.

In the second, 1640 edition of Shakespeare's Sonnets, William Marshall's engraving, adapted from the Droeshout portrait, is followed by lines which parody Jonson's poem to Shakespeare and make a travesty of it by the insertion of question marks.

These lines make mockery of Jonson's tribute to Shakespeare. And instead of 'This Figure', as Ben Jonson called the Droeshout, John Benson refers to his Shakespeare picture as 'This Shadowe'. It looks as if someone is having a game with us.

A Baconian point arises from Jonson's wish that the engraver of Shakespeare's portrait had been able to draw his wit as well as he had 'hit' his face. The same sentiment was expressed on a miniature portrait of Francis Bacon at the age of eighteen, painted by Nicholas Hilliard. Round the top of the oval painting is inscribed, *Si tabula darentur digna animam mallem* (If only his mind could have been depicted this would have been a worthy portrait!) It is possible, therefore, that Jonson was cryptically alluding to Bacon; but it may just be a coincidence. The notion of drawing a picture of someone's great mind was not original, and other poets of the age made use of it.

Jonson's concluding advice to Shakespeare's readers, that they should look 'Not on his picture, but his Booke', directly touches the author and readers of this book. We should, says Jonson, be reading Shakespeare rather than looking at his image and wondering who he really was. That sounds like good advice, but it may not be entirely disinterested. Jonson's intention in the First Folio was to link the plays of Shakespeare to the name of an almost forgotten actor, obscurely buried in Stratford-upon-Avon and beyond easy reach of enquiry. That was his business, but it has nothing to do with us today. We are quite free to ignore his advice, look upon Shakespeare's picture, examine the life of the man it is supposed to represent, and decide for ourselves whether Will Shakspere or someone else is the most likely candidate for the authorship of Shakespeare. Before making that decision, we shall probably have to read Shakespeare.

THE RIDDLE OF THE STRATFORD BUST

Apart from the Droeshout engraving, the only portrayal of Shakspere which has any plausible claim to authenticity is the bust on his monument in Stratford parish church. The monument was erected some time in the seven years between Shakspere's death and 1623, when Leonard Digges made mention of it in his poem for the First Folio.

> . . . when that stone is rent,
> And Time dissolves thy Stratford Monument,
> Here we alive shall view thee soon. This Book,
> When brass and marble fade, shall make thee look
> Fresh to all ages.

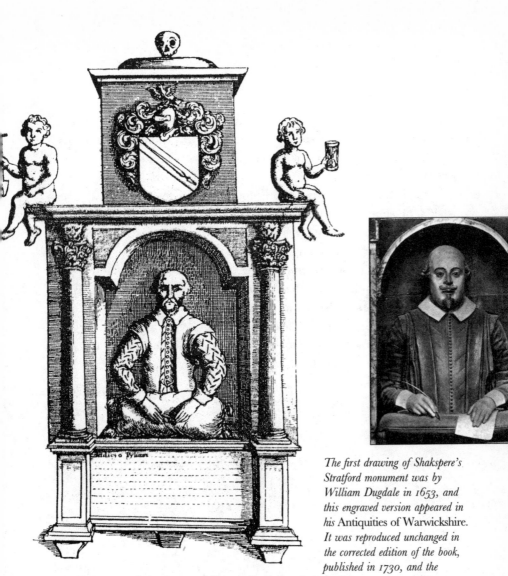

The first drawing of Shakspere's Stratford monument was by William Dugdale in 1653, and this engraved version appeared in his Antiquities of Warwickshire. *It was reproduced unchanged in the corrected edition of the book, published in 1730, and the early Shakespeare editors, Rowe and Hanmer, both showed views of the monument similar to Dugdale's. This early Shakspere is curiously unlike the Stratford bust in its present condition. His features are different, and instead of writing on a cushion he clutches a sack, possibly a symbol of his local trade. The inscription below wrongly states that Shakspere was interred within the monument.*

Time has already affected Shakspere's monumental effigy. On several occasions it has been taken down, repaired and repainted, beginning in 1749 when it was 're-beautified', and there are serious doubts about the extent to which it has retained its original aspect. Its early history has dissolved almost completely. It is not known who commissioned the monument, or paid for it, or composed the lines below it. According to a

89

note, dated 1653, in the diary of the Warwickshire antiquarian, Sir William Dugdale, it was constructed by a stonemason 'one Gerard Johnson', who also made the Stratford tomb of Shakspere's friend and fellow usurer, John Combe.

Shakspere's bust has dismayed generations of pilgrims to his Stratford shrine. This crude, blankly staring image of a portly, middle-aged burgher is a caricature rather than an actual portrait of anyone. Shakespearian biographers are united in their scorn for it. Sir Sidney Lee condemned its 'mechanical and unintellectual expression'. John Dover Wilson saw 'a self-satisfied pork-butcher'. Samuel Schoenbaum criticized its close-set eyes, exaggeratedly high eyebrows, the gaping mouth and 'a nose, too small for the face, placed between plump, sensual cheeks'.

The artificially curled up moustache, separated from the nose by an unnatural gap, is quite unlike the Droeshout's thin stubble. A less appropriate image of any poet, let alone the great Shakespeare, could hardly be imagined. The only reassuring feature of the effigy is the pen in the right hand, held next to a sheet of paper. This alone indicates that a portrait of a literary man was intended.

George Vertue's sketch of 1737 indicates that by that date Shakspere's hand was holding a quill.

There is evidence, however, that the pen and paper were later additions to the effigy. In about 1653, when the monument was still quite new, Dugdale made a drawing of it for his *Antiquities of Warwickshire* (1656). His engraved plate, shown on page 89, shows a monument and bust very different from those seen today. Shakspere's face is gaunt and gloomy, his moustache droops downwards, and instead of holding pen and paper, his hands are spread across a sack or cushion, as if clutching it to his stomach. Both the bust and the monument around it are so unlike their present forms that, if Dugdale was accurate, they must since his time have been considerably remodelled.

In *Murray's Monthly Review*, April 1904, Charlotte Stopes, an indefatigable searcher of records for items bearing on Shakspere's life, drew attention to the

The illustrator of Shakspere's bust in Rowe's 1709 account of his life followed Dugdale in omitting the quill.

discrepancies between Dugdale's representation of the monument and its present appearance. She discovered that, in 1746, a sum of money had been raised at Stratford for the purpose of 'repairing and beautifying' Shakspere's monument, including the bust, which had become 'much impaired and decayed'. After two or three years' delay, the committee administering the fund entrusted the repairs to a local craftsman, John Hall, described as a 'limner' or painter. Mrs Stopes argued that he must have worked with a sculptor to make good the damaged stonework of the monument, and she believed that the two of them had made a radical reconstruction. By skilful insertions of stone and cement, they plumped up Shakspere's face, altered his moustache and remade his clothing. Then they scraped down the cushion to make a desk, placed the paper on it and adapted the right hand to hold a pen. The model for this new Shakspere, she suggested, was a fanciful illustration of the Stratford bust, done by Gravelot for Sir Thomas Hanmer's 1744 edition of Shakespeare. The pen and paper, said Mrs Stopes, were copied from an equally fanciful illustration, made nineteen years earlier by Vertue for Pope's edition. Vertue was the first artist to put a pen in Shakspere's hand (opposite). He showed it again in a sketch made in 1737. Nicholas Rowe, Shakspere's first biographer in 1709, illustrated the bust in the same way as Dugdale, with its open hands grasping a cushion, as shown on page 91.

Charlotte Stopes was a firm anti-Baconian. She had previously written a book against their heresy, *The Bacon-Shakespeare Question Answered*, and she knew their ways. It did not surprise her, therefore, that the greatest support for her theory came from the Baconians and other doubters of Shakspere. They accepted it eagerly, she wrote, 'as they do accept everything that they think can be made to seem derogatory to Shakespeare in any way'.

As inevitably as the Baconians sided with her, the defenders of Shakspere came out against Mrs Stopes and her views on the Stratford bust. The eminent folklorist, Andrew Lang, opposed her in the last of his many books, *Shakespeare, Bacon and the Great Unknown*, a refutation of anti-Stratfordian heresies. 'It is positively certain', he declared, that on the question of the Stratford monument, 'her opinion is erroneous'. Lang pointed out that technically it was quite impossible for a stonemason to have reshaped the stone statue in the way Mrs Stopes suggested. A completely new bust would have had to be made, whereas records show that John Hall, limner, was told to do no more than repaint and restore it as near as possible to the original. Moreover, it was obvious to Lang and other critics that the existing bust was not an eighteenth-century, Georgian artefact, but typically Jacobean.

Andrew Lang's conclusion was that either Dugdale or his engraver had been careless over their illustration of Shakspere's monument in *The Antiquities of Warwickshire*. Dugdale was mainly interested in the heraldic and genealogical aspects of memorials, and in his sketch he faithfully depicted Shakspere's coat of arms, while paying little attention to his effigy or the details of its surroundings. Lang showed a photograph of the Carew tomb in Stratford church, together with the engraving of it in *The Antiquities of Warwickshire*. There are obvious differences between the two, implying that Dugdale was not such a scrupulous draughtsman as his admirers had claimed.

The argument about Shakspere's monument dragged on for years. Mrs Stopes answered Lang and other critics in her book of 1914, *Shakespeare's Environment*, reaffirming her faith in Dugdale. The Carew monument, she found, was not included in Dugdale's original sketchbook, implying that it had been drawn for him by someone else. In other cases, where Dugdale's illustrations differed from existing monuments, she explained that these had since been restored and could not therefore be called in evidence. Tombs which were still in their original state, such as that of Sir Thomas

Lucy at Charlecote, were very accurately represented in Dugdale's book. Dugdale was a Warwickshire man, born during Shakspere's lifetime and acquainted with his family. It was likely, therefore, that he would have been especially careful in drawing Shakspere's monument. His original sketch still exists, and it is apparent that his engraver copied it faithfully.

With the Stratford establishment united against her, Mrs Stopes had to find allies among her natural enemies, the Baconians. Sir George Greenwood, whose candidate for the Authorship, the Great Unknown, often resembled Sir Francis Bacon, came to her aid, producing further evidence that the bust had been considerably damaged and tampered with since Dugdale's time. In the first volume of J. O. Halliwell's sixteen-part *Works of William Shakespeare* (1853), he found it stated that in 1749, when John Hall was working on the Stratford monument, parts of its surroundings were so decayed that they had to be restored. The architraves were remade in marble, replacing the previous white alabaster. Halliwell also noted, though without reference to any original source of his information, that, at the same time, repairs had been made to the thumb and forefinger of Shakspere's writing hand. This proved to Greenwood's satisfaction that Mrs Stopes was right, and Shakspere's monument, including the bust, had been radically altered during John Hall's restoration.

Later, in 1793, the bust was given a coat of whitewash upon the advice of Edmond Malone, the leading Shakespearian of the time, because he thought it looked more dignified that way. In 1861 it was repainted in, as far as could be discerned, the original colours. Several times the bust has been taken down for the making of casts, and has incurred minor injuries, necessitating repairs. After so many known changes, and possibly others unrecorded, Greenwood concluded that, as an actual portrait of Shakspere, the Stratford bust is quite worthless.

Apart from the bald head and clumps of hair around the ears, the Shakspere of the bust has no features in common with the man depicted by Droeshout. If Dugdale's early drawing of the bust is also taken into consideration, then there are three completely different images of Shakspere, all made after his death by artists who had probably never seen him. As a guide to what Shakspere actually looked like, we have no more reliable source than personal imagination.

There is no evidence that Shakspere was ever painted during his lifetime, but many portraits of unknown subjects have been claimed as his authentic likeness. One of them is exhibited in the Birthplace, another in the National Portrait Gallery, and there are examples in prestigious collections elsewhere. Some of them are genuinely old and with interesting provenances, but they are generally very different from each other, and Shakespearian scholars are sceptical about them all.

The controversy over the Stratford bust has little direct relevant to the Authorship question as a whole. Whether or not the bust has been restored out of recognition, whether or not the pen and paper were later additions by Shakespeare cultists, there seems no doubt that the monument was raised in honour of a poet. On a tablet below the bust are inscribed the following lines:

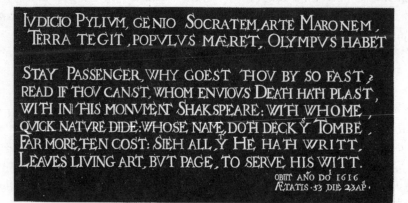

IVDICIO PYLIVM, GENIO SOCRATEM, ARTE MARONEM,
TERRA TEGIT, POPVLVS MÆRET, OLYMPVS HABET

STAY PASSENGER, WHY GOEST THOV BY SO FAST?
READ IF THOV CANST, WHOM ENVIOVS DEATH HATH PLAST,
WITH IN THIS MONVMENT SHAKSPEARE: WITH WHOME,
QVICK NATVRE DIDE: WHOSE NAME, DOTH DECK Y TOMBE,
FAR MORE, THEN COST: SIEH ALL, Y HE, HATH WRITT,
LEAVES LIVING ART, BVT PAGE, TO SERVE HIS WITT.
OBIIT AÑO DOʲ 1616
ÆTATIS · 53 DIE 23 APʳ ·

Both the composer and the sculptor made mistakes, most obviously in the statement that Shakspere lies within the monument. His remains are in fact below the church floor in front of it. There is no name on his tomb-stone, merely the crude rhyme, illustrated on page 57, which has effectively preserved his bones from desecration.

Baconians have tried to make mysteries out of these things, but the inscription is certainly original, or at least early, because it was recorded by Dugdale. It certainly refers to William Shakspere of Stratford, for the year of his birth and the date of his death are given below it, and it praises the man for his literary genius.

The first, Latin lines of the inscription mean, 'A Nestor in judgement, a Socrates in his genius, a Virgil in his art. The earth covers him, the people mourn him, Olympus has him.' The general sense of the last two lines is that Shakespeare's great works have reduced other writers to the level of his pages or servitors. As an implication that William Shakspere was the author of Shakespeare, the inscription could hardly have been clearer.

The Baconians, of course, have not been able to leave it at that. Mrs Stopes stirred them up by a deliberately teasing remark in her *Shakespeare's Environment*, that in Dugdale's illustration Shakspere's hands are laid on 'a

*Most famous of the old pictures with claims to represent Shakspere is the Chandos (top left),
named after a former owner, which in 1709 was copied as the head of the bust in Rowe's edition of
Shakespeare and was the first picture to be acquired by the National Portrait Gallery in 1856.
Below it is the fine portrait attributed to Cornelius Janssen (born 1593) which came to light in 1770.
The Grafton portrait (top right) was found in 1907 in an old inn near Darlington on the Duke of Grafton's
estate. Below, right, is the Felton portrait, bought in a London salesroom for five guineas by Samuel Felton
in 1792. Any one of these, as well as the Flower portrait (see page 17) could possibly be a true likeness
of Shakspere, but no claim has ever been proved.*

large cushion, suspiciously resembling a *woolsack*'. Her reference, of course, was to the Woolsack seat of Lord Chancellor Bacon. The hint was gratefully accepted by supporters of conspiracy theories about the monument. There is no record of Shakspere's family or anyone else having ordered it, so it could have been put up as a subterfuge, to foster the illusion that the Stratford actor was the author of Shakespeare's plays. Suspicious minds have seen more in the inscription than meets the eye. It is fair enough to compare the author of Shakespeare to Nestor, Socrates and Virgil, but they hardly seem appropriate to the local property dealer whom the people of Stratford knew. The learned Bacon was also worthy of those comparisons, and in his case they were in fact made. Francis Carr has pointed out that in 1626, the year of Bacon's death, a volume of Latin verses, *Manes Verulamiani*, was published in tribute to him. In these poems Bacon was compared favourably with Nestor, Socrates and Virgil, and they contain phrases which echo some of those on Shakspere's monument. Then, in poem number 13, Bacon is mysteriously addressed by Nature. She says, in possible reference to his hidden authorship. 'Stay your advance, and leave to posterity that which will delight the coming ages to discover. Something there is, which it is fit should be known to me alone. You, who dare to finish the weaving of this hanging web, will alone know whom these memorials hide.'

A.J. Evans, who in *Shakespeare's Magic Circle* postulated a group led by the Earl of Derby, found a resemblance between the face in Dugdale's drawing and the picture of Bacon in *Sylva Sylvarum*. Bacon was a member of his hypothetical group. The verses on the monument, though ostensibly addressed to 'Shakspeare', could well have been meant for Bacon. Evans suspected that this was part of the general deception.

A.W. Titherley, the Derbyite author of *Shakespeare's Identity* (1952), had his own theory. As a lease-holder of the Stratford tithes, Shakspere was entitled to be buried in the church. His family paid for the monument, including the original effigy in which Shakspere was depicted holding a sack of grain or malt, a symbol of his trade. Some time later, certain literary people in London, admirers of Shakespeare's plays, heard about the death of their reputed author and thought he should be commemorated in his native town. When they discovered that he already had a monument in the church, they composed a suitable inscription and, with the consent of Shakspere's family, engaged a stonemason to carve it beneath the bust. Never having been to Stratford, they did not realize that Shakspere was not entombed within the monument; hence the mistake in their wording. Nor did they realize how incongruous the inscription would look in association with the crude effigy of a small-town tradesman. The locals may have thought it odd, but in a time of political upheavals, under the Commonwealth and with official discouragement of theatrical and cultural activities, there was little curiosity from outsiders. A hundred years after the Civil War, the bust was remodelled and Shakspere's image was adapted to the inscription by the addition of a quill pen. As Titherley saw it, 'the emblem of pen and paper set a final seal, as of truth, on the false equation: Shakspere=Shakespeare'.

The orthodox Shakespearians are unmoved by all these doubts and theories. In their view, the entire discussion has been a waste of time. Modern experts have closely examined the bust which is made from one block of stone, and find no evidence that it has ever been substantially repaired. Dugdale, they say, was wrong, and so was Mrs Stopes, while those who dispute the authenticity of the Shakespeare memorial at Stratford are either misguided or simply out to make mischief.

All the same, it is a very curious fact that in Shakspere's lifetime not a single known document or reference to him by anyone in Stratford associated him with any form of literary activity. It was not until some time after his death that an unknown poet composed the verses for his monument which, for the first time in Stratford, identified him as a famous writer. Most unfortunate is the lack of history or even tradition about the erection of the monument, how it originally looked and who was responsible for the Jonson-like verses upon it. The earliest account of it is infuriatingly uninformative. In 1634, only eighteen years after Shakspere was buried, a Lieutenant Hammond wandered through Stratford church and noted a 'neat monument to that famous English poet, Mr. Wm. Shakespeere'. If only he had thought of asking the locals what they personally knew about their illustrious fellow-townsman.

THE QUESTION OF SHAKSPERE'S LITERACY

If doubts about Shakspere's authorship had to be represented by one fact alone, it could well be the fact that his younger daughter, Judith, was

illiterate: she signed with a mark. She was not alienated from her father; they lived for years in the same town and he remembered her in his will. Yet he gave her no education, not even in reading and writing. His first daughter, Susanna, who married a doctor, could sign her name, but there is evidence that she could do little more than that. If Shakspere was a learned man, the same learned man who wrote the plays, the man whom Jonson punningly described as shaking a lance at Ignorance; if he was even an educated man, he would surely have procured an education for his children.

Shakspere's parents, John and Mary, were also illiterate, so they could not have taught him reading at home. A condition of entry to the Stratford school was that the pupil should know how to read and write. But there is nothing to show that William Shakspere ever was at school, and there is nothing to indicate his degree of literacy. This chink in the Stratfordians' armour has naturally been exploited by their opponents. In *Bacon is Shakespeare* Durning-Lawrence loudly and repeatedly declared that Shakspere could neither read nor write.

Stratfordians laugh at this, but if pressed they turn angry, because it is not an easy proposition to refute. There is no scrap of evidence, no letters, notes or drafts in his own hand, to prove that Shakspere could use a pen. It is not known that he ever read or owned a book. None of the early Stratford legends credits him with any schooling or literary skills.

The only possible evidence of Shakspere's penmanship are four documents bearing altogether six of his apparent signatures. It is disputed whether he himself wrote any of them. If he did, he could scarcely have been the writer who 'never blotted a line'. The signatures are only partly legible, but it can be seen that the name is spelt in several different ways and written in several different styles (opposite). The first, on Shakspere's deposition in the case of *Bellott v. Mountjoy* in 1612, is abbreviated. The next two, also abbreviated to fit over parchment strips, are on the purchase and mortgage deeds of Shakspere's Blackfriars property. These two documents were dated on consecutive days, 10 and 11 March 1613, but lawyers have technical reasons for thinking they were signed at the same time. It seems extraordinary, therefore, that they are in two quite different scripts; this is seen most clearly in the letters 'h', 'a' and 'k'. The last two signatures are from the three on Shakspere's will; the first of the three is so worn it can hardly be seen, and is not reproduced opposite. Opinions differ about whether the other two are in the same hand.

Opinions, in fact, differ on every detail in the question of Shakspere's signatures. Most controversial are those on the will. Their shaky letters, trailing away into a scrawl, can reasonably be taken as a symptom of Shakspere's deathbed weakness. Durning-Lawrence, however, insisted that they were not written by Shakspere but by Francis Collins, his Stratford

*Shakspere's alleged signatures: top, on a
legal deposition of 1612; opposite, on his purchase
deed and (below) mortgage deed of 1613.
The last two signatures are on the second and
third pages of his will.*

lawyer, who wrote out the will. Nor were the three earlier signatures
penned by Shakspere himself, but were added by the law clerks who drew
up the documents on which they appear. By demolishing the signatures
Durning-Lawrence made room for his own contention: 'there is a probability, practically amounting to a certainty, that the Stratford Actor could
not so much as manage to scrawl his own name'.

This notion made little impression at the time. Even Greenwood and the
more moderate Baconians rejected the idea of an illiterate Shakspere and
retained belief in the authenticity of the signatures. Yet there was still the
problem of Shakspere's handwriting. Unlike most educated people of the
age, he never apparently formed a standard signature, but wrote different

versions and abbreviations of his name in different types of script. Many attempts have been made to explain this. Romantics have seen in Shakspere's carelessly scratched signatures evidence of his unworldly genius. Ian Wilson, in his recent *Shakespeare: The Evidence*, revived an old and attractive theory, that Shakspere suffered from 'scrivener's palsy', commonly known as writer's cramp.

A dramatic turn was given to this subject in 1985 with the publication, by Her Majesty's Stationery Office, of a report on Shakespearian documents held by the Public Records Office (*Shakespeare in the Public Records*). The section on Shakspere's will and signatures was written by Jane Cox, the Principal Assistant Keeper of Records. The signatures, she stated, present a problem which Shakespearean literary scholars have often failed to recognize, but which is clear enough to experts on the calligraphy of the period.

> It is obvious at a glance that these signatures, with the exception of the last two (on the will), are not the signatures of the same man. Almost every letter is formed in a different way in each. Literate men in the sixteenth and seventeenth centuries developed personalized signatures, much as people do today, and it is unthinkable that Shakespeare did not. Which of the signatures reproduced here is the genuine article is anybody's guess.

In a letter to *The Times* in 1985, Mrs Cox went even further in the direction of heresy. 'The marked discrepancies between the signatures', she wrote, 'lend credence to the views of most extreme anti-Stratfordians. Could this man write his own name, let alone anything else?'

The solution she proposed for the mystery of Shakspere's signatures was that they were all written, not by him, but by the clerks who drew up the documents on which they appear. This theory, first put forward by Durning-Lawrence, was restated in 1922 in an article by Sir Hilary Jenkinson, an expert on Elizabethan handwriting. He found that it was a practice of clerks in the lawcourts of Shakspere's time to sign statements of evidence themselves, writing the names of the witness in a different hand from that which they had used in the text. Attorneys' clerks probably did the same when drawing up conveyancing documents. Shakspere's name on the purchase and mortgage deeds of his Blackfriars property were likely to have been written by two different lawyers. He himself may not even have been in London at the time of the transaction.

The three signatures on Shakspere's will are equally dubious. Jane Cox gave examples of contemporary wills where the lawyer's clerk had himself written the signatures of the testator and witnesses. In Shakspere's will the signatures of three witnesses, Shaw, Robinson and Sadler, look suspiciously similar. They could have been written by the lawyer who took down the text of the will, and it is possible that he also signed on behalf of William Shakspere. It is not even certain whether the will in the Public Records is the original document or a transcript made for Shakspere's executor to present to the court.

Jane Cox's report left the matter undecided. She had no positive proof that Shakspere did not sign his own will, but by casting doubt on the authenticity of all his supposed signatures she undermined an important bastion in the Stratfordian defences.

Doubts about Shakspere's literacy are by no means set at rest by the evidence of his will. Ever since 1747, when it was discovered in a Stratford archive, Shakspere's will has dismayed and puzzled his biographers. Every word of it has been scrutinized for evidence of Shakspere's character, views and sentiments, but there is nothing in the least personal to be found in it.

The last page of Shakspere's will has the notorious bequest to his wife of his second-best bed inserted above the ninth line. Shakspere's lawyer, Francis Collins, heads the list of witnesses in the left column, and opposite this is the disputed signature, 'By me William Shakespeare'.

It has been called a thorough businessman's will, practical and austere. If only Shakspere had referred, even conventionally, to a 'loving' wife, a 'dear' daughter or a 'faithful' friend, biographers' imaginations would have had something to work on. The will is by far the most personal known document in Shakspere's life, but it gives nothing away and Shakespearians are bitterly disappointed by it.

The Heretics, on the other hand, make the will an important exhibit in their case against Shakspere's authorship. It is not so much what Shakspere included in his will that attracts their interest, but what he left out. Among all his detailed bequests – his clothes to his sister, a silver bowl to his grand-daughter, £1 to his godson, a sword to Mr Combe – there is no mention of a single literary item. It can be inferred from his will that Shakspere pos-sessed none of the trappings of a writer's library, not even books or manu-scripts. Nor did he lay claim to any plays or literary rights. Judged by his will alone, Shakspere was just as the Baconians like to imagine him, a man of humble education, who had become involved in the London theatre and had somehow acquired a large amount of money, enabling him to achieve his greatest ambition of living like a gentleman in his home town.

Shakspere left the bulk of his estate to his respectably married elder daughter Susanna, Mrs John Hall. His less happily married younger daughter, Judith, was appropriately looked after, and various small sums were allotted to each of his family, according to seniority. A soul-saving £10 was left to the Stratford poor, and a number of Shakspere's friends and neighbours received token bequests. The only London friends mentioned in his will were his fellow actors, Richard Burbage, John Heminges and Henry Condell, to whom he left 26s 8d each for the purchase of rings. Strangely enough, this item is the only documented link between Shakspere of Stratford and the Shakespeare of the London stage. It was a later addition to the will, inserted between two lines as if in afterthought.

Another later insertion between two lines, almost at the end of the will, is the notorious bequest to the former Anne Hathwey: 'Item I gyve unto my wief my second best bed with the furniture [bedding, bedcurtains, and so forth]'. This is a unique bequest, but since nothing is known about Mrs Shakspere and the circumstances of her life, it is impossible to be sure what her husband meant by it.

Stratfordian writers have laboured mightily to reconcile the narrow-minded property-owner of Shakspere's will with the noble-minded author of Shakespeare. If the two were identical, then Shakspere must have owned a respectable library, not to mention his manuscripts and rights in such masterpieces as *Hamlet*. The books would have been itemized among his other goods on an inventory submitted to the court by his executors for the grant of probate. Scholars such as F. J. Furnivall, who spent half the nineteenth century sifting through old court records, have searched in vain for this and other documents pertaining to Shakspere's will. Others have researched the wills of people known to have been literate, looking for those in which no books were mentioned, and apparent examples of these have in fact been found. The absence of books from Shakspere's will, therefore, is not conclusive proof of his illiteracy.

It is possible that Shakspere's books were included among the unspecified 'goods and chattels' inherited by Susanna Hall. Her husband the doctor possessed a 'study of books' which, at his death in 1635, he left to his son-in-law with instructions to 'do with them what you please'. Shakspere's books may have been among them, but there is nothing to encourage that idea; John Hall's collection does not seem to have been of much interest or value.

The mystery of Shakspere's non-existent books and manuscripts led to the first occurrence of Baconism. Towards the end of the eighteenth century a distinguished scholar, the Rev. James Wilmot, Rector of Barton-on-the-Heath a few miles north of Stratford, undertook to write a Life of Shakespeare. When he started, he had no doubts about the authorship, and felt sure he would be able to find relics and traditions of Shakspere among his Warwickshire neighbours. Reasoning that Shakspere must have had an extensive library and that some of his books would probably have passed into local collections, Wilmot made a tour of country houses, examining every bookcase within fifty miles of Stratford. Nowhere could he find a single book belonging to Shakspere, and even more surprising was the absence of any note

James Wilmot (1726–1808), the Warwickshire clergyman who first suspected that the true author of Shakespeare was Francis Bacon.

to, from or about him. There were many families in the district who had been there since before Shakspere's time. They retained memories of local legends, striking events and notable people over many generations, but they knew nothing at all about William Shakspere.

Wilmot was further puzzled by the lack of local references in Shakespeare's plays. In the course of his researches among farmers and countrymen he learnt much about the folklore of the Stratford area. He heard memorable tales of spooks, hauntings and supernatural occurrences, which were current in Shakspere's lifetime and must have been the common talk of his childhood. Yet none of this dramatic material was made use of in the writings of Shakespeare.

From his Shakespearian studies Wilmot had concluded that the author was a learned man, a qualified lawyer and expert in scientific and medical affairs. This man could hardly have developed from the uneducated youth of Stratford. Wilmot's other literary enthusiasm was for the writings of Francis Bacon, and it occurred to him that in their minds and expressions Bacon and Shakespeare were so similar that they could well have been the same author.

Wilmot did not publish or even write down his theory, and before his death at the age of almost eighty he commanded all his notes and papers to be burnt. The only record of his Baconian tendency was made by a literary man from Ipswich, James Cowell, who visited Barton-on-the-Heath in search of information on Shakspere. Wilmot let him in on the secret of Bacon's authorship, and in 1805 Cowell repeated what he had heard in a paper to the Ipswich Philosophical Society, who were outraged by this first exposition of the Baconian theory. The subject was dropped, and nothing more was heard of the Rev. James Wilmot and his advanced views until 1932, when Cowell's paper was rediscovered.

In the two hundred years since Wilmot's search, no book belonging to Shakspere or with notes in his hand has ever been authenticated. Many such have been claimed. Shakspere's supposed prayer book and his supposed copies of Bacon's *Essays*, Florio's *Montaigne* and other items have all at various times had their advocates and have all in turn been discredited. The current favourite is a copy of a 1568 legal textbook, *Archaionomia*. Shakspere's name is written upon it, and a later hand has added, 'Mr Wm Shakespeare Lived at No. 1 Little Crown St. Westminster NB near Dorset Steps St James's Park'. The signature was discovered in 1939 in the copy in the Folger Library in Washington DC. Most authorities treat it sceptically, but Eric Sams in *The Real Shakespeare* is confident that the name represents a genuine seventh Shakespeare signature. The book was suitable for a law-clerk, which he believes Shakspere to have been.

Among the many names of Shakspere which have been written in various styles on the flyleaves of old books is this specimen in a legal textbook owned by the Folger Shakespeare Library in Washington DC.

Shakespeare forgeries have been rife over three centuries; even more signatures than portraits of the man have been fabricated, and scholars are naturally suspicious of all claimed examples that lack good provenance. Sams insists that they are just being obstinate, and quotes several experts in favour of the *Archaionomia* signature. The trouble with this and all expert opinion on alleged new Shakspere signatures is obvious. Even if the six conventional but disputed signatures are in fact genuine, they are so shaky and so different from each other that handwriting specialists have no firm basis either for confirming or disputing any alleged specimen of Shakspere's script. Every claim that has been backed by some experts has always been rejected by others.

The traditional orthodoxy, that William Shakspere was the author of Shakespeare, is so deeply established that it seems ridiculous to maintain that he could not even read and write. It is not easy, therefore, to take seriously Durning-Lawrence's contention that he could do neither. His father managed to conduct substantial business, private and civic, without the benefit of letters, but William's generation was better educated. The London actors admired Shakspere's unblotted lines. Even if he was a mask for the real Shakespeare, the conspirators would hardly have picked on a man incapable of writing. Nor would his Stratford neighbour, Richard Quiney, have written him the letter about a loan if he had thought that he could not read it. These, of course, are mere probabilities. In actual fact, the Stratfordians are in the embarrassing position of having no clear, material proof to counter the argument that Shakspere was totally illiterate.

SHAKSPERE AS CANDIDATE: THE PROS, CONS AND THE SILENCES

The case for William Shakspere of Stratford has classical simplicity, giving it an initial advantage over the more complicated cases for all rival candidates. The Stratfordians rely upon firm tradition. Shakspere's name, with adapted spelling, appeared on the title-pages of plays and poems and, even though neither he nor anyone else in his lifetime clearly identified the actor with the author, no one openly challenged the attribution. Two of his poems were dedicated to the Earl of Southampton who never acknowledged the honour, but neither did he repudiate it. Shakspere's family and neighbours neither acclaimed nor disclaimed the great poet in their midst. His fellow actors and impresarios must have known whether or not he was the real author of the plays they were staging. They never expressed doubts about Shakspere's claim, and two of them, Heminge and Condell, certified his authorship of the plays in the First Folio.

The Folio of 1623 is one of the twin pillars of Stratfordian orthodoxy. The other is the poem inscribed below Shakspere's bust in Stratford's Holy Trinity church which was put there soon after his death, and records that Shakspere was the greatest writer of his age. No matter that the bust may have been changed or tampered with; the inscription beneath it is early and unequivocal.

Everyone concerned with the First Shakespeare Folio – the printers who saw the original texts, the two players who edited it, the two earls who received its dedication and the four poets, including Ben Jonson, who wrote verses for it – openly or tacitly accepted the declared authorship. Jonson addressed his poem, 'To the memory of my beloved, the Author, Mr William Shakespeare: and what he hath left us', and he was specific with his pun on the author's name ('shake a lance') and his 'Swan of Avon' epithet. Leonard Digges with his reference to Shakspere's Stratford monument plainly acknowledged his authorship of the Folio's contents.

The most powerful and compelling defence of William Shakspere is that none of the actors and theatre people who must have known him in London ever openly disputed his authorship of plays. This is a serious problem for the anti-Stratfordians, and their responses to it reveal a serious discrepancy in their argument. The true identity of Shakespeare, they say, was a close secret, known to very few people and thus easily maintained. Yet the conspiratorial group inevitably widens. Many cryptic references to the Authorship mystery by many contemporary writers are detected by the Heretics. If they are right, it would seem that almost every writer of the time was in on the secret, and in that case, if the secret was so widely known, it was really no secret at all. The idea of a concealed Shakespeare, someone other than the man from Stratford, is thus made ridiculous.

The orthodox teaching is that, although Shakspere's life is largely a mystery, there is no evidence worth looking at against his traditional claim to the Authorship. Shakspere's twin pillars stand intact. The Heretics may make mysteries, raise doubts and quibble as they please, but unless they can find proof for some other candidate, Shakespeare is respectably identified as Will Shakspere of Stratford-upon-Avon.

It is only when Stratfordians descend into the arena and argue the matter on the Heretics' grounds that perplexities arise. These are inevitably caused by the central paradox of the Authorship question, the discrepancy between the life of Shakspere and the mind of the person who wrote Shakespeare. On the one hand a bookless provincial trader, on the other a universal genius of refined education. How can the two possibly be matched?

This question splits the Stratfordians into two opposite camps, one of which includes the romantics and mystics. These make light of Shakspere's educational deficiencies. They follow Jonson's line, that though Shakspere was far from being a classical scholar, he could defeat the Romans at their own game and outdo all the ancient poets and philosophers. He was a born genius, a child of nature, and such people need no great stock of book learning to be capable of inspired writing, far exceeding anything that a mere pedant or scholar could produce. Shakspere's knowledge came to him directly through mystical channels.

The other, more modern approach to reconciling Shakspere with Shakespeare is by taking a high view of the education provided at the Stratford grammar school, while playing down the classical, legal and other types of rarefied knowledge found in the plays. The Stratford school syllabus has not survived, so if Shakspere went to that school, there is no telling what he might have learnt there. Nor is there any indication of where or what he might have studied during his the 'lost years' of his early manhood. This gap allows room for any amount of speculation, and Stratfordians can take advantage of it to explain any special knowledge attributed to the writer of Shakespeare. Aubrey claimed that Shakspere was once a country schoolmaster, and so he might have been; that would explain his familiarity with the classics. Then again, he could have worked in a lawyer's office, or served in a nobleman's household, studied medicine or theology, enlisted in the army, served in the navy, travelled in Italy. . . . Shakspere could hardly have done all those things, but it is not impossible that he did one or two of them in his early twenties, and with a certain amount of specialized knowledge combined with a quick ear for the characteristic speech of other social and professional types, he could perhaps have qualified himself as a versatile dramatist.

To most of the points raised by the Heretics the Stratfordians have managed to provide more or less reasonable answers. On other points they confess to being mystified. The *status quo* perpetuates their advantage. Unless their opponents can produce new, conclusive evidence, discrediting Shakspere or proving the claim of one or other rival candidate, Stratford has nothing to fear. Even in the barely imaginable event of such evidence coming to light, the Stratford cult is so gainfully established that Shakspere's home town would probably adapt itself to remaining the shrine of whoever was acclaimed as our National Poet.

The life of William Shakspere himself is the main reason why there is a Shakespeare authorship problem. A review of all the known, documented facts about his career gives a picture of a fairly successful local business man who dealt in land, property and rural commodities and arranged small loans upon security. He was also known on the London stage and speculated in the theatre. His will mentioned no books, manuscripts or any other sign of literacy. No one in Stratford ever acknowledged him as a writer, and he never pretended to be one.

There is nothing particularly disgraceful in this life. The anti-Stratfordians are often accused of wilfully denigrating Shakspere, and in some cases that is undoubtedly true. But the point is not that Shakspere was a bad man. Apart from his mysterious years in London, he lived much as his father had before him, and died as a respectable man of property in his own small town. Shakspere's known career was unremarkable, quite consistent with his birth and upbringing; but it is not at all consistent with his posthumous reputation as England's finest, most highly cultured poet and playwright.

This raises a paradox, and one way round it is to suppose that there was a conspiracy. It was designed to conceal the true authorship of Shakespeare by fastening it upon a former actor, living far from London in obscure retirement, who died forgotten and uncelebrated in 1616. Ben Jonson, of course, took part in that conspiracy, and also in it or aware of it were Shakspere's fellow actors and many of the leading people in literature and state affairs.

This idea has several obvious drawbacks. Conspiracy theories have a bad reputation, and respectable people are often unwilling even to consider them. Moreover, in this particular case there are such difficult questions as who organized the conspiracy, why it was necessary in the first place and how it was so efficiently kept secret.

Since there is no agreement on who Shakespeare really was, the chief player in the alleged conspiracy is unidentified. If he was a powerful noble-man or statesman, silence might have been necessary to protect his repu-tation. Writing plays for public performance was not a respectable occupation for such a person. That does not really explain why and how, if the authorship was a secret, that secret was so effectively maintained. A possible reason is that Shakespeare's plays had a hidden meaning and purpose, and that some group or movement used them as a means of instilling their influence secretly into the public mind. The Rosicrucians have been suspected, so have the Jesuits, and some have seen Shakespeare as conveyor of government propaganda.

The greatest difficulty with the conspiracy theory is that many people must have been in the secret, yet no one ever spoke out about it and no reference to it has been found in any private, official or state document. In dealing with this, the theorists emphasize the dangers of free speech in the days of Queen Elizabeth. Theatres, plays and players were all licensed and subject to strict control. Plays were more or less the 'media' of the time; they were censored and made to reflect government policy. Writers and dramatists were constantly under threat of imprisonment or painful death for anything in their works that might be thought seditious. In 1597 Thomas Nashe was sent to the Fleet prison for his part in writing a 'slanderous' play, *The Isle of Dogs*; all copies of it were destroyed and the theatre that showed it was closed. Marston and Chapman, Kyd, Jonson, Daniel and others were arrested on similar charges. It was far easier to enforce silence on a forbidden topic in Elizabethan London than it has ever been since, even in Stalin's Russia.

One way of perpetuating a secret is by the destruction of tell-tale documents. A significant feature of Shakspere's life-history, which has often been commented on, is that virtually all the records that would have referred to him have mysteriously vanished. That is why so little is known about him. No scrap of his own letters or manuscripts has survived, nor have the records of his school years, his theatrical tours or anything he ever said to anyone. The deeds of his Stratford properties are missing, and so is that part of his son-in-law John Hall's diary covering his lifetime. Time and again, as Charlotte Stopes found when she combed the public records in London for evidence of Shakspere's acting career, there are gaps in the record just where his name might be expected to appear. The suspicion is that someone or some agency, backed by the resources of government, has at some early period 'weeded' the archives and suppressed documents with any bearing on William Shakspere and his part in the Authorship mystery.

Then there are the silences, most disconcertingly Philip Henslowe's. According to his biographers, Shakspere probably made his name in the theatre by writing and acting for Henslowe, owner and manager of the Rose and other playhouses. It was therefore an exciting moment when Malone at the end of the eighteenth century discovered Henslowe's working diary, a folio manuscript covering the years 1592 to 1603 with memoranda from before and after those dates. Recorded in it were details of all his theatrical enterprises, his receipts from performances and the sums he paid to dramatists. There were frequent entries for payments to Jonson, Dekker, Chettle, Marston, Middleton, Drayton and a dozen others among the leading theatre-writers of the time, yet Shakspere received not a single mention. This was at the height of Shakespeare's literary career. Henslowe bought and staged a number of plays with the same titles as those later printed in the Shakespeare Folio, including *Titus Andronicus, Henry V*,

*Edward Alleyne (1566–1626) from a portrait
by an unknown artist.*

Henry VI, King Lear, Hamlet and *The Taming of the Shrew*, but none of these was attributed to Shakespeare, nor did William Shakspere receive money for them. For *Troilus and Cressida* Henslowe recorded two part payments to Thomas Dekker and Henry Chettle whom he took to be its co-authors.

Equally silent was Edward Alleyne, Henslowe's stepson-in-law and business partner. He was an educated actor, a theatre owner and the founder of Dulwich College. In his notes and papers he wrote down the names of every notable actor, poet and dramatist of Shakspere's time, and he noted every payment to and transaction with everyone connected with his theatre enterprises. Yet here again, the name of Shakspere or Shakespeare is entirely absent.

Another unexpected silence was Michael Drayton's. Born the year before Shakspere, in the same county of Warwickshire, he was his contemporary in the London theatre world, a poet, dramatist and writer of sonnets. While Shakspere was in Stratford, Drayton often stayed with friends at Clifford Chambers, a village only two miles away. He certainly knew Shakspere's family, for he was a patient of Dr John Hall, who once treated him for a 'tertian' (fever) by dosing him with syrup of violets. Drayton wrote many letters to and about other literary figures, made verses to his fellow poets and received their verses to commend his own works. He should have known Shakspere, but he gave no sign of it and, during the lifetime of his Stratford neighbour, never mentioned his name. Finally in 1627, when Shakspere was many years dead, he produced four lines of tepid, impersonal praise in the Elegies which ended his poem, 'The Battaile of Agincourt'.

> SHAKESPEARE, thou hadst as smooth a comic vein,
> Fitting the sock, and in thy natural brain,
> As strong conception, and as clear a rage
> As any one that trafick'd with the stage.

This says little more about Shakespeare than that he 'trafficked' or had dealings in the theatre. It contrasts with the Elegies in which Drayton celebrates the genius of Spenser and other poets.

Only at the very end of Shakspere's life is there any hint of a link between him and Michael Drayton. Forty-six years after Shakspere's death, the new Stratford vicar, John Ward, noted in his diary a story he had heard locally, that Shakspere had succumbed to a fever after a drinking bout with Drayton and Ben Jonson. Drayton was in fact noted for his temperance; neither he nor Jonson ever referred to the incident, and it is generally supposed to be apocryphal.

The silence of a little-known man, John Chamberlain the letter-writer, is perhaps the strangest of all. His lifespan (1553–1627) bracketed Shakspere's (1564–1616), and he was very interested in the London theatre and its personalities. Many of his letters are

Michael Drayton (1563–1631), the Warwickshire poet.

held in the British Library and Public Record Office. They were written to keep his friends informed about every aspect of life in the capital, and they are valued by historians because they often give details of events otherwise unrecorded. It is almost incredible that Chamberlain said not a word about Shakespeare. James Spedding remarked on his silence in his *Life and Times of Francis Bacon*.

> In the long series of letters from John Chamberlain to Dudley Carleton, scattered over the whole period from 1598 to 1623 – letters full of news of the month, news of the Court, the city, the pulpit and the bookseller's shop, in which court masques are described in minute detail, authors, actors, plot, performances, reception and all – we look in vain for the name of Shakespeare.

Also in vain has been the search for Shakespeare's name in the letters and writings of Sir Henry Wotton (1568–1639), the poet, diplomat and traveller who ended up as Provost of Eton. Throughout his life he was a prolific correspondent, and a great many of his letters to Francis Bacon and other interesting people have been preserved. Among his published works was a 'Collection of Lives, Letters, Poems, with Characters of Sundry Personages etc.' with extensive allusions to the wits and writers of his period, but with the glaring exception of Shakespeare. Even in his detailed account of the burning of the Globe Theatre in 1613, during a performance of Shakespeare's *King Henry VIII*, Wotton never mentioned the playwright.

In this and other cases, where Shakespeare's name was surprisingly omitted from lists of contemporary writers and poets, the Stratfordians offer explanations, and sometimes plausibly. No single silence is entirely fatal to the Orthodox belief. It is the unanimity of silence that is so impressively disconcerting. This has never been explained. Apart from Jonson, whose remarks on Shakespeare are strangely inconsistent, none of his literary contemporaries seems to have known much about him, and whatever they did know they kept to themselves.

The life of William Shakspere, factually examined, gives no independent support to his traditional identification as Shakespeare. Yet successive waves of anti-Stratfordian theorists have broken in vain upon the rock of Orthodoxy. Shakspere may seem an unlikely candidate, but no conclusive case has yet been made for any of his rivals. The following investigation of their various claims is aimed at striking a balance of probabilities rather than at the goal of positive proof. The truth about Shakespeare may one day emerge, but only when new evidence is discovered; and that is most likely to happen when scholars diversify their efforts, and research the lives and claims of other possible candidates with the same obsessive attention that they have devoted to William Shakspere.

V

BACON AS SHAKESPEARE

FRANCIS BACON

Philosopher, scholar, natural scientist, lawyer, courtier, statesman.

1561 22 January. Born in London at York House in the Strand, youngest son of Sir Nicholas Bacon, Lord Keeper of the Seal, and his second wife, Anne Cooke, classical scholar and Puritan, whose sister was married to William Cecil, Lord Burghley. Childhood and education at his father's house, Gorhambury, St Albans. A serious, precocious boy, delicate and sickly.

1573 With his brother, Anthony, went to Trinity College, Cambridge. Disappointment with the quality of scholarship there prompted his life's work of reforming education and learning.

1576 June. Admitted with Anthony to Gray's Inn to study law. September. Went to the Embassy in Paris under Sir Amyas Paulet to study politics.

1579 February. Death of Sir Nicholas Bacon. Francis received no inheritance and was often thereafter in financial trouble. Returned to Gray's Inn. Produced plays for courtly entertainments. Became a barrister in 1582.

1584 Entered Parliament as MP for Melcombe, Dorset. From then on, until raised to the peerage in 1618, served in successive parliaments, representing various constituencies, including Taunton, Southampton, Liverpool, Ipswich, St Albans.

1591 The Earl of Essex, in his early twenties, became Bacon's pupil and patron. Bacon turned to literary work and wrote that he would like to give up the law and study philosophy.

1598 Arrested for debt, relieved by brother Anthony.

1601 Rebellion of Essex, his trial and execution. Bacon took part in his prosecution.

1603 Death of Queen Elizabeth; accession of James I; Bacon knighted.

Francis Bacon from the portrait after Paul van Somer.

1604 Negotiator in the union of England and Scotland.

1606 Married Alice Barnham.

1607 Solicitor General.

1613 Attorney General.

1616 Privy Councillor.

1617 Lord Keeper.

1618 Lord Chancellor; Baron Verulam.

1621 Created Viscount St Albans.
Accused by political enemies of bribery and corruption, Bacon became ill, confessed to some of the charges and was sentenced by the House of Lords to a large fine and imprisonment in the Tower. Ejected from Parliament and his state offices. Released and granted a limited pardon by King James.

1616 9 April. Died in Highgate, having caught cold during an experiment on preserving a chicken by stuffing it with snow. Buried at St Michael's church, St Albans.

TWO GREAT AUTHORS, ONE GREAT MIND

The wide range of specialized knowledge attributed to the author of Shakespeare brings to mind one man in particular. Francis Bacon had most of the qualities listed in Chapter II. Famed throughout Europe for his great mind and learning, he was a born aristocrat, a leading statesman and courtier through two reigns, and a lawyer who rose to the top of his profession as Lord Chancellor. Almost all the learning and expertise discovered in Shakespeare's works are in subjects which Bacon knew well through his education, studies or personal experience. Shakespeare and Bacon stand together as writers of exceptional genius. They were contemporaries and compatriots, members of the same small literary world, known through their writings to the same closely-linked group of readers and theatre-goers. Yet neither of these two remarkable people ever acknowledged or mentioned the other. No one ever saw or heard of them together; no one compared their respective writings. The reason for this, according to Baconian theory, is that they were the same man. Under the name Shake-speare (the spear-shaker, in Latin *hastivibrans*, an epithet of Athena, goddess of Wisdom) Bacon chose to publish the poems and plays which, for personal and political reasons, he was unable to acknowledge as his own.

This is an attractive theory, rationally tenable and, though hotly disputed, not disproved by any of the known facts. On the other hand, despite the vast outpouring of Baconian books and journals, after more than a century of ingenious, dedicated researches, there is still no conclusive evidence that Bacon wrote Shakespeare. The main plank of the theory remains the same today as at the beginning, that Francis Bacon was the only man of his time who was capable of producing such great works.

During the first forty or so years of his life Bacon was constantly studying. Under the supervision of their learned parents, he and his brother Anthony received the traditional form of high education which today is almost unknown. Based on the classical canon of Greek and Roman authors, it included the sciences of number, geometry and astronomy, the arts of music and rhetoric and all branches of ancient learning, as well as history, European languages and literature and Biblical studies. Francis was twelve years old when he and Anthony went up to Cambridge, but he was soon complaining that the professors there had nothing further to teach him.

At an early age Francis Bacon was conscious of his own exceptional abilities and dedicated himself to the highest possible ideal. His life's work was to be nothing less than the salvation of scholarship and civilization. He was to stock his mind with all human learning, ancient and modern, systematize it upon the basis of sound religious philosophy and lay the foundations of an all-inclusive order of science which would raise humanity to a state of rational enlightenment. In a letter to his uncle, Lord Burghley, in January 1592, he stated, 'I have taken all knowledge to be my province.'

Bacon's name for his ambitious project was the Great Instauration, the regeneration of learning. Every subject that the human mind could apprehend was to be categorized and their truths established by direct observations from nature. Bacon is therefore claimed as a founder of modern science. The climax of his work was to be a complete description of human psychology showing how various types of temperaments and passions arise, how they are influenced by sex, age, health, beauty and the like, and how an individual can make himself master of his own mind by recognizing and balancing the opposite urges to which he is subjected.

The section of the Great Instauration dealing with psychology never appeared, but Bacon gave hints in his other writings about how he meant to present it. Of this type of knowledge, he wrote (*De Augmentis*, Book VII), 'the poets and historians are the best doctors'. The lessons of psychology, he wrote elsewhere, should be taught through 'visible representations' and through 'actual types and models, by which the entire process of the mind . . . should be set as it were before the eyes'. These and other remarks seem to imply that Bacon's intention was to demonstrate the interplay of passions and emotions through the medium of historical dramas. The Baconians claim that he actually did so, and that the missing fourth part of the Great Instauration consists of the plays which Bacon published under the name of Shakespeare.

There are some items in the list of Shakespeare's alleged attributes that cannot easily be explained by the hypothesis of Bacon's authorship. Francis Bacon was no professional mariner, nor was he a soldier, and Shakespeare's apparently first-hand descriptions of hunting and the sports and pastimes of the nobility seem rather too robust for someone with Bacon's delicate health and studious habits. There is nothing to show that Bacon had the experience of Denmark which some have attributed to the author of *Hamlet*, nor is he known to have travelled in Italy. These are among the weak points in the case for Bacon as the sole author of Shakespeare. Despite their similarities, the two writers are still not perfectly matched.

The similarities are nonetheless very striking. Bacon and the author of Shakespeare both had the same classically learned, legally attuned cast of mind. Both were conservative traditionalists, supporters of lawful authority and a hierarchically ordered realm. Both writers were linguistically inventive, commanding a wide vocabulary and coining new words and expressions. They each quoted from the same literary sources, often in paraphrase or with slight inaccuracies, as if drawing from learned memories rather than looking up references. They had an equal tendency towards secretiveness and were interested in subterfuges, disguises and hidden communications. There are many examples of these in Shakespeare's plays, while Bacon's addiction to ciphers and coded messages is only too well known to those who have lost themselves in the quest for a cipher in Shakespeare. Finally, both Bacon and, on the evidence of his Sonnets, Shakespeare were lovers of young men.

BACON, SHAKESPEARE AND THE 'GREEK VICE'

The first Baconian writer to assert openly that Francis Bacon was homosexual was the Rev. Walter Begley in 1903. His book, *Is it Shakespeare?*, cautiously published under the name of A Cambridge Graduate, promised in its sub-title *New Revelations*. One of those was found so shocking that the book was anathematized in *The Baconian* magazine and excluded from its list of recommended reading.

The starting-point in this subject is John Aubrey's remark in *Brief Lives*, that Bacon was *paiderastes*, a pederast. He was fair in his judgments, but 'his Ganimeds and Favourites tooke Bribes'. This is confirmed by several letters which his mother, Lady Anne Bacon, wrote to her elder son, Anthony, complaining about Francis's unsuitable companions and servants. One of the friends she objected to was a young Italian adventurer, Antonio Perez, a protégé of the Earl of Essex, who stayed with Francis in his house near Twickenham Park. 'I pity your brother', she wrote, for keeping 'that bloody Perez, yea a coach [or couch] companion, and bed companion, a proud, profane, costly fellow . . .' After Perez, Francis shared his bed and coach with a favourite manservant called Percy. This produced further letters from Lady Anne to Anthony about the disreputable company of servants, many of them Welshmen, who were taking advantage of Francis and exposing him to scandal. Bacon's Victorian editor and biographer, James Spedding, repeated an anecdote by a visitor to Gorhambury when Bacon was living there as Lord Chancellor. The attendants, he noticed, were freely helping themselves to Bacon's money, but when he mentioned it, Bacon merely shook his head and said, 'Sir, I can not help myself.' It may have been that he was open to blackmail by the young men of his household.

In 1601 Bacon was involved in a public quarrel in the Exchequer with Attorney-General Coke who, he complained, made a disgraceful accusation against him. Bacon was left speechless, but when Coke threatened him with a *capias utlegatum* (writ of outlawry), he replied that he could not do so and that 'he hunted upon an old scent'. The misdeed that Coke imputed to Bacon is unknown; Begley suggested that it was probably the old charge of pederasty.

The reason why Begley insisted at such length on Bacon's homosexuality was not to disparage his own candidate for the Authorship, but to strengthen the probability that he was the real Shakespeare. The Baconian movement, however, had made a cult-hero out of Bacon, regarded him as god-like and could recognize no human weakness in his character, least of all the unspeakable 'Greek vice'. Even in the high cause of Baconism, it was felt, the Cambridge Graduate had gone too far.

If Bacon was a lover of boys, so also was Shakespeare. That was the second part of Begley's thesis, and the evidence he found for it was mainly in Shakespeare's poems, the Sonnets above all. He also detected an unhealthy streak in the mind of the great dramatist, in his apparent obsession with cross-dressing and making his young women characters masquerade in men's clothing.

It is almost impossible to speak uncontroversially about Shakespeare's Sonnets. So much has been written about them that a lifetime would hardly suffice to read it all. Even among orthodox Shakespearians there are so many differences of opinion on every aspect of these 154 stylized love-poems that common ground is nowhere to be found. It is not even agreed whether they are genuine expressions of their author's own passions or merely poetic exercises in art for art's sake. As to the characters that feature in them – the poet himself, the Fair Youth, the Dark Lady, and the Rival Poet – guessing at their identities has long been a favourite but fruitless pastime among literary experts.

The suggestion that the Sonnets were no more than literary compositions, of no particular relevance to their author's own life, is mainly due to the difficulty in relating them to the life of William Shakspere. They are supposed to have been written from about 1593, when Shakspere was in the early stages of his London theatre work. Francis Meres referred to them in 1598 as Shakespeare's 'sugared Sonnets among his private friends', and the following year two of them (Sonnets 138 and 144) were published by William Jaggard in a pirated edition of collected poems, *The Passionate Pilgrim*, the whole of which was falsely attributed to Shakespeare. The first complete edition of *Shake-speares Sonnets: Never before Imprinted* was issued in 1609 by another pirate publisher, Thomas Thorpe, who dedicated them to a Mr W.H., mysteriously described as their 'onlie begetter'. The author gave no consent for their publication and, if they were the same sonnets for private friends alluded to by Meres, he probably never intended it. The picture they give of his psychology and passionate inclinations is very intimate. His lover's complaints are generally addressed to a beautiful youth, just approaching manhood, and he is also enamoured of a fickle, dark-eyed lady, whose faults he often compares to the virtues of the lovely boy.

In Sonnet 20 the boy is told that, if it were not for one thing (identified by the pun in the penultimate line), he would have been the poet's mistress. This was the Sonnet that so appealed to Oscar Wilde, and in which he claimed to have found the identity of Mr W.H. The starting-point to his story of 1889, *The Portrait of Mr W.H.*, was the italicized word, *Hews*, in the seventh line of the Sonnet. Taking this as one of Shakespeare's puns, Wilde imagined William Hewes or Hughes as a lovely, effeminate, golden-haired boy-actor in Shakespeare's troupe. He fell in love with the ideal youth he

A Womans face with natures owne hand painted,
  Haste thou the Master Mistris of my passion,
A womans gentle hart but not acquainted
With shifting change as is false womens fashion,
An eye more bright then theirs, lesse false in rowling:
Gilding the obiect where-vpon it gazeth,
A man in hew all *Hews* in his controwling,
Which steales mens eyes and womens soules amaseth,
And for a woman wert thou first created,
Till nature as she wrought thee fell a dotinge,
And by addition me of thee defeated,
By adding one thing to my purpose nothing.
  But since she prickt thee out for womens pleasure,
  Mine be thy loue and thy loues vse their treasure.

The 'Hews' sonnet that excited Oscar Wilde and, in its last lines despite
the 'prick' pun, reassures the orthodox that Shakespeare's love for his young
man-friend was strictly proper.

had dreamt up, and persuaded himself that the author of the Sonnets had loved William Hughes in the same way. 'You *must* believe in Willie Hughes', he told a lecture audience, 'I *almost* do myself!'

The homo-erotic atmosphere that Oscar Wilde detected throughout the Sonnets and Shakespeare's other poems was also apparent to Begley. It was a nasty business, he thought, and painful to admit, but whoever wrote Shakespeare was clearly tainted by an ugly vice, and that was why, in the Sonnets, he depicted himself as the bearer of a brand or blot that besmirched his reputation. William Shakspere could hardly have been so disgraced. By the age of nineteen he was a married man and a father, and according to John Manningham's anecdote he was a keen pursuer of women. In any case, he had no great name or reputation to lose. In Begley's judgement, the boy-loving aesthete who wrote *Shake-speares Sonnets* was most likely to have been Francis Bacon.

BACON WAS NO POET?

The Bacon-as-Shakespeare theory develops easily enough, and up to a certain point it is all plain sailing. Then suddenly it meets an obstacle and is brought to a halt. Standing in its way is the united opposition of all the leading experts on Francis Bacon. From the days of the great James Spedding, who from 1841 devoted the best thirty years of his scholarly life to Bacon studies and finally brought out seven volumes of his complete works followed by a further seven volumes of his life and letters, each successive Bacon authority has rejected the idea that Bacon was Shakespeare.

Delia Bacon (1811–59) of New Haven, Connecticut, whose Philosophy of the Plays of Shakspere Unfolded *was the first substantial anti-Stratfordian publication.*

Spedding was one of the first people to be told about the theory, before it had ever been made public. In 1853, while dining with Thomas Carlyle and his wife in Chelsea, he was introduced to a lively young American woman, Delia Bacon, the pioneer anti-Stratfordian, who initiated him into the secret of Bacon's authorship. He was struck dumb with amazement. Later he pronounced judgment: 'Whoever wrote the Plays of Shakespeare it was certainly not Bacon.'

Throughout his life Spedding remained staunchly anti-Baconian. The styles of the two great writers, he declared, are perfectly distinct and unmistakable. 'I doubt whether there are five lines together which are to be found in Bacon which could be mistaken for Shakespeare, or five lines in Shakespeare which could be mistaken for Bacon with one who was familiar with the several styles, and practised in such observation.' Bacon was a philosopher and no poet, whereas Shakespeare was the exact opposite. Henry James spoke for many other reasonable doubters on the Bacon-Shakespeare question, when he wrote in a letter: 'I find it *almost* as impossible to conceive that Bacon wrote the plays, as to conceive that the man from Stratford, as we know the man from Stratford, did.'

Many wavering Baconians have been put off by these weighty judgments, but the stalwarts point out that they are merely personal opinions. They quote Spedding's own tribute to Bacon's poetic genius. 'The truth is', he wrote, 'that Bacon is not without the fine frenzy of a poet. . . . Had his genius taken the ordinary direction, I have little doubt that it would have carried him to a place among the great poets.' The notable critics who have commented on Bacon's allusive, poetically-attuned mind include Shelley who, in his *Defence of Poetry*, gave reasons for concluding that 'Lord Bacon was a poet'.

The same opinion was expressed by a number of Bacon's contemporaries. John Davies of Hereford, whose lines to 'Our English Terence, Mr William Shakespeare' are quoted on page 55, was more effusive in praise of a great poet when, in his *Scourge of Folly* of about 1610, he addressed an ode 'To the royall, ingenious, and all-learned knight, Sir Francis Bacon'.

The *Bounty* and the *Beauty* of thy Witt
Comprised in Lists of *Law* and learned *Arts*

Each making thee for great Employment fitt
Which now thou hast, (though short of thy deserts)
Compels my pen to let fall shining *Inke*
And to bedew the *Baies* that *deck* thy *Front*;
And to thy health in *Helicon* to drinke
As to her *Bellamour* the *Muse* is wont;
For, thou dost her embosom; and dost use
Her company for sport twixt grave affaires:
So utterest Law the livelier through thy *Muse*
And for all that thye Notes are sweetest Aires
My Muse thus notes thy worth in ev'ry line,
With ynke which thus she sugers; so, to shine.

If Bacon really was a practising poet, capable of writing the verse works attributed to Shakespeare, that side of his life was carefully hidden. The only poetry he is definitely known to have written are some verse translations of the Psalms, done late in life, which are generally considered to be of little merit. It is hinted, however, that Bacon's poetic genius was more actively employed than he cared to admit. According to Aubrey's *Brief Lives*, 'His Lordship was a good Poet, but conceal'd, as appears by his Letters.' The letter which Aubrey must have had in mind was written by Bacon in 1603 to the poet, John Davies, asking for his support and urging him to bring Bacon's name to the favourable attention of King James and the court. His final request, clearly on his own behalf, was: 'So desiring you to be good to all concealed poets . . .'

In his 1604 *Apology . . . concerning the late Earl of Essex* Bacon claimed that, when Queen Elizabeth was coming to dine at his house, Twickenham Park, he wrote her a sonnet, hoping that it would reconcile her to the disgraced Earl. 'Although I profess not to be a poet', he added. The Baconian understanding of this is that Bacon did not profess because he was a concealed poet. His sonnet to Elizabeth might have been one of those which were later published as *Shake-speares Sonnets*.

A possible hint at Bacon's literary concealments is found in the postscript to an undated letter from his intimate friend, Sir Tobie Matthew. 'The most prodigious wit that ever I knew of my nation, and of this side of the sea, is of your Lordship's name, though he be known by another.' This could mean Francis or Anthony Bacon, but in his *Life of William Shakespeare* Lee says that the letter was written from abroad, and the reference was probably to the Jesuit, Thomas Southwell, a teacher of theology in Liège, whose father was a Norfolk man named Bacon.

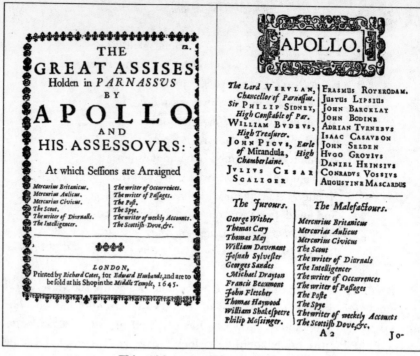

Title and first page of The Great Assises.

Durning-Lawrence in *Bacon is Shake-speare* drew attention to a work, thought to be by George Withers, which was published anonymously in 1645, as *The Great Assises holden in Parnassus by Apollo and his Assessours.* Below the title is a list of twelve arraigned Malefactors (above, left), and the next page (above, right) begins with the names of great men, the assessors under Apollo. Their leader is 'Lord Verulan', Francis Bacon, who is entitled Chancellor of Parnassus, implying that he is Apollo's chosen leader in the realm of poetry.

After the assessors come the names of the Jurors and the corresponding list of Malefactors. Durning-Lawrence showed that the Malefactors' names are simply the styles or titles of the Jurors whose names precede them. Withers is correctly described as Mercurius Britanicus, Cary was Mercurius Aulicus, the Court Messenger, and so on. Shakespeare was called 'the writer of weekly Accounts' because, said Durning-Lawrence, he was responsible for the theatre accounts, which were sent out by his clerk or attorney. The unwarranted reference to Shakspere's professional assistants was enforced upon Durning-Lawrence by his contention that Shakspere himself was illiterate.

The best evidence that Bacon was quietly known to some of his contemporaries as a poet – even as the actual writer of Shakespeare's early poems – is that of Hall and Marston, described in the following section. It is also possible (to Baconians, very probable or indubitable) that Ben Jonson gave a picture of the true Bacon, the youthful scholar, poet and secret dramatist, in his play, *The Poetaster*.

A character in *The Poetaster* is called Ovid Junior. He is supposed to be studying law, but spends most of his time writing poetry. Thus occupied, he is warned by his servant, Luscus, that his father, Ovid Senior, is approaching, and that he had better hide his 'songs and sonnets', put on his academic gown and take up a law book. Luscus rages against his master's 'poetical fancies and furies', but Ovid Junior pays no attention and goes on with his poetry. He comes to the significant couplet from Ovid's *Amores*, which Shakespeare put on the title-page of *Venus and Adonis*.

> *Vilia miretur vulgus, mihi flavus Apollo*
> *Pocula Castalia plena ministrat aqua.*

This is translated by Jonson, through Ovid Junior, as:

> Kneele hindes to trash: me let bright PHOEBUS swell,
> With cups full flowing from the MUSES well.

Ovid Senior and friends then burst into the room, and it is discovered that the young law-student is busy writing verses for the theatre. His father is furious and cries, 'OVID, whom I thought to see the pleader, become OVID the play-maker?' He continues: 'I heare of a tragedie of yours coming foorth for the common players there, call'd MEDEA. By my household gods, if I come to the acting of it, I'le adde one more tragick part, more than is yet expected, to it . . . What? shall I have my sonne a stager now?'

Ovid Junior tries to defend himself, beginning:

> They wrong mee, sir, and doe abuse you more,
> That blow your eares with these untrue reports.
> I am not knowne unto the open stage,
> Nor doe I traffique in their *theaters*.

Like Ovid Junior, Francis Bacon was a younger son, who studied law, not because he was attracted to it but because he needed a profession. Often in letters he complained that his legal duties interfered with his private, literary studies. Also like the young man in the play, Bacon engaged in theatrical enterprises. From his student days at Gray's Inn he produced a regular series of masques for the entertainment of lawyers and courtiers, probably writing much of their verse contents. These, as young Ovid said of his own productions, were not for the public stage and involved no dealings with the commercial theatre.

Up to this point, Ovid Junior and the young Francis Bacon are a close match. Their similarity becomes controversial when Ovid Senior accuses his son of writing a Tragedy for the common players. The young man's defence is that he has not made himself publicly known. If Jonson had Bacon in mind when he created Ovid Junior, his implication is that Bacon had written a play for a company of professional actors, but had not put his own name to it. From there it is but a short Baconian step to concluding that Bacon wrote at least one early play which was performed under the pseudonym of Shakespeare.

Ben Jonson might well have referred to Bacon as Ovid, because that most classically refined of Roman poets was Bacon's great literary model. Shakespeare also was deeply influenced by Ovid. Scholars find Ovidian allusions, quotations and themes throughout his writings, especially in the two early poems, *Venus and Adonis* and *The Rape of Lucrece*. The firmest claim in the Baconian case, supported by the evidence that follows, is that those two poems were the work of Francis Bacon.

The only contemporary illustration of Shakespeare's Venus and Adonis, *painted around the walls of a room in St Albans, was covered up again soon after its discovery, and only a small section is now visible. Below is a detail of the boar's head.*

'VENUS AND ADONIS': THE BACONIAN EVIDENCE

If by some wonderful chance a contemporary painting of a well-known Shakespearian scene were to be discovered in Stratford-upon-Avon, it would cause a world-wide sensation. Up to 1985 no such picture was known, anywhere. But in that year a magnificent specimen turned up. Workmen renovating an old inn removed some panelling from a ground-floor room and uncovered a large old wall-painting. The mural expert, Dr Clive Rouse, was called to see it and gave its date as 1600 or slightly earlier. He called it 'a major national treasure ... priceless'. It was 'a startling find' whose importance he could not overestimate. He knew of no better Elizabethan wall-painting 'outside the great houses like Hampton Court'.

The picture became even more interesting when experts from the Warburg Institute examined it. They recognized the subject and identified it as the end of the hunt scene in Shakespeare's poem, *Venus and Adonis*, first published in 1593, where the young hero is gored to death by a boar.

Unfortunately for the fame of this national treasure, this unique Shakespearian illustration, it is located in the most inconvenient, embarrassing spot that the Shakespeare establishment could possibly have imagined. It is nowhere near Stratford but in the very heart of enemy territory, Francis Bacon's home town, St Albans, Hertfordshire. The fourteenth-century White Hart Hotel on Holywell Hill, where the painting was found, was in Bacon's time the nearest inn to his mansion at Gorhambury, two miles away.

The St Albans mural was immediately annexed to the Baconian cause by Francis Carr, director of the Shakespeare Authorship Information Centre in Brighton (whose legal assault on the Stratford Birthplace Trust is described in Chapter III). As he saw it, Bacon, who was a prominent Freemason and probably a leading member of the esoteric Rosicrucian movement, used the room at his local inn as a convenient place for holding Lodge meetings. The scene in the mural around its walls had a ritual significance for the Fraternity, signifying the solar hero's midwinter death as a stage in his life-cycle. The boar was an emblem of winter, and Francis Carr drew attention to the similarity between the boar's head in the mural and that which Bacon used as his crest. He also found the Rosicrucian symbol, a rose, on one of the horses' heads. An enigmatic building in the mid-dle background of the picture could be a Masonic tem-ple, or perhaps a fanciful picture of Bacon's Gorhambury.

Bacon's wild boar crest.

Only one twenty-foot stretch of the mural was uncovered. It is suspected that more of it lies behind panelling still untouched. The brewery that owned the White Hart was unable to afford the cost of preserving or restoring it; most of it was covered up again, and the room containing it was made into a separate unit as a designer's showroom. Visitors can see a small detail of the picture, exposed under glass.

The Stratfordian response was to belittle the discovery. Marion Pringle of the Shakespeare Birthplace Trust said, as quoted in a newspaper, that it really had nothing to do with Shakespeare. She regretted that there were people who spent their lives trying to undermine Stratfordian Orthodoxy, and she concluded: 'Paintings like this are relatively common, and Venus and Adonis are not exclusive to Shakespeare, it is a common Renaissance theme. Using it to connect Bacon and Shakespeare is not really valid.'

The significance of the White Hart mural is clearly a matter of opinion. Baconians are entitled to make much of it, not only because of where it was found, but because of its subject. If Bacon wrote any of Shakespeare's works, *Venus and Adonis* is reasonably considered to be the most likely. It may be just a coincidence that the climax of that poem was depicted, soon after its publication, round the walls of a mysterious room near Bacon's residence, but it brings to mind another coincidence noted by Baconians. In the entire Works of Shakespeare there is not a single mention of Stratford-upon-Avon, whereas St Albans is named on fifteen separate occasions, with further references to its miracle-working saint. Three of the scenes in *2 Henry VI* are located in or outside the town of St Albans. There was 'my host of St Albans' from whom Falstaff's company of soldiers stole the only shirt they possessed between them (*1 Henry IV*, iv. 3), but unfortunately there is no reason to think that he was the landlord of the White Hart.

At the end of the sixteenth century, two writers of satirical verses, Joseph Hall and John Marston, seem to have indicated that Francis Bacon was recognized by contemporaries as the true author of *Venus and Adonis* and *The Rape of Lucrece*. This was first demonstrated by Walter Begley in *Is it Shakespeare?* H. N. Gibson, Stratfordian author of *The Shakspeare Claimants* (1962), called it 'the one piece of evidence in the whole Baconian case that demands serious consideration'.

The second book of Hall's *Satires* criticizes a certain writer disguised under the name, Labeo. The argument is that this five-letter name, containing b, a, o, is meant for Bacon. It is appropriate because Labeo was a Roman lawyer.

> For shame write better *Labeo*, or write none
> Or better write, or *Labeo* write alone.
> Nay, call the *Cynick* but a wittie foole,
> Thence to objure his handsome drinking bole:
> Because the thirstie swaine with hollow hand
> Conveyed the streame to weet his drie weasand.
> *Write they that can, tho they that cannot do:*
> *But who knowes that, but they that do not know.*

The Satire finishes with the refrain:

> 'For shame write cleanly, Labeo, or write none.'

Hall is reproving Labeo, who was evidently working with a collaborator, for improper writing. Lines 4 to 6 in the above verse are seen as a reference to the two lines of Ovid on the title page of *Venus and Adonis*, where the poet asks for inspiration from the drinking cup at the Muses' spring. The Cynick, who is also presumed to be Bacon, is told that he is a fool for letting another poet, the 'thirstie swaine' (theoretically Shakspere), wet his 'weasand' or throat from the stream, possibly meaning that he has credited himself with the Cynick's poetry. The last two lines, in italics, could be interpreted as a plea for poetry by competent writers rather than by people who cannot write yet pretend to do so. There are those who know about the pretence, but they do not speak out. All this so far is more conjecture, but it gains substance later, when Labeo is convincingly identified.

The following year, 1598, Hall published further *Satires*, and the first one, in his fourth book, alluded again to Labeo and the Cynick:

> *Labeo* is whip't, and laughs me in the face.
> Why? for I smite and hide the galled place,
> Gird but the Cynick's helmet on his head,
> Care he for *Talus* or his flayle of lead?
> Long as the craftie Cuttle lieth sure
> In the black *Cloud* of his thick vomiture;
> Who list complaine of wronged faith or fame
> When he may shift it to anothers name?

No one has ever really understood the meaning of this. Perhaps Labeo or Bacon is laughing because Hall has not succeeded in revealing his galling secret. Labeo has behaved like a cuttlefish, hiding behind a dark cloud of mystery. People cannot complain about his writings because he shifts them to another's name. As for the Cynick's Helmet in line 3, its Baconian interpretation is given by Bertram Theobald in *Enter Francis Bacon* (1932). 'It is tolerably plain that Hall is speaking of the "Honourable Order of the Knights of the Helmet", described in Bacon's *Gesta Greyorum*, produced at Gray's Inn in 1594, and thus pointing to him as the author of *Venus and Adonis*.'

Elsewhere in his *Satires* Hall seems to hint at Labeo's connection with Shakespeare's early poems, but his identity is never disclosed. John Marston, however, Hall's colleague and literary enemy, knew perfectly well who Labeo was meant to be, and he gave the game away in his poem, *Pigmalions Image*, also published in 1598. His appendix to it contains these lines:

> So Labeo did complain his love was stone,
> Obdurate, flinty, so relentless none;
> Yet Lynceus knows that in the end of this
> He wrought as strange a metamorphosis.

The first two lines are a paraphrase of lines 199–200 of *Venus and Adonis*, which occur in a speech by the goddess to her unwilling boy lover:

> Art thou obdurate, flinty hard as steel –
> Nay, more than flint, for stone at rain relenteth?

The metamorphosis in Marston's verse clearly refers to the last episode in the Shakespeare poem, where the slain youth is transformed into a flower.

These clues, and the fact that *Pigmalions Image* is a love poem in the style and metre of *Venus and Adonis*, identify Labeo as the author of Shakespeare's first poem. Yet there is still no indication of who he was meant to be. That secret is finally revealed in one of Marston's *Satires*, number 4, entitled 'Redactio'.

Hall's *Satires* were full of spiteful attacks on his literary contemporaries, either under their own names or, as in the case of Labeo, veiled. Marston's reply to these was published three months later. In 'Redactio' he defended all the prominent writers whom Hall had vilified – but with one exception. Labeo, one of Hall's prime targets, was never mentioned. Yet, as Begley discovered, '*Labeo is there*, but concealed in an ingenious way by Marston, and passed over in a line that few would notice or comprehend. But when it *is* noticed, it becomes one of the most direct proofs we have on the Bacon-Shakespeare question, and what is more, a genuine and undoubted contemporary proof.' The missing Labeo is specifically identified in a line which Marston addresses to Hall:

> What, not *mediocria firma* from thy spite?

Mediocria firma (implying, 'Hold fast to the middle course!') was Francis Bacon's family motto, belonging only to himself and his brother Anthony. So this is the conclusion: Francis Bacon was Labeo, Labeo was the author of *Venus and Adonis*, and Bacon was therefore responsible for at least some of the writings attributed to Shakespeare.

On behalf of Orthodoxy, H.N. Gibson pointed out that it is not quite as simple as that. It is quite likely, he admitted, that both Hall and Marston believed Bacon to be the secret author of *Venus and Adonis*, and thus also of *the Rape of Lucrece* which followed it. But that does not mean that they were right. 'Hall and Marston were not infallible.' He concluded: 'It may prove that Hall and Marston were the first exponents of the Baconian theory, but it does not, and cannot, prove that the Baconian theory is true.'

Strictly speaking, Gibson was right, but Hall and Marston were not just Baconian theorists. They were Bacon's contemporaries, and their evidence disproves the Stratfordian contention that no one in Bacon's time ever hinted that he wrote any of Shakespeare's works.

If, as the Baconians claim, Bacon had powerful support in keeping his Shakespeare writings a secret, Hall and Marston would surely have been persecuted for letting the cat out of the bag. In fact they were. The year after their publication, Hall's *Satires*, Marston's *Pigmalion* and other writings were suppressed and ordered to be burnt by Archbishop Whitgift of Canterbury. There was no obvious reason for this; both satirists were respectable citizens and both became clergymen, Hall a bishop. Yet Bacon was a man of influence, and if he had wanted their work suppressed he could well have called upon Archbishop Whitgift, who was his old friend and tutor.

The Baconian cult at its most luxuriant is an awesome and awful thing. Its adherents credit Bacon not only with the whole of Shakespeare, but with all the great literature of his time, including the works of Montaigne and Cervantes. It is a grand vision, and Bacon's perspective was also grand. It is easy to become immersed in Baconism. But this enquiry is strictly about the authorship of Shakespeare, and Bacon's claim has to be weighed along with those of many others. The strongest and only really substantial part of that claim is that Bacon was recognized by certain contemporaries as the author of Shakespeare's *Venus and Adonis* and *The Rape of Lucrece*.

Rational Baconians do well to concentrate upon these poems, because they present some of the gravest difficulties to the Orthodox case. The first of them was published in 1593, when Shakspere was twenty-eight, and in its dedication to the nineteen-year-old Earl of Southampton the author

Henry Wriothesley, third Earl of Southampton (1573–1624).

called it 'the first heir of my invention', presumably meaning that it was the earliest of his works. Yet several Shakespearian plays are dated to before that time, so Orthodoxy supposes that Shakspere wrote it earlier, even before he had left Stratford to find work in London. A coincidence in their favour is that the printer of both poems was Richard Field who came from Stratford-upon-Avon.

Baconians ridicule the theory that *Venus and Adonis* was written by the young Shakspere of Warwickshire. Though its author was clearly a young man, highly passionate and an admirer of ideal masculine beauty, he was also classically educated, not an inspired rustic. There is no local dialect or turn of phrase in the entire poem. Shakspere, like his father and family a Stratford townsman, would have had a rich Warwickshire accent and vocabulary. If he had been a poet, and true to himself, he could not have avoided expressing himself in terms of his native culture. A born genius he may have been, but he could not, would not, have written in the artful, elevated style of whoever wrote *Venus and Adonis*.

Another puzzle is Shakespeare's intimate and loving dedications of his poems to the Earl of Southampton. This beautiful, auburn-haired young man was a protégé of the Earl of Essex and a favourite of the queen and the court. He was much sought after, both by older, male admirers and by parents who saw him as a perfect match for their daughters. It is quite possible that he indulged in low life and had a relationship with the actor Shakspere, but it seems unlikely that he would have accepted personal dedications from such a person. Nor did he accept them. There is nothing at all, apart from the dedications themselves (shown on pages 52 and 137), to link him with Shakspere. Charlotte Stopes, who spent twenty-eight years researching her 1922 biography of Southampton, hoped to find a link, but she was disappointed and thereafter considered her work to have been a failure. Nicholas Rowe's story, that Southampton gave Shakspere £1000, was written almost a hundred years after Shakspere's death and there is no evidence for it.

It is not unlikely that Francis Bacon was an ardent admirer of young Southampton, that he made advances to him but found his response 'obdurate and flinty'. In that case, assuming that Bacon was the secret author of the early Shakespeare poems, he might well have depicted him as the obstinately chaste Adonis. That would explain the dedications more naturally than by trying to fit Shakspere into the picture.

THE NORTHUMBERLAND MANUSCRIPT: A NEAR MISS

In 1867 a significant link between the names of Bacon and Shakespeare was discovered in the London house of the Duke of Northumberland. The discovery was of twenty-two old manuscript sheets, folded in half for binding and enclosed by another sheet to provide a cover. On the front of the cover was a list of contents, together with many other words and scribblings, but it was ragged, fire-damaged and badly faded. It seemed to have come from the office of Francis Bacon, for most of the enclosed writings were his, and his name was on the top, right-hand side of the cover. It could also have belonged to Bacon's nephew and close associate, Sir Henry Neville, whose name headed the left-hand column, with his punning motto, *Ne vile velis*, repeated below it. The manuscript was dated around 1596.

The Baconian works listed on the cover, and included in manuscript, began with a masque entitled 'of Tribute or giving what is dew'; followed by four speeches, the first entitled 'The praise of the worthiest vertue'; then 'Speeches for my Lord of Essex at the tylt', 'Speech for my lord of Sussex at ye tilt an: 96' and 'Philipp against monsieur' (Sir Philip Sidney's letter of 1580 to Queen Elizabeth advising her against marriage to the Duke of Anjou); also a dissident Catholic pamphlet against the Earl of Leicester, issued anonymously in 1584 under the title, *Leycester's Common Wealth*.

The tattered and stained cover page of the Northumberland Manuscript, discovered in 1867, provides the only written link between the names of Bacon and Shakespeare. Neatly transcribed by F.J. Burgoyne (below), it has been subject to many different interpretations and provoked some exciting theories, but it falls short of proving that Bacon or anyone else was responsible for the writings of Shakespeare.

Several of the items named on the cover were missing from the collection of manuscripts within it. The Earl of Arundel's letter, probably written by Francis Bacon, 'Orations at Graies Inne revell' and the Baconian Essays were not there, nor was there any sign of 'Rychard the second', 'Rychard the third', 'Asmund and Cornelia' and 'Ile of Dogs by Thomas Nashe'.

The writing on the cover page is thought to be in two, possibly three different hands. Mr F.J. Burgoyne, the Lambeth Librarian, took on the task of interpreting it, and in 1904 he published his copy of it in modern script (opposite below), omitting much of the unclear, scribbled writing. A later, less elegant but more detailed transcript was made by A.W. Titherley for his book, *Shakespeare's Identity*. Neither of these versions is useful for answering one of the main questions about this paper: which of the entries belong to the original list of Bacon's writings and which were added as later jottings. That can only be decided from a facsimile of the original (opposite above) by those who can read the handwriting.

The provocative part of the right-hand column begins after the list of items by Bacon, which ends with 'Orations at Graies Inne revell'. The column is then indented to the right, and a line later comes the following enigmatic sequence:

> By mr ffrauncis Bacon
> Essaies by the same author
>   William Shakespeare
> Rychard the second
> Rychard the third
> Asmund and Cornelia
> Ile of dogs frmnt
> by Thomas Nashe
> William Shakespeare

One interpretation of this is that Bacon's secretary, after writing a list of his master's acknowledged works, added others by the same author which had been published in the name of William Shakespeare. These begin with *Richard II* and *Richard III*; then comes an unknown work, *Asmund and Cornelia*, and a fragment of Thomas Nashe's *Isle of Dogs*, the play that landed him in prison. The rest of the column is filled up with various repetitions of the name William Shakespeare.

Whoever wrote and scribbled on the paper clearly had Shakespeare much in mind along with Bacon. Both their names are spelt out or abbreviated many times, and on the left side of the paper is at least one allusion to a Shakespearian work. The words, 'revealing day through every Crany peepes', form line 1086 in *The Rape of Lucrece*, except that in the printed poem the day 'spies' rather than 'peepes' through the crannies. Three lines later in the poem the word 'peeping' occurs, so the writer must have known the verse well but slightly garbled the quotation. The other significant word on the paper is *'Honorificabiletudine'*, an abbreviation of the famous 'long word' in *Love's Labour's Lost*, of which more will be heard later.

Baconians have made much of the Northumberland Manuscript, and it is certainly curious to find the names and respective works of Bacon and Shakespeare so closely and uniquely associated. It is a great mystery, but unfortunately it does not prove anything. The Stratfordians see no great threat in it, and it has been used as evidence for other, non-Baconian candidates. Titherley discussed the Manuscript in an Appendix to his book. By looking closely at the indistinct parts of the writing, as well as the few words on the back of the sheet, he built up a case for his own Authorship candidate, the Earl of Derby. An expert on Derby's handwriting, he recognized it in some of the upside-down words, which must have been added by someone who casually reversed the abandoned paper for jotting notes. As the conclusion of his long, imaginative dissertation on the Northumberland Manuscript Titherley declared, 'One verdict only is possible – Shakespeare's identity with the Earl of Derby.'

This is obviously untrue. Other verdicts are quite possible, and several different ones have been given, with equal emphasis. All that is produced by such proclamations is 'sound and fury, signifying nothing'. The Northumberland Manuscript must signify something, but its message is unclear. It is typical of the clues in this subject, promising much but leading nowhere.

ACROSTICS, ANAGRAMS AND BACON'S SIGNATURE IN SHAKESPEARE

Baconians are often very reasonable, well-informed people, but below the surface of their movement is its underworld, a region of darkness and fantastical illusions. Years, decades, whole working careers have been devoted to the ever-fruitless quest for Francis Bacon's ciphers and hidden messages in the writings of Shakespeare, yet the Shakespeare decoders have made no real contribution to solving the Authorship question. It is tempting to pass them quietly by; but they have published so much, and have been such a powerful influence in the development of Baconian theory, that there is no good excuse for leaving them out. And, for all anyone knows, there may after all be 'something in it'.

In principle, there is nothing absurd in looking for hidden meanings and word-play in Shakespeare or any other author of his period. Writers from classical times onwards have been fascinated by anagrams, acrostics, word-games and the manipulation of letters. Like crossword puzzles today, they provide tests of ingenuity, but they are also used for more serious purposes, for cabalistic divination through letters and numbers or for deceiving the uninitiated. The Elizabethan poets were often necessarily cryptic. Like all good writers under censorship, they developed a system of codes and allusions to communicate with knowing readers, and they enjoyed stretching their wits with literary puns and puzzles. It is not unreasonable to suppose that Shakespeare did likewise.

Nor is it unreasonable to suppose that, if there is any form of cipher in the works of Shakespeare, Francis Bacon put it there. He was a secretive, cunning man. Aubrey was told that he had 'the Eie of a viper'; Ben Jonson spoke of the air of mystery surrounding him. He lived in a world of espionage, court intrigues, family and state secrets, where ciphers and coded messages were a routine part of diplomatic communication. In his writings he displayed an expert knowledge of such things. There is a discourse on the subject in his *De augmentis scientiarum* (1623), where he describes his own invention, the Bi-literal Cipher, which has been the starting-point for many who have looked for a cipher in Shakespeare. Bacon's account begins:

> Let us proceed then to Ciphers. Of these there are many kinds: simple
> ciphers; ciphers mixed with non-significant characters; ciphers containing
> two different letters in one character; wheel ciphers; key ciphers; word
> ciphers; and the like. But the virtues required in them are three; that they
> be easy and not laborious to write; that they be safe . . .; and lastly that
> they be if possible such as not to raise suspicion.

Encouraged by this, a great many Baconians over more than a hundred years have tried their hands at elucidating the cryptic messages which Bacon must surely have incorporated in his Shakespeare writings. Many have published books on what they have believed to be genuine, important discoveries. The scale of their ambitions has ranged from the quest for anagrams and simple arrangements of letters, giving a version of the name Francis Bacon, to lengthy decipherings of entire Shakespeare plays, from which alternative texts have been extracted, with details of Bacon's secret life-story and his reasons for masquerading under the name of Shakespeare.

For all practical purposes, the results of this vast, prolonged industry have been no more than zero. If a regular and consistent cipher could be found in Shakespeare, so that anyone who was given the key could read the same message, that would decide the matter once and for all. Even a phrase or short sentence, such as 'I, Francis Bacon, wrote this play' would be good enough, provided that it was systematically concealed. One way of doing this, much used by Shakespeare's fellow poets, is by means of acrostics. In an acrostic poem the concealed name or phrase is spelt out by the initial letters of each successive verse, or by the last letters or, to make it more complicated and less obvious, by the first letter of the first line, the second of the second line, the third of the third line and so on. The hidden words can be written backwards, forwards, downwards, upwards, with their letters at any regular interval, provided that the system used is maintained throughout. Below is an example from the Friedmans' *The Shakespearean Ciphers Examined*. It is one of the countless acrostics written by the Elizabethan Sir John Salusbury to conceal the name of Dorothy Halsall. Her name is spelt by the letters on either side of the break in each line, beginning on the seventh line and reading upwards, and the name of her husband 'Cvtbert' is concealed in the initial letters; the poet's initials, I.S., appear in the final line as the first letters of the first and last words.

> *T*ormented heart in thral*l*, *Y*ea thrall to loue,
> *R*especting wil*l*, *H*eart-breaking gaine doth grow,
> *E*ver DOLOBELL*A*, *T*ime so will proue,
> *B*inding distres*se*, *O* gem wilt thou allowe
> *T*his fortune my wil*l* *R*epose-lese of ease,
> *V*nlesse thou LED*A*, *O*uer-spread my heart,
> *C*utting all my ru*th*, dayne *D*isdaine to cease,
> *I* yield to fate, and welcome endles *S*mart.

Many researchers claim to have found significant acrostics in Shakespeare, but either they are so short that they would occur by chance in any long text, or the finder has kept to no fixed rule but has picked out convenient letters more or less at random.

Even such a normally level-headed Baconian as Walter Begley was so impressed by an alleged signature of Bacon in Shakespeare's *Rape of Lucrece* that he made it the first item of evidence in *Is it Shakespeare?* He found the gist of it in a book of 1900, written by an unnamed German author, and added some new trimmings.

Beginning with number 26 of *Shakespeare's Sonnets*, Begley pointed to the last line where the poet (presumed to be Bacon) looked forward to the day when he could 'show his head'. The tone of this Sonnet is similar to that

TO THE RIGHT

HONOVRABLE, HENRY
VVriothefley, Earle of Southampton,
and Baron of Titchfield.

THE loue I dedicate to your Lordfhip is without end: wherof this Pamphlet without beginning is but a fuperfluous Moity. The warrant I haue of your Honourable difpofition, not the worth of my vntutord Lines makes it affured of acceptance. VVhat I haue done is yours, what I haue to doe is yours, being part in all I haue, deuoted yours. VVere my worth greater, my duety would fhew greater, meane time, as it is, it is bound to your Lordfhip; To whom I wifh long life ftill lengthned with all happineffe.

Your Lordfhips in all duety.

William Shakefpeare.

A 2

Shakespeare's dedication of The Rape of Lucrece to the Earl of Southampton (left) gives clues for a Baconian message to be wrung from the first and last verses of that poem (below). The first two lines begin 'FR' 'B', and the letters above a line which can be drawn through the end of the last verse spell 'F ba con'.

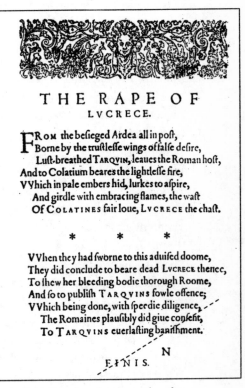

THE RAPE OF
LVCRECE.

FROM the befieged Ardea all in poft,
Borne by the truftleffe wings of falfe defire,
Luft-breathed TARQVIN, leaues the Roman hoft,
And to Colatium beares the lightleffe fire,
VVhich in pale embers hid, lurkes to afpire,
  And girdle with embracing flames, the waft
  Of COLATINES fair loue, LVCRECE the chaft.

*   *   *

VVhen they had fworne to this aduifed doome,
They did conclude to beare dead LVCRECE thence,
To fhew her bleeding bodie thorough Roome,
And fo to publifh TARQVINS fowle offence;
VVhich being done, with fpeedie diligence,
  The Romaines plaufibly did giue confent,
  To TARQVINS euerlafting banifhment.

                          N
    FINIS.

of the dedication at the beginning of *Lucrece*, addressed to the Earl of Southampton (above). The opening sentence of the dedication, 'The love I dedicate to your Lordship is without end: whereof this Pamphlet without beginning is but a superfluous Moity', is not easy to understand. Begley interpreted its phrases as clues to the poem's authorship. In the very first letters of *Lucrece* (right) Bacon 'shows his head', meaning that the large initial F, followed by the capital R and the capital B below it, comprise the monogram Fr. B., which might be called the 'superfluous moiety' of Fr. Bacon. Adding the capital A in the first line of the poem improves it to Fra. B., the exact moiety of Fra. Bacon which, asserted Begley, was how Bacon sometimes signed his name.

Also in the dedication occurs the phrase, 'without end', so Begley turned to the end of the poem and made a cunning amputation to the endings of the last two lines. This mangled the two final words of each line, leaving them as 'con' and 'ba', and by extending his cut to leave only the F in FINIS, Begley achieved the desired name, F. bacon.

This is surely unreasonable. There must be many poems which begin with From, Free, Friend or such, and in which B is the initial letter of the second line. As for the ending, the letters b, a, c, o, n, are among the most common, and examples where they occur close together can be found in any ordinary text. The F of FINIS is an added bonus, but these letters are so artificially gained that no one but a committed Baconian need see them as a genuine mark of Francis Bacon.

The example of Begley has been given, not because his claim to a Bacon signature in Shakespeare is unusually strained, but because it is one of the better efforts. The others are mostly far less convincing. Begley's lapse is odd since he declared himself 'an utter disbeliever in the cryptograms and bilateral ciphers of certain well-advertised American authors, Mrs Gallup to wit, and others'. It shows how strongly the idea of secret messages in Shakespeare has affected the minds of Baconians generally.

A happy hunting-ground for Baconian puzzle-seekers is the strange burlesque scene in *Love's Labour's Lost* (v. 1), involving the bombastic schoolmaster, Holofernes. This play, one of Shakespeare's first, was published in 1698 but is thought to have been written between six and ten years earlier. It is used as evidence by more than one side in the Authorship debate.

The passage here reproduced from the First Folio edition (opposite) has been suspected of holding all kinds of clues and cryptic allusions among its apparent nonsense. An obvious target is the line spoken by Holofernes, 'Bome boon for boon prescian, a little scratcht, 'twill serve.' This, say Shakespeare's editors, has been garbled by the printer, and they suggest various alternative readings for it. Baconians, however, have taken the line as it stands, often seeing the first five words as an anagram. Rearranging their letters, an American interpreter, Dr H.I. Platt in 1897, came up with '*Pro bono orbis F. Bacon é nemo*'. To make it 'a little scratcht' he put a scratch or acute accent on the word 'e', and translated the whole as, 'For the good of all, F. Bacon is nameless'. Platt, however, suffered the fate which threatens all anagrammatical interpreters. Far from being unique, his phrase was proved to be one of many, each making just as good Baconian or non-Baconian sense, which can be made out of the same letters.

In the same passage, in a speech by the clown Costard, occurs the famous long word, *honorificabilitudinitatibus*, and then comes a nonsensical exchange between the pedagogue Holofernes and Moth, a young page.

Page. Yes, yes, he teaches boyes the Horne-booke: What is Ab speld backward with the horn on his head?
Peda. Ba, *puericia* with a horne added.
Page. Ba most seely Sheepe, with a horne: you heare his learning.

In several ways the name, Bacon, can be wrung out of this. The sheep's Ba, together with a horn, or its older, more Latin form, corn, makes Ba-corn, which sounds like the French pronunciation of Bacon.

Line		Number of words in line in ordinary type.
	136 *Loues*	
1	*Curat.* A moſt ſingular and choiſe Epithat ,	6
2	*Draw out his Table-booke.*	=
3	*Peda.* He draweth out the thred of his verboſitie, fi-	9
4	ner then the ſtaple of his argument. I abhor ſuch pha-	10
5	naticall phantaſims , ſuch inſociable and poynt deuiſe	6
6	companions , ſuch rackers of ortagriphie, as to ſpeake	8
7	dout fine, when he ſhould ſay doubt; det, when he ſhold	11
8	pronounce debt;d e b t, not det:he clepeth a Calf, Cauſe:	13
9	halfe, haufe:neighbour *vocatur* nebour;neigh abreuiated	6
10	ne: this is abhominable, which he would call abhomi-	9
11	nable:it inſinuateth me of infamie : *ne inteligis domine,* to	6
12	make franticke, lunaticke ?	3
13	*Cura.* Laus deo, bene intelligo,	=
14	*Peda.* *Bome boon for boon preſcian,* a little ſcratcht,'twil	4
15	ſerue.	1
16	*Enter Bragart, Boy.*	=
17	*Curat. Vides ne quis venit ?*	=
18	*Peda. Video, & gaudio.*	=
19	*Brag,* Chirra.	1
20	*Peda. Quari* Chirra, not Sirra ?	3
21	*Brag.* Men of peace well incountred.	5
22	*Ped.* Moſt millitarie ſir ſalutation	4
23	*Boy.* They haue beene at a great feaſt of Languages,	9
24	and ſtolne the ſcraps.	4
25	*Clow.* O they haue liu'd long on the almes-basket of	10
26	words. I maruell thy M. hath not eaten thee for a word,	12
27	for thou art not ſo long by the head as honorificabilitu-	11
28	dinitatibus : Thou art eaſier ſwallowed then a flapdra-	
29	gon.	**151** Total
30	*Page.* Peace, the peale begins.	
31	*Brag.* Mounſier, are you not lettred ?	
32	*Page.* Yes, yes, he teaches boyes the Horne-booke :	
33	What is Ab ſpeld backward with the horn on his head ?	
34	*Peda.* Ba, *puericia* with a horne added.	
35	*Pag.* Ba moſt ſeely Sheepe, with a horne : you heare	
36	his learning.	

Page 136 in the copy of the Shakespeare Folio owned by Sir E. Durning-Lawrence, with his annotations in the margin. Lines 14–15 contain the 'Bome Boon' enigma; the 'long word' is on lines 27–28 and the 'Ba-horne' words are at the end. Cryptic significance has been seen in the page number and those in the margin.

Alternatively, C is a horned letter, and BA+C+'on his head' spells 'Bacon, his head'. Roderick Eagle in *New Views for Old* says that C) was an old abbreviation for 'con', so Ba-con is once more obtained. This play on the first three letters of Bacon's name, which form the ABC taught by village schoolmasters from a horn-book, may be deliberate, but it does nothing to prove Bacon's authorship.

Baconians have a right to be fascinated by the 'long word', because not only does it occur in shortened form on the Northumberland Manuscript, but it is known that Bacon himself played with it. A pyramid which he made from its letters is among his papers in the British Library.

ho

hono

honori

honorifi

honorifica

honorificabi

honorificabili

honorificabilitu

honorificabilitudi

honorificabilitudini

honorificabilitudinita

honorificabilitudinitati

honorificabilitudinitatibus

It has provided hours of amusement for Baconian anagrammatists, though in defiance of common sense, for the word was not invented by the author of *Love's Labour's Lost* but had been used since the fifteenth century. It is a curiosity with the same appeal to word-lovers as Disestablishmentarianism, which is the longest word in English, or *anticonstitutionellement*, the longest in French, or that small railway station in Anglesey with a Welsh name longer than its platform. Dr Platt had a go at the 'long word' and came up with:

HONORIFICABILITUDINITATIBUS

HI LUDI, TUITI SIBI, FR. BACONO NATI

The translation of this anagram gave the rather unclear meaning, 'These plays, produced by Francis Bacon, guarded for themselves'. Other puzzlers tried to do better. A difficulty in the anagram is that it contains too many of the letters I, and, to get round this, a contributor to *Baconiana* (April 1902) produced 'But thus I told Franiiiiii Bacon'. The explanation for this strange rendering of Bacon's Christian name was that iiiiii spells six in Roman numerals, and *six* in French pronunciation, preceded by Fran, is heard as Francis.

Then came Sir Edwin Durning-Lawrence. From its title onwards, his *Bacon is Shake-speare* admitted no doubts on the question of authorship. Durning-Lawrence was quite certain on every point, including the secret meaning of the 'long word'. It was an anagram, and its unique, correct, indisputable interpretation was:

HI LUDI F. BACONIS NATI TUITI ORBIS

These plays, F. Bacon's offspring, are preserved for the world.

Durning-Lawrence knew that the long word was far older than Bacon's time, but he was not given to doubts and uncertainties, so it never worried him that Bacon could not have designed it to hide his *Hi ludi . . .* anagram. For one thing, he claimed, the line formed a perfect Latin hexameter, and there was further evidence of its esoteric significance. The proof was arithmetical, depending at one stage on calculation of the numerical value of the long word. This is found by the number equivalents of the 24 letters (pairing i with j and u with v) of the old English alphabet.

a	b	c	d	e	f	g	h	i	k	l	m	n	o	p	q	r	s	t	v	w	x	y	z
1	2	3	4	5	6	7	8	9	10	11	12	13	14	15	16	17	18	19	20	21	22	23	24

This makes the combined values of all the letters in *honorificabilitudinitatibus* equal to 287 or 136+151; there are 27 letters in the word, and – here is the marvel – the word is printed on the 27th line of page 136 of *Love's Labour's Lost*, where it is the 151st word set in ordinary as opposed to italic type.

The number of Bacon by the above reckoning is 33, and the 33rd line of the page is the line identifying Bacon: 'What is Ab speld backward with a horn on his head?' As he elaborated his discoveries, Durning-Lawrence worked himself into a state of triumphant amazement. 'It surpasses the wit of man', he wrote, to produce from the long word another anagram with the same qualities. He offered a hundred guineas (worth about £5000 in today's money) to anyone who could do it. The challenge was taken up by a Mr Beevor of St Albans, who made an alternative anagram:

ABI INIVIT F. BACON HISTRIO LUDIT

Be off, F. Bacon, the actor has entered and is playing.

Durning-Lawrence was taken aback, but he was a good loser and paid Mr Beevor his money.

If there was any significance in the placing of the long word, and if Francis Bacon deliberately arranged for it to appear as the 151st word in ordinary type on the 27th line of page 136 in the Shakespeare Folio, he must have worked in close collaboration with his printers. That, declared Durning-Lawrence, was indeed the case. He declared it, as always, emphatically.

> The hour has come when all should know that this the greatest book produced by man was given to the world more carefully edited by its author as to every word in every column, as to every apparent misprint in every column, than any book had ever before been edited, and more exactly printed than there seems any reasonable probability that any book will ever again be printed that may be issued in the future.

This belief, that the production of the First Folio was supervised by Bacon in every detail, down to the precise type-face in which every individual letter was printed, has been held by many Shakespeare decorders. It is the basic assumption behind all attempts at reading the hidden messages that Bacon built into his Shakespeare writings by means of his Bi-literal Cipher.

Bacon revealed the secret of his cipher in 1623. That was the year in which the First Folio was published, so he may have intended to supply the key which would eventually lead to his recognition as the true author of Shakespeare. He began by setting out the 24 letters of the alphabet, each with a corresponding, five-letter combination of a and b.

A	B	C	D	E	F	G	H	I	K	L	M
aaaaa	aaaab	aaaba	aaabb	aabaa	aabab	aabba	aabbb	abaaa	abaab	ababa	ababb

N	O	P	Q	R	S	T	V	W	X	Y	Z
abbaa	abbab	abbba	abbbb	baaaa	baaab	baaba	baabb	babaa	babab	babba	babbb

All that is required to encipher a hidden message in any open text is two different founts of print, sufficiently alike so that only those who look carefully can distinguish between them. All letters printed in one fount represent 'a', and those in the other stand for 'b'. Each letter of the hidden text is spelt out by five consecutive letters in the text actually written, so the open script has to be at least five times as long as the message concealed within it. Bacon gave several illustrations of his method. In the simplest of them the intention is to convey the message, 'Fly!', through a sentence which seems to mean the opposite.

aa   bab   ab   abab   a   bba

do   *not*   go   t*ill*   I   *co*me.

The person who receives this note sees that it is made up of two different sets of characters, one signifying 'a' and the other 'b'. The first five letters stand for aabab, giving the concealed letter F, and the next two groups spell out L and Y. Thus the receiver is apparently asked to do one thing, while secretly told something quite different. Bacon gives another longer example of the same cipher. The interior message is: 'All is lost. Mindarus is killed. The soldiers want food. We can neither get hence, nor stay longer here.' It is hidden in a passage from Cicero's first letter:

In all duty or rather piety towards you I *satisfy every body except myself. Myself* I *never satisfy. For so great are the services which you have rendered* me, *that seeing you did not rest in your endeavours on* my *behalf till the thing was done, I feel as if life had lost all its sweetness, because I cannot do as much in this cause of yours. The occasions are these: Ammonius the King's ambassador openly* be*sieges us with money: the business is carried on through the same creditors who were employed in it when you were here.*

For the purpose of demonstration, the cipher-bearing passages above are printed in a mixture of ordinary and italic type. In practice this would be far too blatant and likely to arouse suspicion. Yet if the two types are so similar that it is hardly possible to distinguish between them, ambiguities arise, confusing the interpreter. Bacon's cipher, in fact, has caused confusion on a grand scale. On the one hand, the type-setters of the First Folio used at least two different founts of print. That is the recognized fact which seems to justify a search for the Bi-literal Cipher. On the other hand, no two investigators, have ever been able to agree on which is the 'a' fount and which is the 'b', nor to which type the individual letters in the text belong. To complete the confusion, it has been shown that the printer of Shakespeare's plays used more than two different founts. The First Folio has been called a printer's pie, composed of types from many different sources. That was inevitable at the time, as print set in different types was broken up for re-use. It is not impossible to imagine that Bacon oversaw the production of the First Folio, standing at the printer's elbow and instructing him on what line and on what page every word should appear. Nor is it totally impossible that he specified the type in which every single letter should be set. It sounds unlikely, but if it was the case, Bacon was far too subtle for his own presumed purpose, to inform posterity through some form of cipher, which when discovered would be apparent to all, that he was the real author of Shakespeare's plays. If that was his intention, it has been defeated by his ingenuity. No one has yet been able to find his cipher in Shakespeare, and the natural, though not inevitable conclusion is that he did not put one there.

BACON'S CIPHER: A LAMENT FOR A LOST THRONE

The reason why it is possible to say with confidence that no one has found convincing evidence of a code, cipher or cryptic writing in any Shakespeare text is that the whole subject has been thoroughly investigated by two people who were ideally qualified to do so. *The Shakespearean Ciphers Examined* by William and Elizabeth Friedman, published in 1957, is almost unique in the Authorship literature. It sheds clear light on one aspect of a subject in which hardly anything else has been finally decided. It sums up and assesses the whole of Shakespearean cryptology, giving professional guidance in a field so large and complicated that open-minded Authorship students were previously confused and uncertain how to judge between its numerous theorists. The Friedmans were impartial experts, with no axes to grind and without emotional attachment to any particular cause. No one is abused or ridiculed in their book. They were well versed in Baconian theory, had some sympathy for it and performed a valuable service for the Baconian movement by delivering it from the obfuscations of the cipher enthusiasts.

Colonel and Mrs Friedman were both professional cryptologists, working for many years in the service of the US Government. During the Second World War Friedman headed the army's cryptoanalytic bureau, where he distinguished himself by cracking the highest-level Japanese cipher. They first met in 1915, when Elizabeth was employed as assistant to Elizabeth Wells Gallup, the most interesting and influential of all the Shakespearian decipherers. Her patron was an American showman, Colonel George Fabyan, who provided her with a research establishment on his estate in Illinois and a team of professional helpers. The Friedmans stayed with her five years, studying her techniques in applying Bacon's Bi-literal Cipher to read his hidden writings in the First Folio and elsewhere. They also knew many of the other Shakespearian code-crackers of the period, gave them respectful attention and kindly pointed out their fallacies. The only researcher whose work they could not easily reject was Elizabeth Gallup.

Born in 1848, Mrs Gallup had a university education and became Principal of a High School in Michigan. There she met Dr Orville Owen, an early interpreter of Bacon's cipher in Shakespeare. She joined in his work, then set up on her own, and continued the research for the rest of her long life. The Friedmans always liked and admired her, finding her 'honest, sincere, gentle, upright and devotedly religious' as well as intelligent and learned. She never wittingly deceived anybody and was totally convinced by her own findings. The first of these were published in 1899 in her book, *The Biliteral Cypher of Sir Francis Bacon Discovered in his Works and Deciphered by Mrs Elizabeth Wells Gallup.*

Elizabeth Wells Gallup, most remarkable and respectable of Bacon–Shakespeare decipherers.

She used the Bi-literal Cipher, exactly as Bacon had specified in *De augmentis*, to read the texts which he had concealed not only in Shakespeare but in works attributed to Marlowe, Peele, Greene, Spenser, Jonson and Burton. The great difficulty was to distinguish between the different founts of print, and she spent many hours peering at the letters with a magnifying glass, concentrating on the italicized passages where the difference was clearer. The Friedmans were amazed at the facility with which she could read the cipher and draw from it long, coherent statements, even though many of her ascriptions of individual letters to one or other fount were later found to be dubious or wrong. The trouble was that, not having her trained eye and special 'feel' for the work, no one else could reproduce or extend her findings, and that has been the case ever since.

From Mrs Gallup's readings of Bacon's cipher, inserted in his own works and those of Shakespeare, Marlowe, Greene and the others, which he had secretly authored, she derived a remarkable story. Bacon repeated his message through all the ciphered books because, she supposed, he had wanted to make sure that some of it survived to be discovered eventually by an alert reader. The gist of it came in her early decipherment of 'A Catalogue of the several Comedies' in the First Folio. It read: 'Queene Elizabeth is my true mother, and I am the lawfull heire to the throne. Find the Cipher storie my bookes containe; it tells great secrets, every one of which, if imparted openly, would forfeit my life. F. BACON.'

The story as it developed was that, while she was in the Tower of London under Queen Mary, Elizabeth secretly married the Earl of

In St Michael's church, St Albans, Bacon's effigy leans on an elbow, providing through this characteristic pose a clue to his decipherers.

Leicester and had by him two sons. Francis was the elder, and the second was Robert, who later became the Earl of Essex. Nicholas and Anne Bacon adopted Francis and brought him up as their own child. He did not learn the truth until he was sixteen, whereupon he confronted Queen Elizabeth, who was angry that he had found out and banished him to France. While he was abroad she arranged things so that he would be barred from his right of succession to the throne of England. Unable to make his grievance public, he expressed it cryptically in his Shakespeare and other writings.

Dr Owen, Mrs Gallup's initiator into the world of cipher, had previously obtained the same information from his own, different method of reading Bacon in Shakespeare. His was called the Word Cipher. The stages by which he discovered it began in the 1880s when he was about thirty years old. He was a doctor in Detroit, and on journeys between patients he liked to read Shakespeare. One day, while reading *King John*, he was struck by the oddity of some words spoken by the Bastard, 'My dear Sir, thus leaning on my elbow I begin . . .' On the evidence of his statue (above), Bacon used to lean on his elbow. Owen recognized a clue, and after eight years' labour, with much help from intuition and occult guidance, he discovered what it was telling him to do.

The Wheel of Fortune, designed under inspiration by Dr Orville W. Owen of Detroit for rapid inspection of the works of Bacon, including those attributed to Shakespeare, Marlowe and other writers. By this means he obtained volumes of deciphered messages.

The spirit of Sir Francis Bacon advised him to construct a 'Wheel'. It consisted of two large spools, around and between which rolled a strip of canvas 2 feet wide and 1000 feet long. Upon the canvas he glued in separate pages the complete works of Bacon, by which he meant the complete works of Bacon, Shakespeare, Marlowe, Greene, Peele and Spenser, together with Burton's *Anatomy of Melancholy*. By cranking the drums in either direction, he could pass the entire Bacon canon under his eyes at any speed required. With the help of secretaries he marked all sentences containing his 'guide words', Fortune, Nature, Honour, Reputation and Pan. These led to certain 'key' words and these in turn to significant phrases or sentences which were then dictated to a stenographer. Colour-coding was used to classify these extracts, and when they were put together in what, according to Owen's system, was the proper order, they formed a more or less coherent text. In a long-winded, dreamy way it told the story of Elizabeth's secret marriage to Leicester and the frustrations of their elder son, Francis, who should have succeeded her as king of England.

The first volume of *Sir Francis Bacon's Cipher Story* was published in 1893. Three others followed, and then Owen sailed for England, leaving his assistants to compile a fifth volume, which they succeeded in doing on their own. His business was to search for Bacon's original manuscripts. By his peculiar means of divination, including the use of anagrams, he learnt that the evidence lay buried in boxes near Chepstow Castle on the River Wye. He and his followers descended upon the place in 1909, and for the next fifteen years they ransacked the area, hiring boatmen and navvies to excavate below the bed of the Wye and causing explosions on its banks. Nothing was ever found, and with the death of Dr Owen in 1924 the search came to an end.

From his Wheel of Fortune Owen learnt that Bacon's manuscripts were hidden beneath the River Wye at Chepstow, and spent several seasons in search of them, hiring workmen for underwater excavations.

Ignatius Donnelly of Minnesota (1831–1901), radical politican, author of the first modern book on Atlantis and the first decoder of Shakespeare.

The story of Dr Owen's extraordinary career, his amazing inventions and his Baconian treasure-hunts on the Wye is told more fully in a previous book, *Eccentric Lives and Peculiar Notions*. It also includes the great Ignatius Donnelly of Minnesota, the Prince of Heretics and a man of many remarkable parts. He was a radical orator, a US Congressman and, finally, a leader of the People's Party. He wrote the first and best book on Atlantis (*Atlantis, the Antediluvian World*, 1882), the first on cosmic catastrophe theory (*Ragnarök: the Age of Fire and Gravel*, 1883), a novel, *Caesar's Column*, foreseeing the tyranny and collapse of capitalism, and other original works. In politics, economics, literature – everywhere he looked – he saw rackets and conspiracies. His was a true Baconian mind. He saw through the racket of Shakespeare, and he determined to bust it by finding the cryptic affirmations of authorship that Bacon must have enfolded in the plays of Shakespeare.

For many frustrating years, Donnelly pored over his replica of the First Folio, seeking, but never finding, the key to Bacon's cipher message. Finally he was illuminated, and in 1888 appeared his massive, two-volume work of almost a thousand pages, *The Great Cryptogram: Francis Bacon's Cipher in the So-called Shakespeare Plays*.

Baconians were eagerly awaiting the revelation which Donnelly had promised them, but when his book came out, reactions were sharply divided. Its first part, setting out the arguments against Shakspere and in favour of Francis Bacon, was much admired. Even today it is regarded as one of the best expositions of the rational Baconian case. The difficulty came with the second volume, where Donnelly explained the workings of his cryptogram, with examples of the messages he had obtained through it.

He first described how he had come across Bacon's Bi-literal Cipher in a children's book. It had sparked his interest, but he had not used it in his deciphering. His method was based on certain key numbers, relating to page numbers and the positions of words in the First Folio. It began simply. He noticed, for example, that the word, Bacon, appears on page 53 of the Histories, and also on page 53 of the Comedies. There seemed also to be a numerical pattern behind the positionings of 'Francis', 'William', 'shake' and 'spear'. Donnelly counted page numbers, line and word numbers, added, subtracted, divided and multiplied, constantly elaborating and adapting his system, until the system itself vanished under the mass of

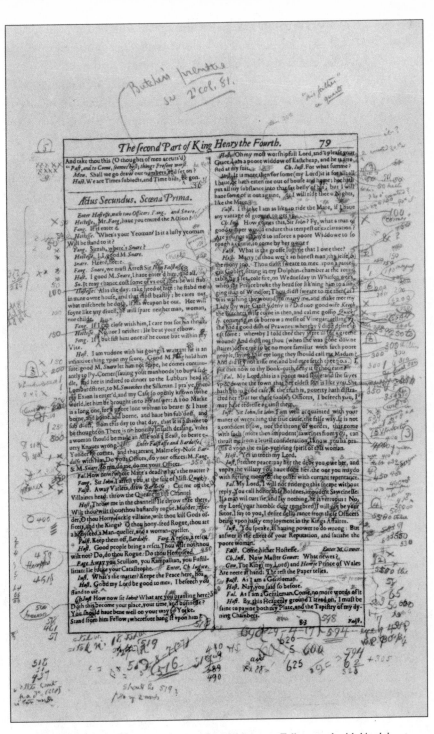

A page from Donnelly's facsimile copy of the Shakespeare Folio covered with his elaborate notes and calculations towards the discovery of Bacon's hidden claims to authorship.

exceptions and special conditions he laid upon it. The end-product was a collection of odd anecdotes about life behind the scenes in the Elizabethan theatre. Donnelly claimed that his work was 'purely arithmetical', not 'a mere hop-skip-and-jump collocation of words', but his critics have taken that last phrase as a good description of it. Those who wanted to believe in Donnelly did so regardless, but the Baconian mainstream moved away from him. Defiantly he followed up his failure with a second book, *The Cipher in the Plays and on the Tombstone*. It made few converts, and even before the Friedmans exposed his fallacies by showing that by the same method of number-juggling almost any message could be wrung out of any Shakespeare play, Donnelly's cryptogram was in discredit.

The Friedmans' work allows no rational alternative to admitting that by the standards of cryptoanalysis and plain common sense, no one has managed to demonstrate a cipher in Shakespeare. Their favourite was Elizabeth Gallup, to whom they devoted over a third of their book. She did some amazing things, such as deriving new translations of Homer's *Iliad* and other classical works out of old books she examined at the British Museum; she was honest and confident in her findings, and the story of Bacon's secret parentage in her decipherings was impressively coherent. A number of people, including professional and high-ranking cryptologists, claimed that they had tested and confirmed her cipher readings, but the Friedmans deny that any of them really did so. Regretfully, since she was their good friend, they had to conclude that only Mrs Gallup could elicit Bacon's testimony in Shakespeare through his Bi-literal Cipher. Scientifically therefore, it was unproven. They came to believe that, quite unknowingly, she was influenced by auto-suggestion. She would find some odd words through the cipher, and then her imagination took over, leading her to identify the different kinds of printed letters by intuition, and causing her to spin out her wished-for life story of Francis Bacon, as she had learnt it from Dr Owen. By strict, rational standards her whole work was a grand, awesome delusion.

Judged otherwise, by its content, the Owen and Gallup cipher work brought out a very interesting and not entirely implausible story. On that level, it deserved and obtained some serious attention. Beginning with Parker Woodward's *The Strange Case of Francis Tidir* (the Welsh spelling of Tudor) in 1901, and up to at least 1948, when Comyns Beaumont produced his entertaining account of *The Private Life of the Virgin Queen*, Baconian writers have had accumulated bits of evidence to support the account of the Queen's secret marriage to Leicester and the fate of her rightful heir, Francis Bacon. Quite possibly the cipher story was true.

Robert Dudley, Earl of Leicester, was Elizabeth's long-lasting favourite and her putative lover. She was infatuated with him, and on acceding to the Throne seemed likely to make him her consort. Amy Robsart, whom he had married when both were eighteen, stood in the way, but in 1560 she was found dead at the foot of a staircase, and it was widely rumoured that her husband was responsible for her murder. It was also reported that the Queen had secretly married Leicester at Lord Pembroke's house, and that she had borne his child. The authorities did all they could to suppress the story, and many people were sent to prison for repeating it. This was naturally taken as confirmation of the rumours.

The Earl of Leicester, claimed by Baconians as Queen Elizabeth's unacknowledged husband and the natural father of Francis Bacon.

In favour of the idea that Francis Bacon was not the real son of Nicholas and Anne is the telling fact that when Nicholas Bacon died his will made generous provision for his widow, his son Anthony and other close relatives, but nothing at all was left to Francis. Then there is the strange matter of the inscription in Canonbury Tower, Islington, where Bacon lived for several years. The medieval tower once belonged to John Dudley, the Earl of Leicester's father. Queen Elizabeth used to stay there, in a room known as the Queen's Lodge. Mrs Gallup's cipher identified Canonbury Tower as one of the places where Bacon's manuscripts could be found – behind a moving panel, the fifth in line, she was told. In the Tower Room, behind the fifth panel, a secret recess was in fact discovered, but it was empty. Years later, however, in the 1930s, something else was discovered to encourage the belief that Bacon was Elizabeth's rightful heir. While the ancient, grimy walls of the top room in the tower were being cleaned, an inscription was uncovered above the door-lintel. It was a list of English sovereigns from William the Conqueror to King Charles. Their Latin names are given in correct order up to Elizabeth, and then follows:

SVCCEDIT FR———JACOBUS

The letters following FR had been thoroughly obliterated by gouging with a chisel. The apparent meaning is that King James succeeded or took the place of FR——— , possibly Francis, the Philosopher-King who could never openly claim his throne.

Even allowing that there is no Cipher in Shakespeare, the phenomenon of the Shakespeare decipherers is still mysterious. One way of looking at them is against the background of their times. The greatest among them, Donnelly, Owen, Gallup and others, were all Americans, active towards the end of the nineteenth century. That was the great age of Spiritualism, a movement that began in the USA in the middle of the century and developed throughout it. The movement for deciphering Shakespeare can be seen as one of the many offshoots of Spiritualism. Through the apparatus of their cipher systems, Donnelly and the others were 'channelling' Bacon's voice in Shakespeare – or some voice from the world of spirits or imagination. The cipher was, as it were, their crystal ball. As is always the case with automatic writing and the other techniques of spiritism, the quality of the message reflects that of the receiver. Thus Donnelly's cipher texts were, like him, rough and ready, full of exclamations and vehement phrases, Owen's were romantically rambling, and Mrs Gallup's were learned and stately. Donnelly and Owen were conscious that, to some extent at least, they were acting as spirit mediums in their decipherings. Mrs Gallup was probably not so aware; as a good Christian she would have resisted the notion of an occult element in her proceedings. To explain her unique success in cipher-reading, she spoke of her long years of experience, her trained eye and, as she put it, her 'inspiration'. Another way of putting it is that she was a channel for automatic writing.

Those who have no interest at all in Spiritualism can dismiss the whole business of Bacon in Shakespeare as as just one more example of its follies. It provides no hard evidence for any side in the Authorship debate. The Baconian movement has been seriously damaged by its discreditable cipher-hunting fringe. To students of mysticism, however, the phenomenon of Bacon's voice speaking through Shakespeare is of rightful interest. Spirit mediums are mostly known for their banalities and gibberish, but the quality of inspiration varies, and some oracles are more reputable than others. If, as seems likely, Mrs Gallup was exercising her unacknowledged gift of mediumship, the quality of what she produced ranks her among the best channellers of her time.

Bacon's spirit messages through Shakespeare do nothing to solve the Authorship question – on the mundane level of this present enquiry. Many Baconians, however, are high-minded mystics. Francis Bacon's cipher story strikes them as a note of truth, and they require no further, literal proof that he wrote the complete works of Shakespeare. Far more than that, they credit him with all the best writings of all the best writers of his age. Like the ideal Shakspere, the sweet country genius as imagined by his romantic biographers, the ideal Bacon, the nobly suffering universal saviour, as his followers depict him, is an attractive idol. The Baconian faith is beguiling, but it is not irresistible, and honest sceptics who feel they have not yet found the true Shakespeare will continue further.

BACON–SHAKESPEARE PARALLELS AND CRYPTIC ICONOGRAPHY

The Baconian movement today seems rather to have faded. The great writers and riddlers of its heyday are long departed, leaving no outstanding successors. It is a grand old movement which, during the course of its long existence, has become dignified and almost respectable as an old-established lost cause. It spreads into many areas, and the bulk and variety of its literature is prodigious. There should perhaps be a Chair of Baconian Studies in some quiet university.

The Baconian case is made up of so many bits and different kinds of evidence that it is impossible to give a complete, fair and short summary of it. Not mentioned so far are the Parallel Passages and the cryptic images in Bacon's and other contemporary publications. Many curious items are repeated in the Baconian literature, for example, the following apparent reference to Bacon or his family in *The Merry Wives of Windsor* (iv. 1), when Mistress Page takes her son, William, to Sir Hugh Evans the Welsh parson, asking him to test the progress of the boy's education. The dialogue that follows is a parody of schoolmasters' proceedings. At one stage Evans turns to Latin grammar.

> *Evans* . . . Well, what is your *Accusative-case*?
> *William. Accusativo hinc.*
> *Evans.* I pray you have your remembrance (childe) *Accusativo hing, hang, hog.*

Mistress Quickly, the servant-girl, then butts in with:

> Hang-hog, is latten for Bacon, I warrant you.

This comic exchange echoes a Bacon family joke, included with other anecdotes in the 1671 edition of Francis Bacon's *Resuscitatio*. It was about his father, Sir Nicholas. At the end of a trial in which he was judge, Sir Nicholas Bacon was about to pass sentence of death when the prisoner asked for his mercy on the grounds that they were related.

> 'Prithee,' said my lord judge, 'how came that in?'
> 'Why, if it please you, my lord, your name is Bacon and mine is Hog,

and in all ages Hog and Bacon have been so near kindred that they are not to be separated.'

'Ay; but', replied Judge Bacon, 'you and I cannot be kindred except you be hanged; for Hog is not Bacon until it be well hanged'.

'Hang-hog is Latin for Bacon' is surely a reference to this joke. Its occurrence in *The Merry Wives* is a mystery, typifying much of the Baconian evidence. It is suggestive and provocative, but leads to no particular conclusion.

A great deal of Baconian scholarship has been devoted to parallelisms – thoughts, phrases and expressions which occur in the writings of both Shakespeare and Bacon. Ignatius Donnelly in 1888 gave almost two hundred pages of 'Identical Expressions, Metaphors, Opinions, Quotations, Studies, Errors, Unusual Words, Characters and Styles'. In 1901 Robert M. Theobald, former editor of *The Bacon Journal*, discussed parallelisms through most of the 499 pages of his *Shakespeare Studies in Baconian Light*, and Baconian writers from that time often listed examples in their books.

The most productive source of parallels between Bacon and Shakespeare is a collection of Bacon's own manuscript notes, first published by

the Baconian scholar, C.M. (or Mrs Henry) Pott, in 1883 as *The Promus* [storehouse] *of Formularies and Elegancies, by Francis Bacon*. A revised version of the text is printed at the end of Durning-Lawrence's *Bacon is Shake-speare*. It consists of quotations and sayings which evidently caught Bacon's eye during his reading, and which he copied down for reference or use in his own works. There are metaphors, aphorisms, Bible texts, proverbs in French, Italian, Spanish and Latin, forms of greeting and turns of phrase. Dates on two of the sheets, 5 December 1594 and 27 January 1595, indicate the period during which Bacon wrote them.

Constance Pott was the first to publish Bacon's Promus. *She claimed that Bacon was founder of the Rosicrucian Society and lived for many years after his supposed death, writing all that was best in seventeenth-century literature.*

From Shakespeare	*From Bacon's Promus*
Every Jack becomes a gentleman. *R.III*	Every Jack would be a Lord.
The latter end of a fray and the beginning a feast *I Hen.IV*	Better to come to the ending of a feast than to the beginning of a fray.
Good wine needs no bush. *A.Y.L.*	Good wine needs no bush.
To hazard all our lives in one small boat *I H. VI*	You are in the same ship.
Your bait of falsehood takes this carp of truth *Hamlet*	Tell a lie to know a truth.
The strings of life began to crack. *Lear*	At length the string cracks.
Out of heaven's benediction to the warm sun *Lear*	Out of God's blessing into the warm sun.
The world on wheels. *Two Gent.*	The world runs on wheels.
Thought is free. *Tempest*	Thought is free.
Fortune governed as the sea is by the moon. *I H. IV*	Fortune changes like the moon.
As if increase of appetite had grown From what it fed on. *Hamlet*	If you eat, appetite will come.
Make use of thy salt hours. *T. of A.*	Make use of thy salt hours.
Can so young a thorn begin to prick? *H. VI*	A thorn is gentle when it is young.
What early tongue so sweet saluteth me? *R. & J.*	Sweet for the speech in the morning.

Many of the items in *The Promus* appeared later in Bacon's published works and, as Mrs Pott demonstrated, many of them were used by the author of Shakespeare. Shown above is a short selection from George Hookham's *Will o' the Wisp or The Elusive Shakespeare* (1922).

In some cases Bacon's notes appear to have been written earlier than the Shakespeare play in which they occur. The Baconian conclusion is that Bacon compiled *The Promus* as a source-book for his Shakespearian and other writings.

The Orthodox arguments against Proof by Parallel Passages are: that Shakespeare and Bacon could have taken similar phrases from the same Biblical, classical and other published sources; that they could have borrowed from each other, and that many of their shared expressions were commonplaces at the time. The same thoughts and phrases were used equally by other contemporary dramatists. That is why the Marlovians, Oxfordians and others can find parallelisms for their own candidates. J.M. Robertson, a formidable defender of Orthodoxy, devoted many pages of *The Baconian Heresy* to showing that Donnelly's and Theobald's parallelisms, taken one by one, are not at all remarkable. There were several good reasons for their occurrence, and it is always likely that two contemporary writers will hit upon the same phrase by simple coincidence.

The most telling point for Orthodoxy is that parallel passages in Bacon and Shakespeare were often repeated by their fellow writers. There was no special relationship between the two great authors other than the bond that linked all literary men of their time. This was clearly demonstrated by Harold Bayley in *The Shakespeare Symphony*, 1906. With scholarly dedication he read through the literature of Bacon's time, finding the same phrases and metaphors in the works of many different authors.

Just a few of Bayley's many examples illustrate the point. Shakespeare, Chapman, Beaumont, Tourneur, Nabbes, Nashe and the anonymous author of *Sir John Oldcastle* all used the phrase, 'grey eyed morn' or morning. The 'gloomy air' was referred to by Spenser, Peele, Marlowe and Greene. Shakespeare, Beaumont and Fletcher, Chapman and Massinger mentioned poverty of spirit. Bacon, Shakespeare, Marston and Chapman repeated the saying that nothing can be made out of nothing, and three of those writers, together with Massinger, Webster, Beaumont and Fletcher and John Ford spoke of putting a girdle round the earth. Shakespeare's observation in *As You Like It*, that 'All the world's a stage', was echoed by Bacon, Lodge, Marston, Nashe, Webster, Chapman, Rowley, Jonson, Massinger, Beaumont and Fletcher and Sir Thomas Browne.

Harold Bayley's demonstration pleased the Stratfordians, but his labours were not actually performed on their behalf. He turned their argument on its head by contending that all the above-named poets and dramatists, and others besides, were schooled by Francis Bacon, who imbued them with philosophy, taught them new words and expressions and oversaw the writings which he allowed them to publish under their own names. Together they formed the Shakespeare Symphony, for the climax of their efforts was, of course, the Works of Shakespeare. Bayley described Bacon's literary orchestra:

> The roulades and cadenzas of John Lyly, the blare of Christopher
> Marlowe, the long slow slope of Shakespeare's violin, the sadder
> sweep of Massinger's viola, the flutings of John Fletcher and Thomas
> Heywood, the harshness of Ford's bassoon, the heroic fanfares of
> Michael Drayton, and the gloom of John Webster's double-bass,
> all blend into an amazing Harmony.

Bayley admitted that his demonstration had reduced the Baconian argument by parallelisms *ad absurdum*. He was a Higher Baconian, not so much concerned with Bacon's authorship of Shakespeare as with his responsibility for all the great literature of his age.

Donnelly, Bayley and Robertson stand for three different opinions on the Shakespeare–Bacon parallelisms. One said that they prove that Bacon wrote Shakespeare; the second that they point to Bacon as the author of all good contemporary literature; and the third that they are only to be expected and mean nothing at all.

Another, highly specialized field of Baconian research is the study of mystical iconography. Continental editions of Bacon's works were given symbolic title-pages, hinting at the presence of a mystery. There are emblems, ornaments and symbolic devices in Shakespeare's and other printed works which may have significance, possibly to the Authorship question. Many books have been written on this topic, but mostly they are penetrable only by initiates in the language of Arcana. One initiate was Harold Bayley. He was a paper-maker who had made a special study of old watermarks, and had come to realize that the strange emblems that paper-makers traditionally etch into their products originated among secret societies, such as the Rosicrucians. This inspired his greatest work, the two-volume *Lost Language of Symbolism*. Earlier, in 1902, he wrote *The Tragedy of Sir Francis Bacon*, showing by means of watermarks, symbolic head-pieces and printers' flowers, that Francis Bacon was a great power in the Rosicrucian movement and was acting on their behalf through his literary productions, including his Shakespeare writings.

Most easily understandable of the Baconian iconologists is Durning-Lawrence. In *Bacon is Shake-speare*, he reproduced the title-page of a book by Gustavus Selenus, *Cryptomenytices et cryptographiae*, published in Lüneburg

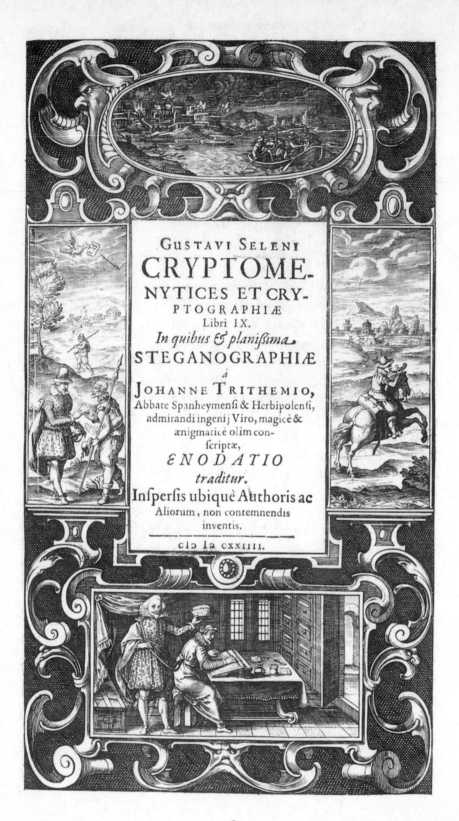

GUSTAVI SELENI
CRYPTOME-
NYTICES ET CRY-
PTOGRAPHIÆ
Libri IX.
In quibus & planissima
STEGANOGRAPHIÆ
à
JOHANNE TRITHEMIO,
Abbate Spanheymensi & Herbipolensi,
admirandi ingenij Viro, magicè &
ænigmaticè olim con-
scriptæ,
ENODATIO
traditur.
Inspersis ubiquè Authoris ac
Aliorum, non contemnendis
inventis.

CIƆ IƆ CXXIIII.

in 1623. Neither Selenus nor his ducal patron had any known connection with Francis Bacon, but the book is about one of his subjects, cryptography or methods of secret writing, and the pictures on its title-page (opposite) can be seen as illustrating Bacon's literary relationships with Shakspere.

In the bottom panel a man in scholar's garb is engaged in writing, while a gaudily dressed actor behind him lifts off his furry headdress, which Durning-Lawrence says is a heraldic Cap of Maintenance. This could represent Bacon writing plays while Shakspere lifts his glory.

In the left-hand panel the Bacon character in his traditional hat is giving a small book to a spearman in actor's boots, who looks somewhat like the Shakspere in Dugdale's drawing of the original Stratford bust (shown on page 89). He has respectfully doffed his hat in which is a sprig of bay leaves. This man is a Shake-spear, and in the background he is seen carrying his spear towards a walled city. The source of the book seems to be the bird, a symbol of spirit, being shot by a bolt in the sky.

The right-hand panel shows the same man, identified by the sprig in his hat. He is mounted with his baggage on a galloping horse, and he is blowing a horn as if to proclaim news. Durning-Lawrence thought that his spur was particularly emphasized and that he was meant to represent Shake-spur.

Above, framed by masks of Comedy and Tragedy, some people in a boat are rowing towards the beacon lights of a harbour. These, said Durning-Lawrence rather weakly, are Bacon lights, because Bacon was pronounced Beacon in the sixteenth century.

It is not known what allegory these pictures were supposed to illustrate, so there is nothing either for or against the idea that they could refer to the Bacon–Shakespeare mystery, which would be appropriate for a book on hidden writings.

Durning-Lawrence recognized the man giving his book to the Spearman in another allegorical figure, the main character on a cryptic title-page to a volume of Bacon's works, published on the continent in 1645 (shown overleaf). His right hand points to a book he is reading, supported on another, and with his left hand he is pushing or restraining a young woman who is striding towards a temple with a smaller book. Baconians versed in symbolism are impressed by this and other illustrations with possible allusions to Bacon's secret, but their interpretations vary from expert to expert, and the uninitiated remain confused or sceptical. There is a strong rational case for Bacon as Shakespeare, but the Baconian symbolists and cryptologists have done little to help it.

FR. BACONIS
De
VERVLAM.
Angliæ Cancellarii
DE
AVGMENTIS
SCIENTIARVM
Lib. IX.

LVGD. BATAVORVM
Apud Franciſcum Moiardum,
Et Adrianum Wijngaerde. *Anno 1645.*

This cryptic title-page to a work by Francis Bacon communicates to subtle Baconian minds that his writings were more extensive and significant than he openly acknowledged.

VI

THE OXFORD MOVEMENT

EDWARD DE VERE
SEVENTEENTH EARL OF OXFORD

1550 2 April. Born at Earl's Colne, Essex, the only son of John de Vere, sixteenth Earl, and Margaret, sister of Arthur Golding, translator of Ovid. Styled Viscount Bolebec during his father's lifetime.

1558 Schooled at Queen's College, Cambridge.

1562 Father died; de Vere inherited estates and title of Great Lord Chamberlain; made a royal ward of Sir William Cecil (later Lord Burghley), lodged in his house in the Strand and tutored there by his uncle, Arthur Golding.
His mother married Sir Charles Tyrell after a short widowhood.

1564 Took a degree at St John's, Cambridge.

1567 Admitted to Gray's Inn to study law.
Killed a servant at Cecil House. Cecil complained about his bad temper and extravagance, but protected him from the law.
Became a favourite courtier of Queen Elizabeth.

1568 Mother died.
Refused leave to serve in the army.

1570 Served under the Earl of Sussex in a campaign against the Scottish Catholic nobles.

1571 Distinguished himself jousting at Westminster before the queen.
Married Anne Cecil, daughter of Lord Burghley who was ennobled for the occasion.

1572 Begged the queen and Burghley to spare the life of his cousin, the Duke of Norfolk, unsuccessfully. Norfolk executed for treason. Refused leave to serve in the navy.

1574 Went abroad without leave, to Flanders. Brought back by the queen's agents.

1575 Given leave to travel. Went to Paris, Strasburg, Padua, Venice, Florence and Sicily. Adopted Italian ways and fashions.
Eldest daughter, Elizabeth, born.

1576 Recalled to England; heard rumours that Elizabeth was not his daughter, left his wife and quarrelled with the Burghleys.
Tired of court life, sought the company of literary and theatrical people.

1579 Sided with the Catholic party over the queen's proposed marriage to the French king's brother, opposed by Sir Philip Sidney and others. Quarrelled violently with Sidney; the queen intervened to forbid their duel.

1580–84 Oxford's theatre company toured the provinces, including Stratford-upon-Avon, then performed in London.

1581 Confessed to the queen his involvement with Catholic party and sent briefly to the Tower.

Reconciled with his wife who later bore him a son (born and died 1583) and three more daughters, one of whom died in infancy.

1582 Wounded in a duel or affray with Thomas Knyvet, uncle of his mistress, Anne Vavasor.

1583 Pardoned by the queen (see 1581); reconciled with Burghley; lost family estates.

1586. Took part in trial of Mary Queen of Scots.

Granted £1000 a year for life from special Government fund.

1588 Equipped and served in a ship against the Armada. Attended the queen at victory celebrations.

Wife died a year after giving birth to their last daughter.

1591 Married Elizabeth Trentham, maid of honour to the queen, who bore him a son and heir, Henry, two years later.

Thereafter, apart from his attendance at state trials and other functions, little is known of his life. He patronized literature and the theatre and supported a company of players. His daughter, Elizabeth, married the sixth Earl of Derby in 1594, and another daughter married Philip Herbert, one of the 'incomparable pair' to whom the Shakespeare Folio was later dedicated.

1596 His wife bought King's Place, Hackney, where he probably lived until his death.

1603 Officiated at James I's coronation.

1604 Died of plague in Hackney and was buried in the parish church, with no memorial and leaving no will.

DR FREUD AND MR LOONEY

Sigmund Freud was a great reader of Shakespeare and admired him for the psychological insights which in many ways anticipated his own. He could not believe that the author of *King Lear*, *Hamlet* and *Othello* was an ill-educated rustic, nor even that he was Anglo-Saxon. The Shakespeare he imagined was dark and Latin-looking, as in the Chandos portrait, and he

Sigmund Freud, the distinguished convert to Oxfordianism.

became interested in a theory, put forward by an Italian, Professor Gentilli, that Shakespeare's name was a corruption of Jacques Pierre, making him of French origin.

From his student days under the influence of his brilliant teacher, Theodor Meynert, who was a Baconian, Freud was fascinated by the Authorship question. Baconism, however, did not satisfy him. If Bacon wrote Shakespeare's as well as his own works, he would have been the greatest genius the world has ever seen, and Freud suspected that several writers must have combined to produce the Shakespeare plays.

The subject of Shakespeare's identity was on Freud's mind throughout his life, but from the age of sixty-seven it was no longer a mystery to him. In 1923 he read a book published three years earlier, by an English schoolmaster, which convinced him that the real Shakespeare was, if not French, a man of Norman blood – Edward de Vere, the seventeenth Earl of Oxford. The cause of his heresy was *'Shakespeare' Identified* by J. Thomas Looney.

In subsequent books and lectures Freud developed the Oxfordian theory and urged his correspondents to adopt it. His followers in the psychoanalysis movement were told that Edward de Vere, the cultivated, passionate wayward aristocrat, who had fallen from his high position in life, was the Shakespeare who reveals himself in the plays and Sonnets. The Oedipal repressions of Hamlet were not, as Freud had first speculated, reflections of William Shakspere's loss of his father and his son Hamnet, but were those of de Vere himself. His beloved father had died when Edward was twelve, and the boy resented it when his mother married again soon afterwards.

In *King Lear*, one of Freud's favourite plays, he was impressed by the correspondence between Lear and Oxford, who each had three daughters. His letter on this topic to his Shakespearian friend, James Bransom, is

Edward de Vere portrayed in typical dandified costume by M. Gheeraedts.

quoted in the *Biography* by his disciple, Ernest Jones, who gives other details of Freud's enthusiasm for the Oxfordian cause. 'The man from Stratford', wrote Freud in 1937, 'seems to have nothing at all to justify his claim, whereas Oxford has almost everything.'

When Freud moved to London at the age of eighty-two to avoid the Nazis in Austria, Mr Looney sent him a letter of welcome, and in reply he acknowledged the source of his Oxfordian convictions. He re-read Looney's book, studied Canon Rendall's *Shakespeare's Sonnets and Edward de Vere* and built up a considerable Oxfordian library. This was greatly to the embarrassment of his English followers, who were already disconcerted by Freud's belief in telepathy; his Oxfordian faith was even less acceptable, particularly in England, and above all because of Mr Looney's name. His editor, James Strachey, warned him about the derision that he would attract through the association. Ernest Jones also disapproved, and they both urged him not to publicize his allegiance. Freud held his ground, properly ignoring cheap jokes about Looney's name and casting a psycho-analytical eye on the English cult of William Shakspere.

'Shakespeare' Identified puts the Oxfordian case clearly and simply, but the name of its author was against it. The original publisher withdrew on that account, demanding a *nom de plume*, but it was finally brought out by Cecil Palmer, who went on to publish many other Oxfordian books. When Looney explained that his name (pronounced 'Loney') was old and honourable in the Isle of Man, his Stratfordian detractors – most recently Schoenbaum in *Shakespeare's Lives* – accused him of snobbery. The same weakness is regularly imputed to supporters of high-born candidates. Freud, of course, was impervious to this charge; he had no ambition to be identified with the English aristocracy.

Looney's conclusion, that Oxford was Shakespeare, was the result of a methodical investigation. First, he read through the plays and poems for clues to the author's characteristics. Nine obvious points emerged, and further studies brought forth nine more. Looney's picture of Shakespeare had these features:

1. A mature man of recognized genius
2. Apparently eccentric and mysterious
3. Of intense sensibility – a man apart
4. Unconventional
5. Not adequately appreciated
6. Of pronounced and known literary tastes
7. An enthusiast in the world of drama

8. A lyric poet of recognized talent
9. Of superior education – classical – the habitual associate of educated people
10. A man with feudal connections
11. One of the higher aristocracy
12. Connected with Lancastrian supporters
13. An enthusiast for Italy
14. A follower of sport including falconry
16. Loose and improvident in money matters
17. Doubtful and somewhat conflicting in his attitude to women
18. Of probable Catholic leanings but touched with scepticism

The next stage was to look for a sixteenth-century poet who wrote in the characteristic Shakespearian rhythm, as in *Venus and Adonis*, where the verses are of six lines, each of ten syllables, and the lines rhyme alternately with a rhyming couplet at the end. Looney went through an anthology of poetry and homed in on a poem which not only had the correct form of stanza but seemed to him to express Shakespearean sentiments. It was Edward de Vere's 'Women'.

> If women could be fair and yet not fond,
>> Or that their love were firm not fickle, still,
> I would not marvel that they make men bond,
>> By service long to purchase their good will,
> But when I see how frail these creatures are
> I muse that men forget themselves so far.
>
> To mark the choice they make, and how they change,
>> How oft from Phoebus do they flee to Pan,
> Unsettled still like haggards wild they range,
>> These gentle birds that fly from man to man,
> Who would not scorn and shake them from the fist
> And let them fly, fair fools, which way they list?
>
> Yet for disport we fawn and flatter both,
>> To pass the time when nothing else can please,
> And train them to our lure with subtle oath,
>> Till, weary of their wiles, ourselves we ease;
> And then we say, when we their fancy try,
> To play with fools, Oh what a fool was I.

This is certainly similar to Shakespeare's view of women as revealed in the Sonnets, and the use of images from falconry in the last two verses

The knowledge of falconry evident in Shakespeare's works is one of the weaknesses in the Stratfordian case and a strong point for Oxfordians.

is also typically Shakespearian. Wild haggards, meaning female hawks caught in the wild when fully grown, are mentioned five times in Shakespeare's plays.

Knowing nothing about de Vere, Looney looked him up in the *Dictionary of National Biography*. The article happened to have been written by the great Stratfordian, Sir Sidney Lee, who thus unwittingly gave aid to the enemy. The sentences about the Earl of Oxford which led Looney on were:

> Oxford, despite his violent and perverse temper, his eccentric taste in dress, and his reckless waste of substance, evinced a genuine taste in music and wrote verses of much lyric beauty. . . .
> Puttenham and Meres reckon him among the best for comedy in his day; but though he was a patron of players no specimens of his dramatic productions survive.
> A sufficient number of his poems is extant to corroborate Webbe's comment, that he was the best of the courtier poets in the early days of Queen Elizabeth, and that 'in the rare devices of poetry he may challenge to himself the title of the most excellent amongst the rest'.

Looney's preliminary list of Shakespeare's characteristics was well answered by what he had discovered so far. Oxford was a high aristocrat, classically educated, an excellent poet, a lover of music and falconry, eccentric, careless with money and cynical about women. He also knew and loved Italy. Looney turned again to Shakespeare and re-read the plays and poems with new, Oxfordian eyes. Everything fell into place. The interests, feelings and experiences of the great author, as deduced from his works, were closely paralleled by the life and character of the Earl of Oxford. There was no doubt in Looney's mind that he had identified the true Shakespeare.

Many people agreed with him. Two years after his book came out, Oxfordian converts founded the Shakespeare Fellowship in London. They were not exclusive but welcomed heretics of other schools. Sir George Greenwood, the agnostic, became the first president, with Looney and the learned Derbyite, Professor Abel Lefranc, as vice-presidents. As the number and quality of Baconian publications declined, a flood of Oxfordian books arose in their place. Leading British writers for the cause included Canon Rendall, Percy Allen, Colonel B.R. Ward, a founder of the Fellowship, and his son, Captain B.M. Ward, who produced a much-needed biography, *The Seventeenth Earl of Oxford*. Eva T. Clark of America in *Hidden Allusions in Shakespeare's Plays* performed the necessary task of re-dating the plays to conform with Oxford's life and early death; Dorothy and Charlton Ogburn expanded the case through 1297 pages in *This Star of England*, and in 1984 their son, Charlton Ogburn, published the most complete summary of the Oxfordian argument, *The Mysterious William Shakespeare*. Oxfordism became the mainstream heresy, and it has remained so ever since.

THE EARL OF OXFORD AND HAMLET

One of the basic concerns in literary studies, particularly in the case of Shakespeare, is the connection between the life and personal experiences of an author and his imaginative writings. From what is known about the career and preoccupations of William Shakspere, it is difficult to identify him with the poet of the Sonnets or with any of the leading characters in the plays. Stratfordians admit this, but deny that Shakspere was necessarily writing about himself. His imagination was transpersonal, so he could enter into the psychology of his characters, reproducing their typical modes of thinking, speaking and acting, without portraying any elements of himself.

Sigmund Freud ignored that view as unrealistic, taking it for granted that in the Sonnets and in plays such as *Hamlet* the author was not just creating pastiches but writing from his inner soul. No serious writer can help giving insights into his own psychology. Nor, if he were true to himself, would Shakespeare or any other writer try deliberately to exclude personal and autobiographical references. He could not and would not avoid drawing upon his own life-experience.

If any character in any Shakespeare play is meant in any way to represent the author, Hamlet is much the most likely. No other part is nearly so long or important. *Hamlet* without the Prince of Denmark is proverbially nothing. He is the only focus and his is the mind in which the tragedy is enacted. Any candidate for the Authorship whose life held parallels to Hamlet's is clearly in a strong position.

When Looney, having identified his Shakespeare, read through the plays again with him in mind, he was struck by the remarkable correspondences between Hamlet and Oxford. Several of the characters in Hamlet's story have their parallels in Oxford's family and close associates. The king who poisoned Hamlet's father and then married his mother is an exaggerated version of Oxford's stepfather. Polonius, Lord Chamberlain in the Court of Denmark and Hamlet's tedious counsellor, is a caricature of Queen Elizabeth's chief minister, Lord Burghley, who was Oxford's guardian.

The daughter of Polonius was Hamlet's Ophelia, while Burghley's daughter, Anne Cecil, was the partner in Oxford's troubled marriage. Anne's brother, Thomas Cecil, was Oxford's rival, as Ophelia's brother, Laertes, was the rival to Hamlet. Horatio, Hamlet's loyal friend, and the soldier Francisco are reminiscent of Sir Horace and Francis de Vere, Oxford's cousins, whom he admired for their military achievements. As Looney saw it, Rosencrantz was Sir Walter Ralegh and Fortinbras James I.

Most convincing is the parallel between Lord Burghley, who, as Elizabeth's chief minister, was charged with maintaining the security of her realm, and Lord Polonius who had the same position under the king of Denmark. The famous words of advice from Polonius to his son, as Laertes was about to leave for France (i. 3), are much the same as the maxims which Burghley drew up for the benefit of his son, Thomas.

> *Polonius.* See thou character. Give thy thoughts no tongue,
> Nor any unproportion'd thought his act.
> Be thou familiar, but by no means vulgar.
> Those friends thou hast, and their adoption tried,
> Grapple them to thy soul with hoops of steel;
> But do not dull thy palm with entertainment
> Of each new-hatch'd, unfledged comrade. Beware
> Of entrance to a quarrel, but being in,
> Bear 't that the opposed may beware of thee.
> Give every man thy ear, but few thy voice;
> Take each man's censure, but reserve thy judgment.
> Costly thy habit as thy purse can buy,
> But not express'd in fancy; rich not gaudy;
> For the apparel oft proclaims the man,
> And they in France of the best rank and station
> Are most select and generous chief in that.
> Neither a borrower nor a lender be;
> For loan ofte loses both itself and friend,
> And borrowing dulls the edge of husbandry.
> This above all: to thine own self be true,
> And it must follow, as the day the night,
> Thou canst not then be false to any man.
>
> *Burghley.* Let thy hospitality be moderate.
> Beware that thou spendest not more than three or four parts of thy revenue.
> Beware of being surety for thy best friends; he that payeth another man's debts seeketh his own decay.

With thine equals be familiar yet respectful.

Trust not any man with thy life, credit, or estate.

Be sure to keep some great man for thy friend.

Similar precepts were given in John Lyly's *Euphues and his England*, published in 1580 and dedicated to his 'very good lord and master', Edward de Vere, Earl of Oxford. Lyly's fine writing is said to have been a great influence on Shakespeare, but Looney saw it the other way round. Three years younger than Oxford, Lyly was his private secretary and companion. It was Oxford, said Looney, who inspired Lyly's play-writing and who doubtless passed on to him Burghley's heavy words of wisdom.

Oxford makes a convincing Hamlet – or *vice versa*. Hamlet was a royal prince of Denmark, Oxford a premier nobleman at the English court. They both lost their beloved fathers and felt dispossessed by the men who married their mothers. They both suffered under the tyranny of father-figures – the usurping king and Lord Burghley; and they were both sensitive and rebellious, seeing through other people's pretensions and having no faith in women. Like Hamlet, Oxford maintained a company of actors, was skilled in music, knew Italy, fought a duel and killed a man in his guardian's house. Hamlet stabbed Polonius whereas Oxford's victim was one of Burghley's servants, but with the help of Freud it can easily be supposed that he fantasized about murdering Lord Burghley.

Comparisons between Anne Cecil and Ophelia are also reasonably close. Anne was a little girl when the young Lord Oxford came to live in her father's house as his ward. She fell in love with him, and they were married when he was twenty-one and she barely fifteen. It was a grand wedding, attended by the queen, but the marriage became a tragedy. Oxford was ambitious, proud of his ancient lineage and determined to emulate the great deeds of his ancestors. He knew he had married beneath him – the Cecils for all their political power were not an aristocratic family. It may have occurred to him that Lord and Lady Burghley had trapped him into the match, which had put him even more firmly under the control of his substitute father. After his marriage Oxford began petitioning the Queen for leave to travel abroad, to serve in the army or the navy, and when each time he was refused he saw the frustrating influence of Lord Burghley.

Finally, without permission, Oxford escaped to the continent. The authorities had him brought back, but it was plain by then that he could not be restrained for ever, and at the age of twenty-five he was given leave to travel. While he was away, his wife gave birth to a daughter. He did not hear about it for several months, and the news reached him together with rumours that he was not the real father. This was probably only court gossip, but it was a blow to his fragile self-esteem, causing him to sever relations with Lady Oxford, and with her parents who he thought had deceived him. It was not until four or five years later, when he and Anne came together again, that he saw how deeply he had hurt her. It marked his life as well as hers. After she died, he married again and retired into the state of mysterious seclusion where, according to the Oxfordians, he wrote the plays of Shakespeare.

All's Well That Ends Well provided the evidence which Looney regarded as conclusive for the Oxfordian case. In his summary, the story of Bertram is seen to be virtually identical with Oxford's early life.

> Bertram, a young lord of ancient lineage, of which he is himself proud, having lost a father for whom he entertained a strong affection, is brought to court by his mother and there left as a royal ward, to be brought up under royal supervision. As he grows up he asks for military service and the right to travel, but he is repeatedly refused or put off. At last he goes away without permission. Before leaving he had been married to a young woman with whom he had been brought up, and who had herself been most active in bringing about the marriage. Matrimonial troubles, of which the outstanding feature is a refusal of cohabitation, are associated with both his stay abroad and his return home.

This is so like Oxford's history that, if he himself was not the author of *All's Well That Ends Well*, it must surely have been someone who knew him well. After he had identified Bertram as a portrait of Oxford, Looney came across an item which seemed to confirm it. In the play, Bertram is tricked into sleeping with his own wife, Helena, when she takes the place of a woman with whom he has made a nocturnal assignation. In the dark he cannot tell one from another. According to Wright's *History of Essex*, exactly the same story was told about Oxford. 'He forsook his lady's bed, but the father of Lady Anne, by stratagem, contrived that her husband should unknowingly sleep with her, believing her to be another woman, and she bore a son to him in consequence of this meeting.'

A similar story was told by Boccaccio in the fourteenth century and it is evidently archetypal. Neither the version in *All's Well That Ends Well* nor the account in Wright's *Essex* is likely to be a literal description of the reconciliation between the Earl and Countess of Oxford, but they certainly seem to link Oxford to the Shakespeare play. Helena, who admits that she is socially inferior to Bertram, is described as small, sweet, loyal and loving, which is exactly how Anne de Vere was described by her contemporaries. As in the story, Anne produced a son after making peace with her husband.

Another Shakespearian character, Berowne or Biron in *Love's Labour's Lost*, was seen by Looney as another aspect of the Earl of Oxford. He, Bertram and Hamlet form a composite picture of one man, and that man is likely to have been the author of the plays. That means that Oxford is the likely candidate. If one follows Looney's advice, becomes familiar with Oxford's biography and then reads *Hamlet* and the other plays with him in mind, numerous references to him and his associates can be identified. It is all very well for Samuel Schoenbaum in *Shakespeare's Lives* to comment sarcastically that, according to the Oxfordians, 'the Earl can hardly restrain himself from putting in appearances everywhere in the [Shakespeare] canon'; but the Stratfordians are always searching the plays for personal, autobiographical allusions to William Shakspere, more or less in vain. For them to cavil at the apparent references to the Earl of Oxford seems like a case of sour grapes.

THE OXFORD GROUP

Like every Authorship theory, the case for Oxford is lacking in one respect. No single item in all the evidence assembled for it amounts to positive proof. To make up for that, Oxfordians since Looney's time have greatly expanded the case, adding so many new, suggestive points of interest that it has grown cumbersome. As in the case for Bacon, it can no longer be briefly and completely summarized. This section gives some of the main, most commonly quoted examples of Oxfordian evidence.

First of all, there is an objection to be raised. The Stratfordians' one-line rebuttal of the Oxford theory is that Oxford died in 1604, but new Shakespeare plays kept on appearing. He died before the first stagings of *King Lear, Macbeth, Antony and Cleopatra, Timon of Athens, Coriolanus, Pericles, Cymbeline, The Winter's Tale, The Tempest* and *Henry VIII*. Oxford was too old and died too early to have been the real Shakespeare. The first Shakespearian poem, *Venus and Adonis*, generally considered to be the work of a young poet, was published when he was forty-three.

Looney's answer was that Oxford must have died with several plays unfinished, and these were later completed by his followers. *The Tempest*, which he criticized on stylistic grounds and because he disliked the 'negative' philosophy in it, was not by Shakespeare or Oxford but a work of some inferior dramatist. That last suggestion has not been well received, even by Oxfordians. Their contention is that Shakespeare's plays were all written long before their conventionally accepted dates, and none of them after 1604. It is not too difficult, in fact, to challenge the supposed date of any Shakespeare play. The evidence is generally so weak and arguable that even the most orthodox experts cannot agree among themselves.

Exemplifying this uncertainty is the case of *All's Well that Ends Well*, whose first printing was in the Shakespeare folio of 1623. Sidney Lee in the *Dictionary of National Biography* 'tentatively assigned' it to 1595, the editors of *The Henry Irving Shakespeare* placed it as early as 1590–92, while Edmund Chambers in the *Encyclopaedia Britannica* considered it to have been written as late as 1602. Other authorities have given different dates within this twelve-year span.

The positive case for Oxford begins with the possible genesis of the name under which he is presumed to have written the plays. His subsidiary title, Viscount Bolebec, entitled him to bear arms with the crest of a rampant lion brandishing or shaking a broken spear. This implies Break-spear, Shake-shaft and finally Shake-speare. Allusions to that name were made by the scholar and poet, Gabriel Harvey, in 1578 in some Latin verses addressed to the Earl of Oxford, who was attending the

The crest of de Vere as Viscount Bolebec was a lion shaking a broken spear.

Queen on her progress to Cambridge. While urging him to take up arms on behalf of his country, Harvey included some significant phrases, here translated:

Thy splendid fame, great Earl, demands more than that of any other the high-flown eloquence of a poet . . . . Mars will be thy servant, Hermes thy messenger, *Pallas striking her shield with her spear-shaft* will attend thee . . . . Phoebus Apollo has long cultivated thy mind in the arts. English poetic measures have long enough been sung by thee. May your Courtly Epistle – more polished than the writings of Castiglione himself – witness how greatly thou dost excel in letters. I have seen many Latin verses of thine, yea, even more English verses are extant; thou hast drunk deep draughts not only of the Muses in France and Italy, but hast learnt the manners of many men, and the arts of foreign countries. . . . Neither in France, Italy nor Germany are such cultivated and polished men. . . . Now is the time for thee to *sharpen the spear*. . . . Thine eyes flash fire, *thy countenance shakes a spear*, who would not swear that Achilles had come to life again?

The Earl of Oxford depicted in 1572 as Great Lord Chamberlain bearing the sword of state before Queen Elizabeth.

There were many 'hidden poets' at the Court of Queen Elizabeth and Oxford was their leader. That was stated in a book of 1589, *The Arte of English Poesie,* by an anonymous author, thought to have been George Puttenham, who wrote:

> I know very many notable gentlemen in the Court that have written commendably, and suppressed it again, or else suffered it to be published without their own names to it: as if it were a discredit for a gentleman to seem learned. . . . And in her Majesty's time that now is are sprung up another crew of Courtly makers [poets], Noblemen and Gentlemen of Her Majesty's own servants, who have written excellently well as it would appear if their doings could be found out and made public with the rest, of which number is first that noble gentleman Edward Earl of Oxford.

Several other contemporary writers named Oxford as a leading poet and author of comedies. His known poems were all written before he was twenty-six, and no plays under his name have survived. Yet most of his literary work is likely to have been done after he was forty, had married again and retired from public life. That was his main period as the writer of Shakespeare.

He did not write alone but as the leader of a secret group. That is the general conclusion of Oxfordians since Looney's time. The evidence for it was discovered in 1928 by the Oxfordian writer, Captain B.M. Ward, in the form of a Privy Seal Warrant, signed by Queen Elizabeth on 26 June 1586. It commanded the Treasury to pay the Earl of Oxford the annual sum of £1000. This huge allowance was paid throughout Elizabeth's reign, was confirmed by King James and continued up to Oxford's death. No reason was given for it, and Oxford performed no obvious public service that might have justified such a large salary. The Queen was notoriously mean when it came to money, preferring to reward her deserving subjects with titles and grants that cost her nothing. Ward's researches showed that the only annuity exceeding Oxford's during her reign was the £1200 paid to the Master of the Posts for running the country's postal services.

The form of the grant, said Ward, was typical of the Secret Service. Oxford was being paid to set up and manage a sort of Government propaganda department, producing plays such as Marlowe's *Edward II* and the *King John* and *Henry V* of Shakespeare to encourage patriotic sentiments during the wars with Spain. All the main Authorship candidates were members of this group, including Marlowe, whose place after his death in 1593 was taken by William Shakspere.

This amiable theory should satisfy most people. It would certainly explain the occurrence of parallel phrases and metaphors in the works of so many contemporary dramatists. The only point of dispute is the main one, the identity of the group leader, the Master Mind behind the plays. The Oxfordians of course have their answer, but so do the Baconians, Derbyites and all others who allow a Groupist element into their theories. Stratfordians are sceptical about Oxford's propaganda department. His state allowance, they suggest, was for maintaining him in respectable style after his financial ruin. Moreover, when *Richard II* was staged on the eve of the Essex rebellion, it was in order to stir up trouble for the administration. The queen would hardly have gone on paying Oxford's group of propagandist playwrights after they had produced a scene showing the deposition of a monarch. Shakespeare's historical plays can be seen as encouraging patriotism, but it is difficult to accept that they were no more than vehicles for government propaganda.

If Oxford had left a will, it would no doubt have shed light on the mystery of his life. Unexpectedly, in view of his hereditary, state and family affairs, he died intestate. At least, no will was found. Struck by this anomaly, Oxfordian Randall Barron investigated further and discovered something very curious, which he reported in the Shakespeare Oxford Society

Newsletter (Fall, 1993). Oxford died on 24 June 1604, and that same day there was a panic in King James's Court. What happened is described in G.P.V. Akrigg's *Shakespeare and the Earl of Southampton*. The king ordered his heir to keep to his chambers and sought the protection of his loyal Scots guards. Southampton and other associates of the Earl of Oxford were suddenly arrested and taken for questioning to the Tower, while their private papers were seized and examined. Next day they were released without charge. Wild rumours swept through the court, but the authorities kept silent, no explanation was given and all documents on the incident were suppressed. As Barron concluded, it looks as if there was a search for Oxford's will to stifle any embarrassing disclosures it might have contained.

The Oxford Group theory seems more attractive than the case for any lone individual; it combines the strong points for each candidate and overrides their weaknesses. William Shakspere is allowed his place in it, and it accommodates almost any candidate whose supporters clamour for his inclusion. Bacon's place is as archivist and editor-in-chief after Oxford's death. This theory appealed to the anti-Stratfordian members of the Shakespeare Fellowship, whose first President, Sir George Greenwood, stated their conclusion that the Shakespeare Folio was the work of 'many pens and one Master Mind'.

This is a soothing idea, and its only drawback is its vagueness. A composite, all-talented Shakespeare is the dream candidate, but his substance is also dream-like. Apart from his £1000 a year, there is no evidence that Oxford ran a propaganda agency, nor that anyone else belonged to it, nor that such a thing even existed. Yet if there was a Shakespeare group, for a patriotic, esoteric or some other purpose, it is easy to imagine the Earl of Oxford as its leader.

OXFORD AND THE SONNETS

The author of *Shakespeare's Sonnets* wrote from the heart, exposing his emotions and inner nature, but without ever revealing the one thing that everyone would like to know about him, his identity. He provided many clues, or apparent clues, together with puns and allusive wordplay, but they are all equivocal and have been interpreted in dozens of different ways. Even a simple outline of the author, drawn directly from his own words in the poems, is bound to be controversial, so the following can be claimed as no more than an honest effort.

The Sonnet-writer was a senior man in both rank and age. He was cultured, sensitive, fastidious and inclined to self-pity. He cast himself as an outsider. Physically he had been lamed or wounded, but the main reason for his suffering was his deep sense of disgrace and failure. For some reason he had become a social outcast. For the sake of his lover's reputation he could not openly declare his love. He was fated to die in ignominy, leaving a dishonoured name behind him, but one day the lover would be proud of him and would become famous by association with him. Finally, in two Sonnets he insists repeatedly that 'my name is "Will"'.

The Sonnets are about love. The first 126 are mostly addressed to a fair youth, beginning with a series of seventeen in which he is urged to marry so as to perpetuate his beauty and lineage through children. In the final sequence, apart from the last two, the poet is bewitched by a dark-eyed, dark-skinned woman. He is passionately aroused by her, but she is treacherous and entices the youth away from him.

The lovely Anne Vavasor, Oxford's dark lady, in a sixteenth-century portrait.

Oxfordians have no difficulty in seeing Edward de Vere in the Sonnet-writer. Anne Vavasor, his mistress who had a son by him, fills the role of the dark lady. The beloved youth is generally identified as Henry Wriothesley, Earl of Southampton. In 1590 when he was seventeen, he was urged by his guardian, Lord Burghley, to marry Oxford's eldest daughter, Elizabeth, who was Burghley's granddaughter. If Oxford was the author of the Sonnets, he was giving the same advice, as a prospective father-in-law. Southampton refused the engagement, and Elizabeth later married the Earl of Derby.

The poet's references to his lameness, which seems to be more than a metaphor, can be explained by the wound Oxford received in 1582, when Anne Vavasor's kinsman, Thomas Knyvet, assaulted him. Expressions of shame and failure were also appropriate to Oxford. He had not lived up to the military traditions of his family, but had squandered his fortune in foreign travels, lost his ancestral estates, made a disaster of his marriage and failed to provide properly for his daughters. As well as these public causes of shame, there were probably others, more personal, as indicated in the Sonnets.

Oxford was a known writer of sonnets and was one of the first poets to use that form of verse. Shakespeare's sonnets were in private circulation before 1598, and the earliest were perhaps written in about 1590 when Oxford was forty and William Shakspere twenty-six. The older man is clearly indicated by many self-references, for example:

> But when my glass shows me myself indeed,
> Beated and chopp'd with tann'd antiquity
> > (Sonnet 62)

> That time of year thou mayst in me behold
> When yellow leaves, or none, or few, do hang
> > (Sonnet 73)

> Thus vainly thinking that she thinks me young,
> Although she knews my days are past the best
> > (Sonnet 138)

In Sonnet 3 the poet hints that he knew the youth's mother in the 'lovely April of her prime', and in the preceding Sonnet he may be thinking of his own age in telling the young man that 'When forty winters shall besiege thy brow', his beauty will have faded away.

Sonnet 125, beginning 'Were't aught to me I bore the canopy', carries a good Oxfordian clue. The only sense that can be made of this is that it was a reference to the canopy which protected the queen on state occasions. As hereditary Lord Great Chamberlain, Oxford was probably one of the senior noblemen who bore the canopy at the celebration of the defeat of the Spanish Armada, and again at the queen's funeral.

In character with Oxford is the poet's constant lament that he must die in obscurity and without honours.

> Your name from hence immortal life shall have
> Though I, once gone, to all the world must die
> > (Sonnet 81)

> My name be buried where my body is,
> And live no more to shame nor me nor you
> > (Sonnet 72)

Oxford was buried quietly in Hackney church; there was no monument, his grave is unknown and he left no will.

The 'Will' sonnets (135, 136, 143) with their elaborate wordplay on 'Will', a name in inverted commas, and 'will', meaning something else,

seems to imply that the poet was called William. This is good for supporters of William Shakspere and William Stanley, Earl of Derby, but the
Oxfordians have found evidence that Edward de Vere was known to his
fellow-poets as Willy. These sonnets are incomprehensible until read
through the eyes of Dr A.L. Rowse, who sees that 'will' means the sex
organs of the man and woman. Other lascivious puns occur in the Sonnets,
most obviously in 151, where the very name of his mistress makes the
poet's flesh rise and point her out. Shakespeare by these clues could have
been anyone.

As a self-declared lover of boys – or of one in particular, the writer of
the Sonnets has earlier been compared with the pederastic Bacon. On the
other hand, the final couplet in the notorious Sonnet 20 shows that the
writer's love for his young man was strictly Platonic. This sounds like the
romantically imaginative Oxford rather than Bacon. The love of Oxford's
life was probably his dark lady, Anne Vavasor. He was once accused of
homosexuality, but by a prejudiced and unreliable witness. It is quite possible that he conceived a jealous passion for Henry Wriothesley and was
distressed to see the lovely youth being petted and spoilt by worthless
courtiers. Yet here the Oxfordian case becomes confused. If Oxford's love for young Henry was as intense and personally covetous as the Sonnet-writer's for the fair youth, he would hardly have preceded his passionate addresses with seventeen sonnets pressing him to marry his eldest daughter. No self-respecting father would try so blatantly to force his daughter upon an unwilling suitor.

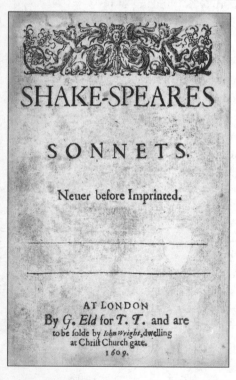

Title-page of Shakespeare's Sonnets, published for Thomas Thorpe in 1609.

THE OXFORD ANAGRAM

The strongest link in the Oxfordian chain is that Edward de Vere was the author of the Sonnets. In contrast, their conventional attribution to William Shakspere is weak, largely derived from the title under which they were published. They were issued in 1609 by a small-
time operator in the book trade, Thomas Thorpe, who called them *Shake-speares Sonnets*, using the suspiciously impersonal, hyphenated name. Thorpe's edition was pirated. Somehow

he had obtained possession of the manuscripts which, in days before copyright laws, meant that he owned the literary rights. He published without the author's consent or prior knowledge, presumably to make a quick profit. Shakespeare's sonnets had been talked about for at least eleven years, and two had previously been published, so there was a likely market for the complete collection.

Adding to the mystery, Thorpe prefixed a publisher's dedication to the *Sonnets* (right). In the thirty or so words above his initials he set up an enigma that has perplexed scholars and attracted theorists ever since. The main questions are about the dedicatee, Mr W.H., who he was and in what sense he was the 'onlie begetter' of the *Sonnets*.

Sir Sidney Lee in his *Life of William Shakespeare* shed light on these questions. The dedication was not, as had commonly been supposed, to the fair youth who inspired most of the Sonnets,

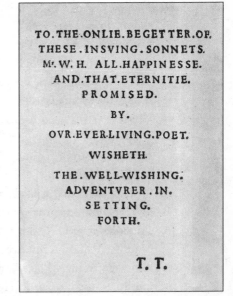

TO.THE.ONLIE.BEGETTER.OF.
THESE.INSVING.SONNETS.
Mr.W.H. ALL.HAPPINESSE.
AND.THAT.ETERNITIE.
PROMISED.

BY.

OVR.EVER-LIVING.POET.

WISHETH.

THE.WELL-WISHING.
ADVENTVRER.IN.
SETTING.
FORTH.

T. T.

The dedication to Mr W. H. from the 1609 edition of Shakespeare's Sonnets. Sir Sidney Lee identified Mr W. H. as William Hall, and in 1922 Colonel Ward discovered a link between Hall and the Earl of Oxford.

but to their begetter in another sense, meaning the person who got or procured them on Thorpe's behalf. By his initials and the name, Mr W. H. ALL, hidden in the dedication, Lee identified him as William Hall, one of Thorpe's occasional collaborators and, like him, a minor figure in the printing-publishing business. He was a dealer in literary properties, acquiring manuscripts by whatever means he could, and either printing them himself or passing them on to another publisher. By some means he got his hands on Shakespeare's famous sonnets, and then made a deal with his friend, Thorpe, who perhaps at the time was better able to pay for their printing.

A significant link between William Hall, the *Sonnets* and the Earl of Oxford was discovered in 1922 by Colonel B.R. Ward and described in his book, *The Mystery of 'Mr. W. H.'* The clue he followed was that in 1606, three years before he found the Sonnets, William Hall had acquired and published another manuscript, *A Foure-fold Meditation*, a poem by Robert Southwell. He had it printed by George Eld (who later printed *Shake-speares Sonnets*). Its author was an illegal Jesuit missionary to England, who was arrested in 1592, tortured for three years in the Tower and then executed at Tyburn. His earlier place of refuge was the house of Lord Vaux at

Hackney. After his retirement Oxford also lived at Hackney, which was then a suburban village. In 1596 his second wife, Elizabeth, bought a large house there, King's Place, which was probably where Lord Vaux had sheltered Southwell. It could also have been the place where, after Southwell's death, William Hall found the manuscript of his poem, and perhaps he found the Sonnets there too. Suspecting that Hall was a Hackney man, Colonel Ward went to investigate.

He found the very evidence he was looking for. It was an entry in the Hackney church register: 'William Hall and Margery Gryffyn were joyned in matrymonye on the 4th Aug. 1608.'

This suggested a likely series of events. William Hall was a parishioner of Hackney and was married at the church near King's Place. He knew someone in the Oxford household and was thus able to acquire the Southwell manuscript when it turned up there. A few months after his marriage, King's Place was sold, and Oxford's widow took charge of the family estates at Castle Hedingham in Essex. As the Hackney household broke up, Oxford's manuscripts of the Sonnets came to light. They are not the sort of poems by which a widow would care to remember her husband, so Hall was allowed to take them. Perhaps they were thrown out, no one thinking that they might fall into the hands of an opportunist publisher. Hall placed them with Thorpe, and Thorpe expressed his gratitude through the dedication. In wishing him 'all happinesse and that eternitie promised by our ever-living poet', the publisher was congratulating the begetter on his recent marriage and wishing him the benefit of offspring. The 'book called *Shakespeares Sonnettes*' was entered on the Stationer's register on 20 May 1609, nine months after the wedding of William Hall and the scrivener's daughter, Margery Gryffyn. It may have marked the birth of their first child.

The most strikingly odd feature of Thorpe's dedication to Hall is the phrase which he applies to the author of the *Sonnets*. 'Our ever-living poet' is not appropriate to a person still living. Oxfordian researchers have looked far and wide for examples of 'ever-living' in literature, and found that in virtually every case it refers to someone who is no longer alive. Its one occurrence in Shakespeare's plays is in *1 Henry VI* (iv. 3), where the former monarch is called 'that ever-living man of memory, Henry the Fifth'.

In 1609 when the *Sonnets* appeared, William Shakspere still had seven years to live, Bacon, Derby and Rutland were flourishing, but Oxford was five years dead. Apart from Marlowe, Oxford is the only one of the major candidates whom Thorpe could properly have referred to as 'our ever-living poet'.

Thorpe certainly knew who his author was, and in a sure but subtle way he conveyed that knowledge through the phrase, 'our ever-living'. Those words do not just say that the poet is dead, but have a further, more specific meaning. As Bacon was known by his personal motto, *Mediocria firma*, so was Oxford by his *Vero nil verius*. This was a pun on his name and on the town of Ver in Normandy where his family originated before the Conquest. It means, 'Nothing is more true than Truth itself'. Sometimes the middle word was written *nihil*, and the order of the words is unimportant. Thorpe took Oxford's motto, shifted its thirteen letters around to make an anagram, and by substituting a final 'G' for the final 'S' he obtained 'our ever-living'.

NIL VERO VERIUS

OUR EVER-LIVING

The words of Thorpe's dedication, commented Lee, are fantastically arranged and in odd grammatical order. The reason for that is now apparent. Thorpe wanted to bring in two bits of wordplay. The first was quite simple, the concealment of the name, W. Hall, but the second was more important. Thorpe could not resist weaving in a clue to the identity of the author, so he made an anagram out of Oxford's motto, and from *nil vero verius* obtained 'our ever-living'. It was almost too appropriate, because it gave the game away by implying that the author was dead. It was an awkward phrase, bound to attract attention. Yet 'our ever-living' was the best possible anagram for identifying the author of the *Sonnets* as '*Nil vero verius*, poet'. Thorpe's meaning is that the poet was the Earl of Oxford.

The likelihood of the anagram being significant has three points in its favour. 'Our ever-living' is the only epithet which Thorpe or any other contemporary applied to the author of the *Sonnets*; it was inappropriate to the still-living Shakspere and seems in context awkward and contrived; it applies perfectly to Oxford, both openly as written and esoterically as an anagram of his motto. If Thorpe intended to conceal the author's name, while allowing anyone who looked shrewdly at his dedication to perceive it, he could hardly have done better.

There is an extraordinary parallel to this anagram in the second edition of the *Sonnets*. They were not reprinted until 1640, when all but eight of them, newly ordered and grouped under titles, were included with other poems and tributes to Shakespeare in *The Poems of Wil. Shakespere, Gent.* Some of the strange features of this volume have already been noticed (page 86), particularly in the introductory address 'To the Reader', signed with the initials of John Benson, I.B., and there are others.

I.B.'s preliminary address 'To the Reader' in the second, 1640 edition of Shakespeare's Sonnets has some strange, possibly cryptic references to the author.

Benson's short address (above) contains words and phrases, such as 'ever-living' and 'these ensuing Lines', which echo phrases in Thorpe's original Dedication of the sonnets, and his reference to the author of the poems is similarly preceded by a puzzling epithet. Whereas Thorpe called the poet 'ever-living', Benson wished glory to the 'deserved Author'. This phrase is just as awkward as Thorpe's, and commentators have drawn attention to it. A writer can be called deserving, but it is hard to understand what a 'deserved' author might be. Benson has copied Thorpe by identifying the true Shakespeare through a near-anagram. The rearranged letters of DESERVED spell out ED. DE VERS.

Elsewhere in 'To the Reader', Benson gave a more open hint that de Vere rather than Shakespeare was the author of the Sonnets. The poems, he wrote, 'had not the fortune by reason of their Infancie in his death' to become as famous as the rest of the Author's works. This implies that the poems were finished shortly before the author's death. Shakspere lived on for many years after the Sonnets were first mentioned and published, but they were indeed in their infancy when Oxford died in 1604.

Oxfordians suspect that Edward de Vere put anagrams or near-anagrams of his own name into his writings, particularly the Sonnets. In his known poems he was often alliterative, and in one of his 'echo verses' he made play with 'Vere', its anagram, 'ever', and other words which echo its sound.

From sighs and shedding amber tears into sweet
    song she brake,
When thus the Echo answer'd her to every word
    she spake:

> Oh heavens! who was the first that bred in me this
>   fe*ver*? Vere.
> Who was the first that gave the wound whose fear
>   I wear for *ever*? Vere.
>
> What tyrant, Cupid, to my harm usurps thy golden
>   qui*ver*? Vere.
> What wight first caught this heart and can from
>   bondage it deli*ver*? Vere.

From this base, Oxfordians have gone on to examine Sonnet 76, where the poet almost gives away his own name:

> Why is my verse so barren of new pride,
> So far from variation or quick change?
> Why with the time do I not glance aside
> To new-found methods and to compounds strange?
> Why write I all still one, ever the same,
> And keep invention in a noted weed,
> That every word doth almost tell my name,
> Showing their birth and where they did proceed?
> O, know, sweet love, I always write of you,
> And you and love are still my argument;
> So all my best is dressing old words new,
> Spending again what is already spent:
>   For as the sun is daily new and old,
>   So is my love still telling what is told.

The poet is saying that the theme of love is always the same, so he is not going to change his way of expressing it. In the fifth line he becomes cryptic. 'Ever the same' is *Semper eadem*, the motto of Queen Elizabeth. A 'noted weed' means a well-known disguise. His name is almost told by 'every word'. This suggests a near-anagram, and the letters of EVERY WORD do indeed form EYWORD VER, which is fairly close to Edward Vere or Ver as he sometimes spelt it. Then again, an anagram of A NOTED WEED and EVERY WORD together is YE NOTED EDWARD VERE with WO left over.

It is impossible in this world of delusion to survive without humour and scepticism, so it must be pointed out that the above anagram could just as well be WO! NOT YE EDWARD DE VERE.

One of the longest words that can be made from the letters in *Nil vero verius* is 'envious'. In Mrs Cowden-Clarke's *Concordance to Shakespeare*, 'envious' is paired with 'sliver'. The only occurrence of the latter word as a noun in Shakespeare is in *Hamlet* (iv. 7), where the queen brings news of Ophelia's drowning. As she climbed into a willow tree, 'an envious sliver broke', throwing her into the water. That is a strange way of describing a snapping twig, but the reason for the expression could be that 'envious sliver' is a near-anagram (with an S for a R) of *Nil vero verius*. Ophelia is supposed to be Anne Cecil, Oxford's first wife, whom he publicly accused of infidelity, bringing grief and scandal upon her and her family. Oxford knew he had let her down, just as the 'envious sliver' or *Nil vero verius* let down Ophelia.

Another possible Oxfordian anagram is in a curious emblem on the title-page of Henry Peacham's *Minerva Britanna* of 1612 (left). Beneath the title is the proscenium arch of a theatre. The scene within it is of a hand mysteriously emerging from behind a curtain and writing with a quill pen.

In the tittle-page emblem to Peacham's work of 1612, a mysterious hand inscribes letters forming a significant Oxfordian anagram.

The letters, upside-down to the reader, are MENTE VIDEBORI. This is an incomplete sentence. The hand is in the process of writing MENTE VIDEBORIS, meaning 'In the mind thou shalt be seen'. The omission of the S allows an anagram. After taking out the letters DE VERE, the remaining letters are NOMTIBI. This seems to be the only arrangement that makes sense: NOM (a conventional abbreviation of *nomine*) TIBI DE VERE means THY NAME IS DE VERE.

The Latin sentences which twine around the encircling laurel wreath mean, 'His genius abides' and 'All the rest will be wiped out by death'. Dorothy and Charlton Ogburn who explain this in their book, *This Star of England*, point out that Henry Peacham was known for his interest in anagrams and that he greatly admired Oxford as a poet. In 1622 he published another book, *The Compleat Gentleman*, praising the Elizabethan age for the unrivalled quality of its poets. He named those 'who honoured Poesie with their Pennes and practice', beginning with the most high-ranking, the Earl of Oxford, and continuing with Buckhurst, Paget, Sidney, Dyer, Spenser and Daniel. He made no mention of Shakespeare. The Ogburns suspected that through the emblems of his earlier book Peacham was hinting to the initiated that Edward de Vere was the real Shakespeare.

THE OXFORD ASCENDANCY

There are still Bacon societies, Marlowe and other candidates still have their followers, but by far the most active and organized students of the Authorship question today are the Oxfordians. They give the best parties and events, circulate newsletters with details of new discoveries and attract a glamorous following. Sir John Gielgud is a recent convert. Their leading spokesman, Lord Burford, a scion of the de Vere family, makes a career from lecturing on the case for Oxford. William Shakspere and Edward de Vere are now the leading contenders for the Authorship.

Oxford appears to be the ideal candidate. Everything known about him conforms to the mind and character of Shakespeare, as deduced from his works. He was a nobleman of high rank and culture, classically educated under Burghley's strict regime and tutored by Arthur Golding, the translator of Ovid. This is significant because Shakespeare made great use of Ovid, sometimes drawing from the original Latin but often from Golding's version. From his early childhood on his father's estate at Castle Hedingham, Edward de Vere was familiar with the terms and customs of hunting and hawking, and with games such as bowls and tennis to which there are so many informed references in Shakespeare. He was schooled at Cambridge University and studied law at Gray's Inn. Military and naval terms were well known to him through experience. He travelled widely on the continent, and lived for some time in Italy, where he adopted the Italian style of dress and manners that caused him to be laughed at in England. With his lifelong interest in the theatre, his patronage of acting companies, his musical accomplishments and his reputation as a poet and writer of comedies, de Vere has almost all the characteristics attributable to Shakespeare.

Sigmund Freud was by no means infallible, but he is an impressive witness in the case for Oxford. In his judgment, Oxford's early life and the tragedies of his later career, his mind, temperament and apparent psychology imply that Hamlet was his own self-portrait. This and the many other probable references in the plays to Oxford's life and family add up to the near-certainty that he was either very close to Shakespeare or was the author himself.

Modern Oxfordians feel that things are going their way, and they are constantly finding new evidence to augment their case. A recent addition is the study by the Shakespeare scholar, Roger Stritmatter, of Oxford's copy of the Geneva translation of the Bible, belonging to the Folger Shakespeare Library in Washington, DC. This has been identified as the translation from

*Many of the marked passages in Oxford's copy of the Bible,
preserved in the Folger Library, were reproduced in the plays of Shakespeare.*

which Shakespeare drew the many Biblical allusions in his plays. In his copy, Oxford marked in coloured inks hundreds of phrases and verses that were used by Shakespeare. Many of them are obscure and rarely quoted. As just one example, in 2 Samuel 21: 19, an Israelite hero 'slew the brother of Goliath the Gittite, the staff of whose spear was *like a weaver's beam*'. Oxford underlined the italicized phrase, and in *The Merry Wives of Windsor* (v. 1) Falstaff says wittily, 'I fear not Goliath with a weaver's beam; because I know also life is a shuttle'. The second part of this is a paraphrase of Job 7: 6, 'My days are swifter than a weaver's shuttle.'

This makes up for Oxfordian disappointment over the Ashbourne portrait. This fine painting, now exhibited in the Folger Shakespeare Library, turned up in the middle of the nineteenth century when it was

A detail from the Ashbourne portrait, thought to represent Shakespeare,
which Oxfordians identify as a portrait of de Vere.

acquired by a schoolmaster of Ashbourne, Derbyshire. He identified the
three-quarter-length figure as William Shakspere, and found some contemporary experts who agreed with him. The main evidence was the sitter's
lofty brow and the inscription top left:

ÆTATIS SUAE 47

A°: 1611.

This fitted Shakspere who was forty-seven in 1611. The skull below the
man's right arm (illustrated on page 261) was surely a reference to the
grave-digger scene in *Hamlet*.

In 1939 Charles Wisner Barrell was allowed by the Folger to examine
the portrait with X-ray and infra-red photography, and in January the
following year his sensational conclusions were announced in *The Scientific
American.*, January 1940. The portrait, he found, had been doctored to
make it resemble the conventional Shakspere. Beneath the overpainting
Barrell discerned an original portrait of the Earl of Oxford. The device on
the signet ring was Oxford's wild boar, and below the inscription could
faintly be seen a shield with the armorial bearings of the Countess of
Oxford. An even fainter monogram beneath it identified the artist as the
Dutch portrait painter, Cornelius Ketel, who died in 1616.

These results have not stood up to later scrutiny. Barrell was a committed Oxfordian and this evidently coloured his interpretations. The Folger's
own experts could see no monogram, and the opinion of heralds was that
the arms were not those of Lady Oxford nor of any other woman. Samuel

A neuer writer, to an euer reader. Newes.

Ternall reader, you haue heere a new play, neuer stal'd with the Stage, neuer clapper-clawd with the palmes of the vulger, and yet passing full of the palme comicall; for it is a birth of your braine, that neuer vnder-tooke any thing commicall, vainely: And were but the vaine names of commedies changde for the titles of Commodities, or of Playes for Pleas; you should see all those grand censors, that now stile them such vanities, flock to them for the maine grace of their grauities: especially this authors Commedies, that are so fram'd to the life, that they serue for the most common Commentaries, of all the actions of our liues shewing such a dexteritie, and power of witte, that the most displeasd with Playes, are pleasd with his Commedies. And all such dull and heauy-witted worldlings, as were neuer capable of the witte of a Commedie, comming by report of them to his representations, haue found that witte there, that they neuer found in them selues, and haue parted better wittied then they came: feeling an edge of witte set vpon them, more then euer they dreamd they had braine to grinde it on. So much and such sauored salt of witte is in his Commedies, that they seeme (for their height of pleasure) to be borne in that sea that brought forth Venus. Amongst all there is none more witty then this: And had I time I would comment vpon it, though I know it needs not, (for so

¶ 2   much

The oddly phrased preface to the 1609 edition of Troilus and Cressida
provides Oxfordians with a puzzle but no solution.

Schoenbaum in *William Shakespeare, Records and Images*, says that the shield identifies the sitter as most probably Sir Hugh Hamersley, Lord Mayor of London in 1627. In the portrait his brow has been heightened, and the date has been altered to 1611 from the painter's original 1612, the year when Hamersley was forty-seven. Oxfordian experts may disagree, but even if the original portrait was of their candidate, and even if it was altered to represent Shakspere, nothing more significant need be inferred than that someone adapted it for commercial reasons.

Apart from turning Freud's psychoanalytical methods against them and calling them snobs, the Stratfordians have made a poor response to the Oxford theorists. This is partly because the theory is still vague and diffuse. It is one thing to present a highly credible candidate for Shakespeare, but it is far more difficult when it comes to establishing him. The Stratfordians have their own candidate, and they are perfectly satisfied with him. They need no Earl of Oxford or any other interloper.

Against the Oxford theory are several references to Shakespeare, later than 1604, which imply that the author was then still alive. These include Davies's epigram (page 55) and the anonymous preface in certain copies of the quarto edition of *Troilus and Cressida*, published in 1609 (opposite). Headed 'A never writer to an ever reader. News', this ironically grandiloquent text seems almost calculated to tease the Oxfordians. On the one hand it indicates a living Shakespeare, but on the other hand its heading is obviously playful. It repeats the recurrent pun on Oxford's abbreviated name, . . . an E. Ver writer . . . an E. Ver reader. This is one of those vertiginous semi-clues that warn sensible people against involvement in the maddening question of 'Who Wrote Shakespeare?'

Idolizers of Shakespeare object to Oxford because of his character. He was neither the merry English country lad enshrined in Stratford legend, nor the grave, wise, judicial Shakespeare imagined by Baconians and others. The one thing everyone knows about him is the ludicrous anecdote in Aubrey's *Brief Lives*. 'This Earle of Oxford, making his low obeisance to Queen Elizabeth, happened to let a Fart, at which he was so abashed and ashamed that he went to Travell, 7 yeares. On his returne, the Queen welcomed him home, and sayd, My Lord, I had forgott the Fart.'

Oxfordians never mention this story – understandably, because it is a low blow to the dignity of their candidate. Even William Shakspere with his malt-dealing and money-lending was never so degraded. Oxford was a puzzle to his generation, and malicious gossips made fun of him. Short in stature, ever ready to feel slighted, he was moody, rebellious, quarrelsome and dissolute. His matrimonial and love affairs were awkward and convoluted. He might quite naturally have seen himself as Hamlet. In Colin Wilson's sense of the word, he was an outsider, and in the betting sense he is still an outsider as far as his chances go of being recognized as Shakespeare.

VII

EARLS AND OTHERS

WILLIAM STANLEY, SIXTH EARL OF DERBY

1561 Born in London, according to some authorities; others say born in 1560 at main family seat, Lathom House, Lancashire.
Father: Henry, Lord Strange, who succeeded his father in 1572 as fourth Earl of Derby.
Mother: Margaret Clifford, great granddaughter of Henry VII and granddaughter of Queen Marie of France.
Childhood at Meriden Manor, Warwickshire.

1572 With elder brother, Ferdinando, and a younger brother who died early, admitted to St John's College, Oxford.

1582 Given leave to travel abroad with tutor Richard Lloyd. Went to France, Spain, Italy, Mediterranean countries and, according to legend, much farther afield.

1587 Returned home to Lancashire, became occupied with the theatre and the family company of players.

1593 Appointed Governor of family kingdom, the Isle of Man.
25 September. Father died; Ferdinando became fifth Earl of Derby.

1594 Studied law at Lincoln's Inn.
16 April. Ferdinando died, rumoured to have been poisoned by Jesuits whose agent he had betrayed. William became sixth Earl of Derby.
A lawsuit over family property with sister-in-law, Ferdinando's widow, which was to drag on for years at ruinous cost to both sides. Francis Bacon involved in the litigation.

1595 26 January. Married Elizabeth de Vere, daughter of the seventeenth Earl of Oxford, at Greenwich Palace in the presence of the queen.

1597 Left the court and London to administer great estates in and around Lancashire. His marriage disturbed by mutual jealousies.

1599 Nominated with the Earls of Southampton and Rutland to campaign with Essex in Ireland, also for an expedition to the Low Countries, but seems not to have left England.

1601 23 April. Elected Knight of the Garter.

1603 Member of the Privy Council.

1607 Lord Lieutenant of Lancashire and Cheshire.

31 January. Eldest son, James, born at Knowsley.

1608 Reported on training and conditions of troops to be sent to Ireland.

1610 Officiated at installation of Henry, King James's heir, as Prince of Wales.

1612 Kingship of the Isle of Man, exercised by the English Crown since 1593, restored to the Earl of Derby, ruling jointly with the Countess.

1617 Councillor for Wales.

Visited by King James at Lathom House.

Disbanded company of players.

1626 James, Lord Strange (son) married Charlotte, daughter of le duc de La Trémoille.

1627 Countess of Derby died away from home.

James, Lord Strange took over rule of the Isle of Man.

By this year had retired into private life, living on £1000 a year.

1642 29 September. Died aged eighty-one.

THE EAGLE AND THE EARL OF DERBY

Upholders of Orthodoxy often complain that anti-Stratfordian theorists have no grounding in Elizabethan literature and are not qualified to give opinions on the Authorship question. This objection did not apply to Professor Abel Lefranc of the Collège de France, the renowned authority on Rabelais, Molière and the literature of Shakespeare's period. Unlike Looney and other Heretics, he was no dilettante scholar but a weighty professional. When Lefranc declared that William Shakspere could not possibly have been the great Shakespeare, poet and dramatist, his opinion was accepted by many of his compatriots, and a succession of books by French writers supported his conclusion, that the real Shakespeare was William Stanley, sixth Earl of Derby.

The first volume of Lefranc's *Sous le masque de 'William Shakespeare'* was published in 1918 and was followed the next year by the second. After his thirty-five-year study of Shakespeare, Lefranc had found nothing in the plays and poems to favour the Stratfordian case. There was no correspondence between the life and the works. In every other case known to Lefranc, even in works of pure fantasy, the author inevitably left his personal mark on the text, betraying something of his own mind, character and experiences of life. Shakspere seemed to be the only exception. This

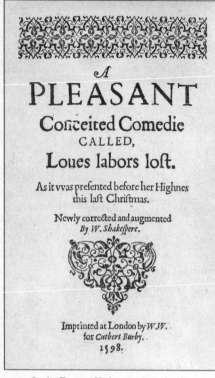

A
PLEASANT
Conceited Comedie
CALLED,
Loues labors loſt.

As it vvas preſented before her Highnes
this laſt Chriſtmas.

Newly correĉted and augmented
By W. Shakeſpere.

Imprinted at London by *W.W.*
for *Cutbert Burby.*
1598.

Set in France, Shakespeare's early play,
Love's Labour's Lost, *is a leading exhibit in
the case for William Stanley.*

was so incredible that it negated his claim to the Authorship. The true Shakespeare, as revealed through his writings, was an English nobleman who wished to conceal his identity.

In the early Shakespeare play, *Love's Labour's Lost*, Lefranc recognized an author who understood the spirit of France, spoke cultured and colloquial French and knew at first hand the manners of court life. He must have spent some time at the Court of Navarre, for his allusions to it showed intimate knowledge available only to the privileged few. The play was evidently not written for public performance but for entertaining the English court, where these allusions would be recognized.

In his search for the real Shakespeare, Lefranc found himself drawn towards the Earl of Derby. He was a great traveller and patron of the theatre, maintaining his own company of players, but little else was known about his life. There was no entry for him in the *Dictionary of National Biography*, merely a brief mention under the name of his son and heir, James, who was executed by Cromwell. Nor was he known for any literary work. Some letters from the later part of his life have survived, but any plays or poems he may have written would have been destroyed when the Cromwellians burnt the Stanley stronghold, Lathom House in Lancashire. The case for his being a playwright is based on a discovery by the pioneer Derbyite, antiquarian James Greenstreet, who wrote three articles on the subject in *The Genealogist* (July 1891; January, May 1892). He found that on 30 June 1599 a Jesuit spy in England, George Fenners, reported in two letters, intercepted by the Secret Service, that the Earl of Derby was 'busyed only in penning commodyes for the commoun players'.

The evidence that confirmed Lefranc in his theory was Edmund Spenser's poem, *Colin Clouts come home againe*, completed in 1594. In it are verses to contemporary poets, mostly disguised under names which Spenser gave them. On one page (shown overleaf) the poet Daniel is named openly, and critics have identified other references. The Shepherd of the Ocean is Sir Walter Ralegh; Amyntas is Ferdinando, fifth Earl of

And to what courfe thou pleafe thy felfe aduaunce:
But moft, me feemes, thy accent will excell,
In Tragicke plaints and paffionate mifchance.
And there that fhepheard of the O C E A N is,
That fpends his wit in loues confuming fmart:
Full fweetly tempred is that Mufe of his,
That can empierce a Princes mightie hart.
There alfo is (ah no, he is not now)
But fince I faid he is, he quite is gone,
A M Y N T A S quite is gone and lies full lowe,
Hauing his A M A R I L L I S left to mone.
Helpe, ô ye fhepheards, helpe ye all in this,
Helpe A M A R I L L I S this her loffe to mournc:
Her loffe is yours, your loffe A M Y N T A S is,
A M Y N T A S, flowre of fhepheards pride forlorne:
He, whilft he liued, was the nobleft fwaine,
That euer piped on an oaten quill:
Both did he other, which could pipe, maintaine,
And eke could pipe himfelfe with paffing skill.
And there, though laft not leaft is A E T I O N,
A gentler fhepheard may no where be found:
Whofe Mufe, full of high thoughts inuention,
Doth like himfelfe heroïcally found.
All thefe, and many others moe remaine,
Now after A S T R O F E L L is dead and gone.
But while as A S T R O F E L L did liue and raigne,
Amongft all thefe was none his Paragone:
All thefe do florifh in their fundry kind,
And doe their C Y N T H I A immortall make:
Yet found I liking in her royall mind,
Not for my skill, but for that fhepheards fake.

Lines in Spenser's poem, Colin Clouts, *suggest that William Stanley was the Aetion or Eagle man whom many critics have identified as Shakespeare.*

Derby and William Stanley's elder brother, who died in 1594; Alice, his widow, is the mourning Amarillis; Astrofell is Sir Philip Sidney and Cynthia Queen Elizabeth.

The controversial identification is of Aetion in the four lines:

And there, though last not least is AETION,
A gentler shepheard may no where be found:
Whose Muse, full of high thoughts invention,
Doth like himselfe heroically sound.

Since Malone in the eighteenth century, critics have taken Aetion to represent Shakespeare. Thomas Fuller in 1662 noted the 'warlike sound' of his surname. Lee in his *Life of Shakespeare* found it 'hardly doubtful' that Spenser was greeting Shakespeare under the name of Aetion, a Greek epithet meaning Man of the Eagle.

This interpretation has been disputed, largely because of the difficulty in equating Shakespeare-Aetion with Shakspere the actor. Spenser knew all the people alluded to in his poem, but his visits to London were few and brief, so it is unlikely that he had met Shakspere at the beginning of his theatrical career. Nor would he have called Shakspere 'gentle', which in his time meant 'noble'. His lines to Aetion follow directly after those to Derby's family connections, the Amarillis, Phyllis and Charillis of his poem. These were the three daughters of Sir John Spencer, the first of whom married Ferdinando, Earl of Derby. After his lament for Ferdinando and his call to other shepherds (poets) to comfort his widow, it would be natural for Spenser to turn next to the brother, the new Earl, William Stanley. He would then be Aetion.

If the sixth Earl of Derby was the Eagle Man, Spenser must have had some reason for the name. It occurred to Lefranc that perhaps his family crest was an eagle. Consulting the Peerage, he was delighted to see that the Stanley crest, borne by the Earls of Derby, was an eagle and child (right). It commemorated the foundation legend of the Stanleys, that they were descended from one who as a baby was abducted by an eagle. No other noble family had an eagle crest. It was the unique badge of the Stanleys; the Eagle Tower was the citadel of Lathom House (below), and known as the Eagle's Nest.

The Stanley coat of arms has as its crest a baby being carried off by an eagle.

This is a strong case. Spenser's Amyntas is undoubtedly Ferdinando

Lathom House in Lancashire, stronghold of the Stanleys.

because, in a letter to Spenser, Thomas Nashe referred to the fifth Earl of Derby as 'Jove's Eagleborn Ganimed, thrice noble Amyntas'. Aetion, the Man of the Eagle is therefore most likely to be his brother, William, who succeeded him as head of the family. The name could hardly apply to anyone else. The authorities identify Aetion as the poet Shakespeare, so Spenser seems to have recognized Shakespeare as the sixth Earl of Derby.

Lefranc and his followers examined all contemporary references to Shakespeare, open and
implicit, and found that they applied more
naturally to William Stanley than to William
Shakspere or any other candidate. For instance,
in an earlier poem, *Teares of the Muses*, Spenser
made Thalia lament the recent death of 'our
pleasant Willy', saying about him,

> But that same gentle spirit, from whose pen
> Large streames of honnie and sweete nectar
>   flowe,
> Scorning the boldnes of such base-borne men
> Which dare their follies forth so rashlie throwe,
>   Doth rather choose to sit in idle cell
>   Than so himselfe to mockerie to sell.

*William Stanley's brother, Ferdinando,
fifth Earl of Derby.*

This has often been taken as an allusion to Shakespeare, his death being
meant figuratively. Lee disagreed, claiming that Willy was a term of familiarity applied to other poets, including Sir Philip Sidney. He suggested that
the allusion was to the recently dead comedian, Richard Tarleton. Looney
took advantage of the confusion by proposing Willy as the Earl of Oxford.
The poem was written in 1691, when nothing had yet been published
under the name of Shakespeare. Spenser then would probably never have
heard of the Stratford actor. William Stanley at least had the right
Christian name; he was 'gentle' rather than 'base-born', and he was more
likely than Shakspere to avoid mockery by not publishing his own verses.
Spenser dedicated the poem to his distant cousin Alice, wife of Ferdinando,
the fifth Earl of Derby, the Amarillis of his later poem. It would be appropriate among the family to refer to her brother-in-law, William Stanley, as
Our Willy.

The initials and Christian name of William Stanley make it easy for the
Derbyites to claim on his behalf the 'Will' sonnets and anything published
by 'W.S.' In *Shakespeare's Vital Secret* one of Lefranc's American followers,
Richard Lucas, saw William Shake-speare as a nickname, adopted by
William Stanley, who enjoyed the coincidence that one of the minor
players in his theatre company was called Will Shakspere.

Interpreting the possible, unspecific allusions to Shakespeare is an unsatisfactory business, even for Stratfordians. If a writer of the time meant to be
enigmatic, no one today can claim that his meaning is clear. There are
many cases, including those mentioned above, where a contemporary

writer seems to be referring to Shakespeare the poet, but in a context which rules out Shakspere the actor. In such cases it is legitimate to look for a candidate who answers the description better.

An allusion which applies more readily to William Stanley than to Shakspere or anyone else is the epigram by John Davies of Hereford, quoted on page 55, 'To our English Terence, Mr Will. Shake-speare'. The hyphenated name and the comparison with Terence, the mask-name for hidden Roman poets, arouse suspicions, and the lines that follow make no sense if addressed to Shakspere. He may have played some kingly parts on the stage, but hardly in sport since he was a professional. It is not clear how his acting would have affected his qualifications to be a companion of royalty, and there was never any prospect of his becoming a king.

If Davies's tribute was meant for Derby, his lines are understandable. The Earl of Derby, with vast estates in northern England and Wales, had almost royal status. He was indeed the hereditary king of the Isle of Man. By virtue of his mother's direct descent from Henry VII, he had a legitimate claim to the throne. Though scrupulously loyal to the reigning sovereign, Elizabeth, he and his brother before him were courted by the Catholics, who saw both the earls as secretly of their party and as potential rulers after the deposition of the queen. To forestall the conspiracy, Elizabeth may have considered making the Earl of Derby her consort. Against that, however, were his excessive interest in the theatre and his appearances on stage as an amateur actor. Davies was saying that, had the Earl of Derby not demeaned himself by associating with common players, he might have been co-ruler of the kingdom.

Yet he would only have been king among the 'meaner sort'. In one chapter in his *Shakespeare's Vital Secret*, Lucas gave reasons for interpreting this to mean that Derby's right to sovereignty arose from his descent from royalty on his mother's side. Another possible meaning is that Derby could only have been the queen's consort, a meaner sort of king than one ruling in his own right.

The Earl of Oxford is also thought to have caught Queen Elizabeth's eye as a possible husband. He too had the right qualifications, but he can hardly have been the Shake-speare whom Davies was addressing in the poem. The sixth line ('Thou hast . . . a raigning Wit') implies that Shake-speare was still alive in 1611, when Davies's poem was published in his *Scourge of Folly*, whereas Oxford was seven years dead. Moreover, John Davies was a close friend and protégé of the Earl of Derby. He shared the theatrical interests of his patron and, if the plays Derby wrote were those of Shake-speare, he would certainly have known about it.

There are many other possible allusions to Derby as Shakespeare, but the Derbyite case is better supported by the internal evidence of the plays. Many scholars have been impressed by the strength of this evidence, and Lefranc's converts have produced a large international body of literature. Lefranc himself went on to publish further books and articles for the cause. His French followers added many others; Derbyite books appeared in Swedish and Dutch, and the movement spread to the Anglo-Saxon world. In England its most energetic supporter was Dr A.W. Titherley, a professor of science at the University of Liverpool. His series of Derbyite books, beginning in 1939, reached its climax with *Shakespeare's Identity*, a volume of several hundred thousand words published in 1952. More concise and readable is A.J. Evans's *Shakespeare's Magic Circle*, where the Earl of Derby is seen as the master-mind behind a Shakespeare group including Oxford, Rutland, Ralegh, Bacon and the Countesses of Pembroke and Rutland. New impetus was given to the movement in 1988, when Cecil Cragg published his well-meant but sadly literal translation of Lefranc's heresy-founding *Under the Mask of William Shakespeare*.

SHAKESPEARE AT THE COURT OF NAVARRE

In 1582 William Stanley was given leave to travel, and embarked on a long, educational tour of Europe. He was then about twenty-one, and his father arranged for a tutor, Richard Lloyd, to accompany him. They went first to Paris, where the fourth Earl of Derby had been the queen's ambassador when she bestowed the Order of the Garter upon Henri III. After a splendid reception at the French court, they continued their journey south-west, visiting Orleans, Blois, Samur and Angers, and eventually reached Spain. The young nobles at the Spanish court were quick-tempered; Stanley had to fight a duel, killed a man and escaped disguised as a friar. His adventures became legendary. He was said to have travelled through Italy and Greece to the Holy Land, through northern Europe and as far as Russia. It is not known for certain where he went nor exactly when he returned home, only that his extensive tour lasted about five years.

On their way either to or from Spain, it is very likely that William and his tutor visited the court of Navarre at Nérac near the Spanish border. The king of Navarre at that time was Henri Bourbon, later Henri IV of France. As a Protestant ruler he decided to reform his court on ideal religious lines. It became a centre of learning and culture, attracting young aristocrats, both Protestant and Catholic, from all over Europe.

Henri of Navarre was separated from his wife, Marguerite de Valois, sister of the French king with whom he was on bad terms. The king had not paid his sister's dowry, which included lands situated in the province of Aquitaine, and this together with their religious differences had led to battles and bloodshed. In the cause of peace and reconciliation with her husband, Marguerite returned to Navarre in 1578. Her methods of diplomacy were based on glamour and seduction. Besides her mother, the politically active Queen Catherine of France, she brought with her a train of beautiful, high-spirited maids of honour, known as the *escadron volant*. They travelled

Marguerite de Valois, whose exploits at the Court of Navarre were reflected in Love's Labour's Lost, *and were later described in her* Mémoires *of 1626.*

through France, finding parties and entertainments wherever they stayed, and paraded into the court at Nérac, where they succeeded brilliantly in everything they had set out to do. In an atmosphere of gaiety and courtly love, personal and political differences were soon settled. The religious idealism of Henri's court was transformed into something more completely ideal, and he and Marguerite were happily reunited.

In that idyllic period, the Court of Navarre was visited by an Englishman who afterwards wrote *Love's Labour's Lost*. Included in that play are scenes, characters and events, which only someone with intimate experience among those people at that place and time could have known about. Abel Lefranc was a specialist in that period. From contemporary records, particularly the *Mémoires* of Marguerite de Valois in which the life of the court is described in great detail, he proved that the author of *Love's Labour's Lost* was better informed on what went on there than any outsider could have been – at least until 1626 when Marguerite's book was published.

In the Shakespeare play the King of Navarre is given the name of William Stanley's elder brother, Ferdinand. He and his three companion lords, Biron, Longaville and Dumain, agree to form a sort of Platonic

*A painting from around the 1580s by Bunel the
Younger of a troupe of Commedia dell' Arte actors
at the Court of Navarre recalls the masque of the
Nine Worthies in* Love's Labour's Lost.

academy, seeing no women, sleeping and eating as little as possible and
spending their time in study. Their resolve is frustrated by the arrival of
a princess of France, sent by her father the king to settle a dispute which
has to do with Aquitaine. With her come three charming young ladies-in-
waiting. The king and his three companions entertain them, and after
much teasing flirtatiousness and fast, witty conversation, the result is four
pairs of lovers.

The only differences between this and the true history of Navarre are
that in Shakespeare's play the king is Ferdinand rather than Henri, and
the visitor is the daughter of the French king rather than his sister, Henri's
estranged wife. The three lords are given almost their actual names.
Lefranc identified Biron as le baron de Biron, who was the same age as
William Stanley and a famous wit at the Court of Navarre; Longaville is le
duc de Longueville, a close ally of Navarre; Dumain is probably le duc du
Maine, who was a good friend of Henri before becoming his enemy.

Close counterparts to most of the characters in the play were found
among the courtiers of Navarre. Originally the correspondence was even
closer, for in the first version of the play the visiting princess was, as in real
life, the queen. That version no longer exists, but traces of it remain in the

Quarto edition, published in 1598, where certain stage directions were left unchanged and refer to the queen rather than the princess. This change, together with a different name for the king, must have been for diplomatic reasons, to avoid open representation of living rulers on stage.

Adding further weight to his opinion that the author of *Love's Labour's Lost* had first-hand experience of French high society and was familiar with its ways, resorts and even its gossip, Lefranc quoted Montégut, the French translator of Shakespeare.

> It is extraordinary to see how faithfully, even down to the most minute detail, Shakespeare represents historical truth and local colour. In the same way as all the details in *Romeo and Juliet*, *The Merchant of Venice* and *Othello* are Italian, so all the details of *Love's Labour's Lost* are pure French. In their conversations his ladies and gentlemen are completely French – lively, alert and full of spirit. It is an endless game of battledore and shuttlecock, a skirmish of witty remarks, a miniature battle of to-and-fro repartee. Even their bad taste is totally French, while their language is sharpened and exaggeratedly refined to that degree of affectation which has never displeased the French, especially those of the higher classes.

Love's Labour's Lost was the first play to be published with the name W. Shakespeare on its title-page. The orthodox view is that it was written in about 1589–90, when Shakspere was no more than twenty-six and either still in Stratford or newly arrived in London. He could not possibly have been received into the Court of Navarre, where birth and breeding were the essential qualifications. At that point Lefranc and his French colleagues lost patience with the Stratfordian theory. It made a mockery of their historical and literary scholarship, and Lefranc felt almost insulted by the obstinacy of Anglo-Saxon scholars who persisted in believing that William Shakspere wrote the play.

Anthony Bacon was an honoured guest at the Court of Navarre for about six years up to 1590, and wrote detailed accounts of it to his brother Francis. Lefranc, however, ignored this Baconian point. His researches convinced him that only one Englishman was in the right place at the right time and had all the other necessary qualifications to have written *Love's Labour's Lost*. William Stanley could and almost certainly would have been at the Court of Navarre around 1583 – it was on the direct route between France and Spain. One thing virtually confirms it and points directly at Stanley as the author of *Love's Labour's Lost*. A memorable character in that play is Holofernes, a ridiculously pedantic schoolmaster, and he is a cruelly accurate caricature of Richard Lloyd, Stanley's irksome tutor.

In the play (v. 1) Holofernes proposes to entertain the court with a performance of the Nine Worthies. This turns out to be an absurd, stilted production, in which each of the Worthies – heroes of ancient history – appear in turn on stage, announce their names and declaim verses about what they did. The court wits make fun of the show, the actors join in the badinage and only the first half, presenting five of the Worthies, is completed.

Then suddenly the mood changes. The lovers decide to part for a year, to leave the enchantment of court and go into the world, where the men will prepare themselves by meditation or good works for their final reunion. The actors come back on stage and two of them, representing the spring cuckoo and the winter owl, give those beautiful songs that begin, 'When daisies pied and violets blue' and 'When icicles hang by the wall'. On that wonderfully mystical note *Love's Labour's Lost* is brought to an end.

The masque of the Nine Worthies, as Holofernes presents it, is an obvious satire on a work published in 1584. It was a poem of about 1200 lines with a long title beginning, *A briefe discourse of the most renowned actes and right valiant conquests of those most puisant Princes, called the Nine Worthies* .... The nine heroes who each give formal accounts of themselves and their legends are: Joshua, Hector, King David, Alexander the Great, Judas Maccabeus, Julius Caesar, King Arthur, Charlemagne and Guy of Warwick. The author of this tediously stiff and old-fashioned work was none other than Richard Lloyd, William Stanley's tutor and companion during his tour of France.

It is quite clear that the farce of the Nine Worthies in *Love's Labour's Lost* is based on and makes mockery of Lloyd's poem. The five Worthies shown in the play, Hector, Pompey, Alexander, Hercules and Judas Maccabeus, are (with Pompey for Caesar, and Hercules brought in from comic effect) similar to Lloyd's, and Lefranc noted several parallels between the corresponding speeches. For example, one of Lloyd's ponderous lines goes,

a Lyon Wich sitting in a chaire hent a battel-axe in his paw argent.

In wicked parody of this, one of the Worthies in the play is given the line,

your lion, that holds his poll-axe sitting on a close-stool.

Assuming William Stanley to be the author of *Love's Labour's Lost*, it would be perfectly natural for him to ridicule his tutor in this way. Lloyd, sixteen years older than William, was not just his boring preceptor, responsible for his education, but an agent of the authorities back home. He must have been a most tiresomely inhibiting companion for a young man on his first trip abroad. It would be no wonder if William resented him, despised him and wrote him into his first play as the pompous fool, Holofernes, with his stupid old Nine Worthies.

The Nine Worthies idea was not Lloyd's invention but derived from a traditional summer play put on by the people of Chester, the local town patronized by the Earls of Derby, so it is possible that Lloyd went to a performance there with the Stanley family. It is also possible that William Shakspere saw the Nine Worthies at Chester; he may have gone there on a provincial tour with a theatre company. As a modern actor from the capital, he would have laughed at the rustics with their old-fashioned play, and perhaps he wrote the parody of it in *Love's Labour's Lost*. In that case he would unwittingly have parodied Lloyd's version of the original.

Lefranc was not the first to correlate the characters in *Love's Labour's Lost* with historical figures at the Court of Navarre. Most of the identifications are orthodox and uncontroversial. His really significant discovery was the correspondence between Holofernes and Richard Lloyd. That has never been refuted, and it turns the Authorship spotlight fully upon William Stanley. It is more than likely that he went to Navarre, but there is no positive proof of it. Even if he did go there, and had to drag his embarrassing tutor along with him, there could have been other English writers at the court, one of whom was amused by the ill-assorted couple and caricatured Lloyd as Holofernes in a play which he later wrote as *Love's Labour's Lost* by W. Shakespeare. There is a case for Francis Bacon, informed by his brother Anthony. It is not quite necessary, therefore, to conclude that William Stanley was the secret author of that play, but after studying the many subtle proofs in Lefranc's *Sous le masque de 'Shakespeare'*, it seems highly probable.

While studying the history of the Court of Navarre, as described in the *Mémoires de Marguerite de Valois*, Lefranc came across a remarkable story, an almost exact parallel to that of Ophelia in *Hamlet*. It was a favourite story of Queen Marguerite, and if William Stanley was at her court he would doubtless have heard it.

One of her ladies-in-waiting had a daughter, Hélène, who went to stay with her married sister and there fell in love with the marquis de Varembon, the brother of her sister's husband. He wanted to marry her, but he was already destined for the Church and his brother objected. Hélène went sadly back to her mother, who was unkind to her. Meanwhile, de Varembon gave up the idea of becoming a priest, and he and his brother came to Hélène's district with the queen's court. Marguerite invited her to stay with them at Namur, but the young man acted coldly towards Hélène and left abruptly. The poor girl was so heart-broken that she could only breathe by crying out in pain. Some days later she died of grief.

A great funeral was arranged, and, just as the flower-decked coffin was approaching the grave, a disturbance arose. A few days after he had left, the marquis realized that he was deeply in love with Hélène, and hastened back to propose marriage. He entered the town to find the streets crowded with mourners. Pushing his way up to the coffin, he asked whose it was, and on hearing the story fell off his horse in a dead faint. As described in the *Mémoires*, his soul, '*allant dans le tombeau requérir pardon*' (going into the grave to ask forgiveness), he appeared for a time lifeless.

This is the familiar story in *Hamlet*. Ophelia loves Hamlet and he at heart loves her, but he leaves her cruelly and takes ship for England. Ophelia goes mad with sorrow and drowns in a stream. Hamlet returns unexpectedly, and encounters the funeral as the flower-strewn coffin is lowered into the grave. He asks whose funeral it is, and upon hearing that it is his true love who had died for his sake, he leaps bodily into the grave, rather than spiritually like the Frenchman. When challenged by Laertes he cries out:

> I lov'd Ophelia: forty thousand brothers
> Could not, with all their quantity of love
> Make up my sum.

There is no other source for the tragedy of Ophelia and Hamlet than this beautiful old French love-story. It was known to Shakespeare, because there is an allusion to it in *Love's Labour's Lost* (v. 2), where Rosaline reminds Katharine how Cupid killed her sister, and Katharine remembers how she died of love. It was this allusion which, when Lefranc discovered its source, led him to discover the origin of the Ophelia story.

This is highly convincing, but it is not the only convincing identification of Hamlet and Ophelia. As described in the previous chapter, Freud and Looney were convinced that Hamlet was a self-portrait by the Earl of Oxford, with his mistreated wife Anne portrayed as Ophelia. A.J. Evans in *Shakespeare's Magic Circle* built a bridge between the two noble candidates. As he saw it, William Stanley returned from his travels at the age of about twenty-six, and brought with him the sad love-story which he had heard directly from Marguerite de Valois at the Court of Navarre. He went to see Oxford, his future father-in-law, for literary advice, and became his collaborator in writing *Love's Labour's Lost*, *Hamlet* and other plays. Their partnership then expanded into a group, the complete Shakespeare Circle.

The only known likeness of William Stanley,
sixth Earl of Derby.

In the 1920s Lefranc and Looney came together as members of the
Shakespeare Fellowship, and thrashed out their differences. They came to
agree that there was a Shakespeare group, in which both their candidates
were prominent. Most easily settled was the authorship of *The Tempest*. It
was written some years after Oxford was dead, and Looney was pleased,
therefore, to allow Lefranc to annex it to his case for the Earl of Derby.

THE MAGICIAN
OF 'THE TEMPEST'

The Tempest is set on rocky island, the domain of a noble magician who rules by enchantment. Prospero is an initiated philosopher, who has studied the arts which lead beyond mere knowledge to a state of understanding and freedom. By mastering himself he has gained powers beyond the reach of any tyrant. He represents divine intelligence, the principle that, in a properly ordered constitution, controls its energetic spirit (Ariel) and its gross, corporeal element (Caliban).

The grave and mystical John Dee, painted by an unknown artist.

Prospero's order of government, both of himself and of his realm, is the ideal as described in Plato's *Republic*. The author of *The Tempest* recognized and accepted this ideal; Prospero is a model of the perfectly realized individual. He is a portrait, not of Shakespeare himself, but of his highest aspirations.

Recent Shakespearian writers, more aware than their predecessors of the mystical, philosophical ideas which entered English minds in the latter part of the sixteenth century, have recognized *The Tempest* as a product of the perennial esoteric tradition that resurfaced to create the Renaissance. From antiquity, through the Mystery schools, the Hermetic philosophers, neo-Platonists and alchemists, that tradition has inspired many cultural revivals. Its influence on Shakespeare is very apparent, particularly in the later plays, *The Tempest* above all.

Frances Yates, in a series of books including *Majesty and Magic in Shakespeare's Last Plays*, draws attention to the commanding figure of Dr John Dee, the learned magus, astrologer and wise counsellor to Queen Elizabeth. He was the principal heir in England to the occult tradition in its Rosicrucian form. Renowned throughout Europe as a teacher of science and esoteric knowledge, John Dee was a catalyst in the transformation of English literature and its poetic flowering in the time of Shakespeare.

Shakespeare must have been familiar with Dee and his philosophy, because they are so accurately reflected by the wise Prospero and his magical realm. Frances Yates was always careful to avoid casting doubts on Shakespeare's authorship, but she nevertheless added to them by acknowledging that the author of *The Tempest* was a profound student of the esoteric sciences taught by Dee and an active abetter of his Rosicrucian revival. She asked herself a bold question: 'Dare one say that this movement reaches a peak of poetic expression in *The Tempest*, a Rosicrucian manifesto infused with the spirit of Dee, and using (like Andraea) theatrical parables for exoteric communication?'

This view of Shakespeare, as agent for an ideal philosophical revival, was seen a hundred years before Frances Yates by another brilliant woman, Delia Bacon. She, however, drew the conclusion that more than one person must have been involved in this great undertaking. Her eye was not upon Will Shakspere but on the noble wits and poets of the Elizabethan Court. Sir Walter Ralegh was her favourite, and in her heresy-founding book of 1857, *The Philosophy of the Plays of Shakspere Unfolded*, she identified him as leader of the Shakespeare-writing group, along with Bacon, Sidney and a few others.

One of the first to see Dr Dee as the inspiration for Prospero was Abel Lefranc in 1919. *The Tempest* is thought to have been written in about 1611, three years after the death of Dee, so it may have been in tribute to him. It was Lefranc's favourite Shakespeare play, the one in which the author most clearly revealed himself. 'I cannot help repeating', he wrote, 'that if any work of literature has ever revealed, in every one of its details and as a whole, a patrician origin, it is this one.'

The author of *The Tempest* must have been a powerful nobleman, otherwise the play could never have been performed or published. Magic and mysticism had flourished at the Court of Queen Elizabeth, but under James I the tone was completely different. The new king was fanatically opposed to anything to do with magic, spiritualism or the supernatural. Mystical and Rosicrucian philosophy were no less abhorrent to him than fairies and witchcraft. At the same time as *The Tempest* appeared, witches were being burnt in Lancashire. James had no sympathy for Dr Dee, but allowed him to be persecuted and die in poverty.

Whoever wrote *The Tempest* was uniquely privileged; no other author dared to treat the subject of spirits and occultism other than with disapproval or mockery. Lefranc gave examples: the magician in Marlowe's *Faust* comes badly to grief; in Greene's *Friar Bacon* he is taken by the devil; Jonson's *Alchemist* is about the impostures and punishments of magical charlatans. Only Shakespeare could present at court a play which delighted in spirits and enchantments and glorified the late disgraced Dr Dee.

This Shakespeare, this patrician philosopher who knew John Dee and was an inner member of his mystical fraternity, was easy for Lefranc to identify. He was, of course, William Stanley, known after 1594 as the Earl of Derby. Dee was in contact with most of the literary aristocracy and had deep influence on Sidney, Spenser, Ralegh, Oxford, Dyer and many others. He seems, however, to have been most intimate with Derby. In an account of William Stanley's travels by J. Nuttall of Liverpool, it is said that he met Dee in Russia and was admitted into his circle. In Dee's diary, Lefranc found many entries recording meetings with William in London, and when in 1595 the queen made Dee Warden of Manchester College, the Earl and his family often visited him there.

Prince Ferdinand, the romantic hero in *The Tempest* who marries Prospero's daughter, has almost the same name as William's elder brother, Ferdinando the fifth Earl. There is, in fact, an instance in the Folio edition of the play where Ferdinand is written Ferdinando. William's brother was king of the Isle of Man, but that large, fertile, populous island in the Irish Sea is nothing like Prospero's rocky, almost inaccessible islet.

There is, however, a small, uninhabited island five hundred yards off the southern tip of Man which closely corresponds to the island in *The Tempest*. The Calf of Man is roughly circular, about a mile wide, grassy, with caves, inlets and fresh water. Many ships have been wrecked on its rocks. It has the ruins of an ancient chapel and traces of former habitation.

The only inhabitant of the island before the arrival of Prospero and his daughter Miranda was Caliban. He is the Calf-man, and in the play he is several times referred to as a 'moon-calf', which is the only occurrence of that word in Shakespeare. When Caliban curses Prospero for making him learn his language (i. 2), he could be echoing the complaint of the native, Celtic-speaking Manx, that their masters were making them learn English. Another unique word in *The Tempest* is 'calf-like'. Its only appearance in Shakespeare is in *The Tempest* (iv. 1) where Ariel reports on how he has dealt with the 'varlets' who escaped the wreck:

> so I charm'd their ears
> That calf-like they my lowing follow'd through
> Tooth'd briers, sharp furzes, pricking goss and thorns.

Consciously or not, the author of *The Tempest* seems to have had the word 'calf' on his mind, as if he were thinking of the Calf of Man as the ideal philosopher's retreat, where nature provides rocky shelters and the simple necessities of life. It was in fact used for that purpose. On the death of Francis Bacon in 1626, his pupil, Thomas Bushell, retired to the Calf of

A view across the Calf towards the main island of Man. As a former hermitage surrounded by dangerous seas, the Calf of Man is very like Shakespeare's description of Prospero's island.

Man and spent three years alone there, following the method which his master had recommended for a healthy life by subsisting on a diet of herbs, oil, mustard, honey and spring water.

Bushell's sojourn on the Calf was too late to have inspired *The Tempest*. There was, however, a previous hermit there. Manx folklore tells of his doing penance for having killed a young woman in a fit of jealous rage. According to Joseph Train's *History of the Isle of Man*, he was 'a person who by his splendour and affluence had been distinguished in the Court of Queen Elizabeth'.

It is often claimed – most emphatically by believers in Sir Walter Ralegh as the author of *The Tempest* – that the island is a picture of one of the Bermudas. That cannot be so, because Ariel was sent away from the island to the 'still-vex't Bermoothes' when Prospero needed some dew. The royal ship was wrecked on a voyage from Tunis to Naples, but Prospero's magic could have transferred the scene from the Mediterranean to the Irish Sea and the Calf of Man.

Continuing in the Derbyite interest this identification of Prospero's island with the Calf of Man, it is easy to see Prospero as the Celtic sea-god or Poseidon, whose Manx name is Manannan. In the *Book of Fermoy* of about 1400, Manannan is described as 'a pagan necromancer who possesses the ability to envelop himself and his island in a mist, to make them invisible to strangers and enemies'. Like Prospero he has a magical cloak and can raise or calm storms by enchantment.

Prospero's familiar spirit is Ariel, who is said to move within each of the four elements: earth, air, fire and water. Like Merlin, he was once imprisoned within a tree by a witch's spell. Theorists have derived his name from those of the two angelic beings, Uriel and Aniel, invoked by Dr Dee in his magical operations. In fact Ariel in the Old Testament (Isaiah, 29) is a spiritual name for the holy Jerusalem. Ariel is told by the Prophet, 'thy voice shall be, as of one that hath a familiar spirit, out of the ground'. Those that fight against Ariel 'shall be as a dream of a night vision'. Like so much in Shakespeare, Ariel is drawn from the Bible, and he retains in *The Tempest* his original character, as the spiritual element in Prospero's kingdom.

Caliban represents the gross, material, mundane aspect of the Calf of Man, the rigours of life there, the gathering of fuel, the hauling of water. He is a 'moon-calf', which literally means an ill-begotten monster. It is also an anagram of Calf o' Mon, Mon or Mona being archaic names for the Isle of Man. As the calf follows the cow, so the Calf of Man follows its mother-island. This is unmistakably referred to in Ariel's line, 'That calf-like they my lowing followed.'

If there is any substance in the above, it points to a Shakespeare who knew the Isle of Man, or to William Stanley who ruled it. In his insular subjects he saw something of Caliban, the unteachable brute, and something of Ariel, the true but imprisoned spirit of their lovely island. He wanted, like Prospero, to release that spirit, to use it as his agent for an ideal reformation. Yet the absolute ideal, the simple, primordial way of life, is only possible in a place like the Calf of Man. Gonzalo, the 'honest old Counsellor' in *The Tempest*, gave a picture of it in the famous lines which Shakespeare adapted from Montaigne's essay *Of Cannibals*, in John Florio's translation of 1603:

> I' the commonwealth I would by contraries
> Execute all things; for no kind of traffic
> Would I admit; no name of magistrate;
> Letters should not be known; riches, poverty.
> And use of service, none; contract, succession,
> Bourn, bound of land, tilth, vineyard, none;
> No use of metal, corn, or wine, or oil;
> No occupation; all men idle, all;
> And women too, but innocent and pure;
> No sovereignty.

The natural men and women in this anarchist's heaven would have no need of moral teaching, but be 'all idle: whores and knaves'.

The Earl of Derby, however, was a born ruler and had to take on the responsibilities of his position. The anarchist's ideal is impossible in elaborate, civilized societies. A wise lawgiver is needed, one who can devise a just constitution which his successors can honourably maintain. Thus Prospero dismisses Ariel, gives up his magical powers and prepares himself for death, leaving his well-trained daughter and her husband to administer the earthly kingdom he has regained for them. In the same way, William Stanley, following the precepts of Dr Dee, prepared his son, James, for his brilliant rule over the Isle of Man, as the Great Stanley. As a philosophical guide for his successor he wrote *The Tempest.*

To sum up the case for Derby: there is nothing much against him as a possible candidate for Shakespeare. He went to college, studied law, travelled abroad and spoke excellent French, probably also Spanish and Italian. He is likely to have attended the Court of Navarre during its great years, and he was a good friend of John Dee. Contemporary allusions to the poet Shakespeare could often have been meant for William Stanley. His brother Ferdinando, Lord Strange, took over the company of players, formerly patronized by the Earl of Leicester, to which Shakspere belonged. When Shakspere was twenty-three, the company played in Stratford-upon-Avon before going directly to Knowsley, one of the great Derby mansions in Lancashire. The Stratford actor may well have spent his 'lost years' in the north of England, working for successive Earls of Derby in their constant theatrical activities. When Leicester's company became Strange's in 1588, Shakspere and William Stanley were brought into close contact. If there was a conspiracy over the Authorship, they had plenty of opportunities for hatching it.

In *Shakespeare's Magic Circle*, A.J. Evans pointed out how many of the topographical references in Shakespeare's plays are to places around north Warwickshire, where William Stanley grew up. His childhood was spent at one of the family houses, Meriden Manor, between Birmingham and Coventry. Meriden in the Forest of Arden, is said to be at the very centre of England. Nearby, at Polesworth, lived Holinshed the chronicler, from whom Shakespeare derived many of his plots and histories. Places around there or on the road from there to London, mentioned in the plays, are Tamworth, Sutton Coldfield, Hinckley, Greet (for Greece), Barston, Coventry, Kenilworth, Rugby, Warwick, Southam, Dunsmore Heath and Daventry. Wincot where Sly drank in *The Taming of the Shrew*, is identified by Stratfordians as Wilmcote, a hamlet near Stratford, but it is just as likely to be Wincot in the north of the county. Wilmcote in 1712 was found to consist of just two cottages and there was never an ale-house there.

The case for Derby is plausible on all levels. The candidate has the right qualifications and no obvious drawbacks. The Derbyite authors are dignified and scholarly, and have collected many significant points of evidence. None of it is conclusive, but that is the case with all other candidates. The weakness is that the sixth Earl of Derby is not known to have written a single play or poem, and showed no signs of doing so up to his death in 1642. The only mention of him as a writer, the report by Fenners that he was busy penning plays for the common players, could have been a spy's code-phrase. Above all, why in the last thirty years of his life was there no follow-up to his 'Rosicrucian manifesto' *The Tempest* ? The Derbyite answer is that, like Prospero, he retired from the world when his great work was accomplished.

JUST ONE MORE EARL

Bacon, Oxford, Derby; need we go on? As alternatives to William Shakspere, each of them has qualifications enough to attract a firmly committed following. Eventually, perhaps, evidence will emerge to prove one or other of their claims – or to confirm William as the unchallenged title-holder.

This brings a loud objection from the continent. French, German and Belgian writers each have their own favourite Shakespeare. We cannot close the list of entries before hearing the most convincing case of all, that of Roger Manners, fifth Earl of Rutland. Then there is another Earl to consider, Southampton; and then there is Sir Walter Ralegh, and Christopher Marlowe; and after them come a host of other candidates, some with interesting points in their favour and some in the 'why-not?' category. The floodgates are opened, sweeping away the certainties of Baconism and such, and everything that looked like becoming established is set adrift. This is the time for patience and a cool head. Since Roger Manners too has a confirmed, academically respectable following, his claims must be examined with the rest.

As Oxford has his Looney and Derby his Lefranc, so Rutland has his Demblon. Célestin Demblon is the man who read 5000 books while researching Shakespeare's Authorship. He hailed from Liège, which he represented in the Belgian Chamber of Deputies, and was a professor of French literature at the University of Brussels. After his heroic course of reading, and travels to England, Italy, France and Denmark in the footsteps of Roger Manners, he published *Lord Rutland est Shakespeare* in 1912 and *L'Auteur d'Hamlet et son monde* two years later. They contain everything known and imaginable about Rutland and his right to be regarded as Shakespeare, but they were by no means the last word on the subject.

Nor were they the first word. The pioneer Rutlander was Burkhard Herrman, writing under the name of Peter Alvor. In *Das neue Shakespeare-Evangelium* of 1906 he deduced that Rutland was the author of Shakspeare's comedies, leaving the tragedies and histories to Southampton. The first claim for Rutland as the total Shakespeare was by Carl Bleibtreu in the introduction to his play, *Der wahre Shakespeare*, published in 1907. *Die Lösung der Shakespearefrage* followed in 1909, and Bleibtreu returned to the subject with *Shakespeares Geheimnis* (Shakespeare's Secret) in 1923, by which time the theory was well established. Rutland books were published by writers in Germany, Belgium and other European countries, as well as in America, both North and South.

ROGER MANNERS, FIFTH EARL OF RUTLAND

1576 6 October. Born at Belvoir Castle, eldest son of John, fifth Earl.

1587 Entered Queen's College and later Corpus Christi, Cambridge. Studied there for seven years.

1588 21 February. Father died. Roger inherited vast but debt-ridden estates in the Midlands and North of England. Made a royal ward under Lord Burghley, whose duties as guardian were mostly taken on by Francis Bacon.

1595 Given leave to travel abroad, but his mother died that spring, so spent most of the year at Belvoir, administering estates. Left for the Netherlands that autumn.

1596 To France, Germany, Switzerland and Italy.
28 March. Entered Padua University.

1597 Sailed with Essex on his expedition to the Azores.

1598 February. Entered Gray's Inn as a law student.

1599 April. Went on the Essex campaign in Ireland.
June. Recalled from Ireland. Went to Bath to treat swollen legs.
Autumn. Married Elizabeth, aged fifteen, only daughter of Sir Philip Sidney. They had no children.

1600 July. Went to the Netherlands with the Earl of Northumberland to help the Dutch against the Spanish.

1601 8 February. Imprisoned in the Tower and threatened with execution for his part in the Essex rebellion. Gave evidence for the prosecution, and fined £30,000.
6 August. Released into the care of his great-uncle, Roger Manners, squire of Uffington. Lawsuit with Lord Roos over family estates began and continued throughout the rest of his life.

1602 Spring. Allowed to return to Belvoir.

1603 King James visited Belvoir, was entertained by a Jonson play, remitted Rutland's fine and appointed him Lord Lieutenant of Lincolnshire.

June: Made ambassador to Denmark for the christening of the royal heir. Visited Elsinore.

December. Took part in entertaining King James at Wilton House.

1605 Entertained the king of Denmark in London.

1612 26 June. Died at Belvoir after years of ill health. Buried at Bottesford, Leicestershire.

In contrast to the battery of Baconian lawyers, the Rutlanders have had only one legal luminary on their side, and he was a Russian. Pierre S. Porohovshikov of Moscow University, Judge at the St Petersburg High Court of Justice and with many other imperial honours, had good reasons after the Revolution to emigrate to America, where he became Professor of History at Oglethorpe University and threw himself behind the Rutland cause. He was no extremist, not claiming that Rutland had written the whole of Shakespeare, but allowing Bacon the poems, *Venus and Adonis* and *Lucrece*, and Oxford the Sonnets. Nor, for reasons made obvious below, did he attribute the earliest Shakespeare plays to Rutland. His book, *Shakespeare Unmasked*, was published in 1940.

The latest known Rutland book, *Alias William Shakespeare?* by Claud Sykes of 1947, has the rare feature of being prefaced by a man who did not believe in it. In its opening pages the conservative historian, Sir Arthur Bryant, stood firmly on the side of Orthodoxy, insisted that the plays were written by a simple English countryman and offered to eat his hat if he were proved wrong. Politely doing his best, he allowed that Sykes's book was 'absorbing, erudite and ingenious'.

Also unusual was the author's idea on how to identify Shakespeare. He called in Sherlock Holmes. The great detective took on the commission and proved an exemplary Authorship investigator. He read through the complete works of Shakespeare, studied Elizabethan literature in the British Museum Library and joined a repertory company on a few weeks' tour of the provinces. Following clues he had found in the plays, he visited Italy and Denmark. Finally he went to Belvoir Castle in Rutland, ancestral home of the Manners family, and announced his solution by pointing to a portrait of the fifth Earl of Rutland.

The characteristics of Shakespeare which, as Sykes imagined it, Sherlock Holmes deduced from the plays were mostly the same as those discerned by supporters of other noble candidates. Shakespeare was a courtier, a wealthy nobleman, a qualified lawyer and a classicist, speaking fluent French and Italian. He was a huntsman and falconer, had travelled in France, Denmark and northern Italy, experienced military service and nautical life and had witnessed a great storm at sea.

The real Shakespeare had studied at Cambridge University. To prove this point, Rutlanders quote Professor F.S. Boas in *Shakespeare and the Universities*, where the author of the plays is shown to have been familiar with several terms which were used only at Cambridge in his time. No one but a Cambridge man would have known or cared much about Dr John Caius, founder of Caius College, who appears in *The Merry Wives of Windsor* under his own name. This is not a great point for Rutland, who was born three years after the death of Caius in 1573, whereas the Earl of Oxford, whose Cambridge days were in 1564, would probably have known the man, and the Bacon brothers, Francis and Anthony, would at least have heard about him when they went up to Trinity College in the year he died. More significant are the lines spoken by Polonius in *Hamlet* (ii. 1).

> Inquire me first what Danskers are in Paris;
> And how, and who, what means, and where they keep.

The word, 'keep', meaning 'lodge', occurs about a dozen times in Shakespeare, but the *Oxford Dictionary* says that its use in that sense is peculiar to Cambridge University. William Shakspere, who was never at a university, would not naturally and casually have used Cambridge jargon. Nor would he have referred to 'Danskers', which is the Danes' word for themselves and must have been written by someone who was familiar with them or had been to their country. Rutland's experience of Danes and Denmark is the main point in his favour.

A marked tendency in Shakespeare's plays is for two brothers to hate each other. Psychologists may see in this an unconscious autobiographical influence. William Shakspere had three younger brothers, but there is nothing to indicate his personal relations with them; they had all died by the time he made his will. Rutland also had three, and he was on very bad terms with at least one of them. His younger brother, Sir Oliver

Torture and cruel deaths threatened dissidents in Shakespeare's time, as shown by this engraving of the executions after the failed Gunpowder Plot of 1605.

Manners, was a sponge, a spendthrift and, worst of all, an active Roman Catholic dissident. He allied himself with the Jesuits, was mixed up with the Gunpowder Plot and tried to involve his brother in the affair. After many embarrassments and demands for money, Rutland set the seal on their quarrel by confiscating Oliver's share of the family estate. This was just how Oliver, the elder brother in *As You Like It*, treated his younger brother, Orlando.

The most learned of Rutlanders, Célestin Demblon, went through all the works of Shakespeare, and from each play and poem deduced the author's temperament, circumstances and mood when he wrote it. These he compared with the biography of Roger Manners, and found that in every case the two sets of data perfectly or adequately matched each other. Shakespeare's writings illuminate the life of Rutland, and *vice versa*. Demblon set out to retrace the routes taken by Rutland in his travels, beginning at Belvoir Castle, where he found that the library contained rare books which Shakespeare is known to have used. Records show that the bulk of Shakespeare's source-literature was in the sixteenth-century Belvoir library.

Also at Belvoir, in fresco on the ceiling of the Elizabethan Salon, is a copy of Correggio's picture, *Io and Jupiter*. This is recognized as the picture referred to in the Induction to *The Taming of the Shrew*, where a great lord takes Sly, the drunken tinker, into his mansion and tricks him into believing he is the real owner. Showing him some of the luscious works in his art collection, he says:

> We'll show thee Io as she was a maid,
> And how she was beguiled and surprised,
> As lively painted as the deed was done.

At Padua University Demblon made a striking discovery. Rutland studied there during his Italian tour, and in the same register that records his entry on 28 March 1596 are the names of his two Danish fellow-students, Rosencrantz and Guildenstern.

As Demblon piled up his evidence, item by item, his case for Rutland became a mighty edifice. The only trouble with it was its foundations. Many people have dismissed the case and considered it no further upon discovering the basic premise on which it rests. Rutland supporters have to presume something for which there is no external evidence at all, that Roger Manners was a very exceptional specimen of a child prodigy.

Born in October 1576, Rutland was only sixteen-and-a-half when the first Shakespeare work, *Venus and Adonis*, was published. That means he must have written it at the age of fifteen or so. By the time he was twenty, about fourteen of Shakespeare's plays are thought to have been completed. Roger Manners certainly did not waste his youth if he was so productive, and he was precociously cunning to prevent elders and contemporaries from noticing his remarkable talents.

Faced with this difficulty, Porohovshikov gave up and admitted that someone else must have written the early poems and plays of Shakespeare. Demblon, however, insisted that the thing was possible, and Sherlock Holmes, speaking through Claud Sykes, agreed with him. There are many well-known examples of infant prodigies. Rutlanders parade them: Raphael, Burns, Byron, Chatterton, Sir Philip Sidney, Victor Hugo and, of course, Mozart whose first opera was commissioned when he was fourteen. Shakespeare, whoever he was, must have been a quick developer to have accomplished what he did. In his time there was no special indulgence of children, and they grew up earlier than they do now. Rutland's education, backed by the great library at Belvoir, must have been exceptional since he was admitted to Cambridge at the age of eleven. Far from being impossible that he wrote *Venus and Adonis* in his mid-teens, it is actually quite likely. Many critics have regarded that poem as a product of adolescent passions inspired by a classical theme.

Sonnet 111, containing the words, 'manners' and 'Dyer', is found significant by supporters of two Shakespeare candidates.

Other critics, Oxfordians in particular, insist that Shakespeare's early poems were the work of a mature genius. Nothing about Shakespeare is ever agreed on by everybody. Most difficult for the Rutlanders are the Sonnets, where the poet clearly describes himself as an older man. Yet Rutland was only twenty-two when Meres mentioned that Shakespeare's sonnets were in private circulation, and it is generally believed that they were composed some years earlier. Sykes plays the usual game among theorists, urging the significance of the word 'manners' in Sonnets 85 and 111 (above), and explaining that, like the poet, his candidate was lame – and in two senses, since Rutland suffered from swollen legs and was rumoured to be impotent. These arguments are defensive and do nothing to disturb the evidence that the author of the Sonnets was nearer the age of forty than twenty when he wrote them.

Nevertheless, Rutland's candidature has been taken seriously by several of the later and better anti-Stratfordian writers, who have seen his hand in at least some of the Shakespeare plays. Gilbert Slater made him one of his *Seven Shakespeares* group, and he was a member of *Shakespeare's Magic Circle* assembled by A.J. Evans. His most likely contributions arose from his travels in Italy and in particular to Denmark. These, examined below, are the highlights in the case for Rutland, but behind them are many lesser gleams of evidence. They are too numerous to be more than exemplified; one of the most interesting is about Rutland's part in the sad story of the Earl of Essex.

This story is very important to the Authorship question as a whole, because it describes the only known occasion in Shakspere's lifetime when that question was openly raised. It came up during the massive investigation by state security agents which took place after the Essex rebellion. On 6 February 1601 the Earl of Essex mustered his followers and co-conspirators at his house on the Thames and prepared them to march on the City, rally the disaffected citizens and lead them to depose the queen – or, as he later put it, to request her to change her advisers. As part of the plan, his agents bribed the actors at the Globe Theatre to put on the Shakespeare play, *Richard II*, on 7 February, the evening before the rebellion was due. The same play, it appears, was also at the same time acted in other parts of London.

The theatre was the popular medium at that time, and these performances were meant to have an immediate effect on popular sentiments. The climax of *Richard II* is the deposition of the monarch, but that scene could never normally be shown on stage. Nor was it included in the first version of the play, published in 1597. The queen and her censors would have regarded it as an incitement to rebel against the established order. Two years before the Essex rebellion, she had sent an author, Dr John Hayward, to the Tower for life, his offence being to have published a book, dedicated to the Earl of Essex, which described the unmentionable deposition scene. She suspected Hayward of being a front for someone more dangerous, and instructed Francis Bacon to discover if he was the real author.

After the failure of Essex, when he and his followers had been arrested and put to interrogation, the authorities began immediately to enquire into the circumstances behind the provocative showing of *Richard II*, deposition scene and all. They questioned Augustine Phillips, manager of the Globe, whose answer, that the performance was commissioned by Essex's agents, was apparently found satisfactory. At the trial of Essex and his fellow

Robert Devereux, second Earl of Essex, painted four years before his execution. Baconian theorists regard him as the son of Queen Elizabeth and Leicester and brother to Francis Bacon.

conspirators, Francis Bacon for the prosecution made much of the treasonable playing of *Richard II*. Essex and others were dealt with by the headsman or hangman, and nothing more was heard about the theatre scandal — except from the queen herself.

That summer, while looking through some records brought to her by the archivist at the Tower, Elizabeth saw a reference to Richard II and cried out angrily, 'I am Richard II, know ye not that?' The archivist replied soothingly, and evidently with reference to Essex rather than to the author of the play, 'Such a wicked imagination was determined and attempted by a most unkind gent, the most adorned creature that ever Your Majesty made.' To this the queen said, 'He that will forget God will also forget his benefactors; this tragedy was played forty times in the open streets and houses.'

Following her suspicions about Hayward's authorship, it seems certain that the queen would have insisted on knowing who wrote *Richard II*. The deposition scene, though suppressed during her reign and not published in the play until 1608, is thought to have been part of the original version, so the author was a potential trouble-maker. Shakespeare's name did not appear on the title-page of the first, 1597 edition of the play, but it was known in the theatre as a Shakespeare work. It seems extraordinary, therefore, that Shakespeare never testified or was even mentioned during the Essex trial. Shakspere the actor was neither arrested nor questioned. No one seemed curious about the author whose play had caused such scandal and had so infuriated the queen.

This is highly mysterious. The anti-Stratfordian conclusion is that the authorities paid no attention to Shakspere because they knew that he was not the real author of the plays. But who then was? And why did nothing happen to him? Within the mystery, however, one thing is made clear. The only person who could not possibly have written *Richard II* was Francis Bacon. Essex or one of his sympathizers would have known his secret, and the perfect answer to Bacon's charge, that they caused a seditious play to be performed in public, would have been that they saw no harm in staging a play written by the learned counsel for the prosecution!

There is more than one possible explanation for this: for example, that the play was by Marlowe, and he was dead. Another solution is put forward by the supporters of Rutland. Shakespeare, they say, was indeed recognized, and indeed punished. The Earl of Rutland played a minor part in the Essex affair. He was not one of the core conspirators, but as an old friend of Essex and Southampton he was asked to join them at the last minute. For this he was sent to the Tower with the others, and his execution seemed likely to follow. Fortunately he had an old uncle in the country who had once been a friend of the queen. This good gentleman went up to court and persuaded Elizabeth that it would be easier for everybody if he took the young rebel back home and kept him out of trouble. The condition was that Rutland should pay an enormous fine of £30,000. This was later reduced, and in the reign of King James it was remitted altogether.

Rutland's severe punishment seems out of proportion with such a light offence, especially since he turned queen's evidence and betrayed friendships by testifying against Essex and Southampton. An explanation is that the crime for which he was almost executed was writing *Richard II*. Rutland then was the real Shakespeare.

When Rutland was in the Tower, fearing for his life, Shakespeare began writing gloomy plays. This seems more or less true, and it typifies the Rutland case. It is not an easy case because it is accumulative and has to be studied in its many details. The assertion is that Rutland wrote Shakespeare, because everything that is known about his life and personality corresponds perfectly with the Shakespeare revealed through his plays. Porohovshikov summed it up. 'The facts are simple. The plays do not harmonize with Shakspere's life; the plays are a faultless reflection of Rutland's career.'

This requires a demurrer, as Bacon would have put it. It can undoubtedly be seen, since Porohovshikov, Demblon and others have seen it, that the life of whoever wrote Shakespeare ran parallel to that of Rutland. The significance of this fades away when the cases for other candidates are considered. A feature in all of them is the claim that their respective lives and characters match those of Shakespeare – as deduced from his works. These works are so universal that many different minds, careers and experiences of life can be read into them. Everyone's life, not just Rutland's, is reflected in Shakespeare's plays.

There is, however, one thing that distinguishes Rutland from all the other possible writers of *Hamlet*. He actually went to Denmark, and the castle at Elsinore.

King Frederick II and his son, the future Christian IV, with Kronborg Slot at Elsinore in the background. This is a detail of a tapestry from the famous series showing all the kings of Denmark which Shakespeare may have alluded to in Hamlet.

SHAKESPEARE IN DENMARK

The first quarto edition of *Hamlet, Prince of Denmark* was published in 1603, and in the following year there appeared a second edition, revised and enlarged. Shakespeare's play was based on an earlier version of Hamlet, but he added certain Danish touches. Rossencraft and Gilderstone, as spelt in the first (Q1) edition, were the names of two well-known families in Denmark, Rosenkrantz and Gyldenstjerne. Young men from both families attended the University of Wittenberg, where Shakespeare made them Hamlet's fellow students.

Shakespeare must have heard about Kronborg Slot, the castle at Elsinore, from someone who had been there. This was deduced by Jan Stefannson in *The Contemporary Review*, January 1896. Part of his evidence was the line, 'Look upon this picture and on that' (iii. 4), spoken by Hamlet as he points to a portrait of his father, the late king, contrasting it with a picture of his uncle the usurper. The scene takes place in the queen's chamber, but Stefannson saw a reference to the famous tapestry series (detail above), showing all the one hundred and eleven kings of Denmark, which hung in the Hall of Knights at Elsinore's castle.

In the year between the publication of Q1 and the second (Q2) edition of *Hamlet*, Shakespeare had learnt much more about Elsinore and the Danish court. In Q1 the chamberlain was called Corambis, not Polonius as in Q2. Polonius is the Latinized form of Plönnies, the name of a Swedish family that traditionally served the Danish crown. The chamberlain's servant, Montano in Q1, became Reynaldo (the Scandinavian Ranald); the anonymous Gentleman acquired a Danish name, Osric; the queen, originally Geruth, was properly renamed in Danish Gertrude, and another new Danish name in Q2 is Yaughan (Jörgen) the innkeeper. The two courtiers became more correctly Rosencrans and Guyldenstern. The Danish word, *Danskers*, appears in Q2 but nowhere else in Shakespeare, and so does *crants*, a floral garland, mentioned by the priest at Ophelia's funeral.

The opening scene of *Hamlet* suggests that, after writing the first version, Shakespeare visited Kronborg Slot at Elsinore. In Q1 there is no stage direction, but in Q2 the place where the sentries stand guard and where the Ghost appears is 'a platform before the castle'. According to Claud Sykes, this platform, a stone-paved area enclosed by battlements on top of an earth bank, is still to be seen in front of Kronborg Slot. It is guarded by a sentry, and it is known locally as the Ghost Walk.

The writer of Q1 evidently did not realize that there are no mountains in Denmark, for at the end of the opening scene Horatio said,

> But look, the morn in russet mantle clad,
> Walks over yonder mountain top.

Standing on the platform at Elsinore, Shakespeare must have seen his mistake. But he also saw how he could adapt his line, for, looking east across the water towards sunrise and the Swedish coast, he would have noticed a tall hill, the Karlkulle. Thus in Q2 Horatio spoke more appropriately:

> But look, the dawn in russet mantle clad,
> Walks o'er the dew on yon high eastern hill.

It should be possible now to identify the author of *Hamlet*, the man who rewrote the original version to produce the 1604 edition. It must have been someone who went to Denmark for the first time in the second half of 1603, visited Elsinore and was received in the royal castle. The Rutlanders have had no difficulty in recognizing this figure. Soon after his accession, James I had need of an ambassador in Denmark, where the infant heir to the throne was about to be christened. To head the large English delegation, attend the ceremony and confer the Order of the Garter on the Danish king, he chose the Earl of Rutland.

One reason for the appointment may have been that Rutland had Danish acquaintances, including the young noblemen he studied with at Padua. There was certain to be a Rosencrans and a Guyldensterne at the christening. On 28 June 1603 the ambassadorial party set sail for Elsinore, and arrived there nine days later. King Christian IV was in Elsinore to greet them, and he and Rutland conversed in Italian, their only common language. After two days they proceeded to Copenhagen for the ceremony.

Features of the Danish court, accurately recorded in the 1604 Quarto of *Hamlet*, included the king's Swiss bodyguards and the drunken banquets, where every toast was accompanied by an artillery salute. After the christening, the English party returned to Elsinore and stayed in Kronborg Slot. The Danish king and court went there too, and the drinking began in earnest. This upset Rutland, as it did Hamlet, and after a few days he made excuses to leave early for home. On the return voyage the ship was threatened by a terrible storm, as in the play, and Rutland was forced to land at Scarborough rather than at Gravesend where he had embarked.

Once again, as Demblon, Sykes and the Rutland school of writers often remark, the Earl of Rutland was in the right place and at the right time to qualify as the author of Shakespeare. This Danish episode is the strongest item in the case for Rutland, and it is certainly very impressive. On the strength of it several theorists have allowed him a place among a Shakespeare-writing group. Another possibility is that he told William Shakspere about his adventures; or Shakspere himself could have gone to Denmark. English actors in his time made tours of that country, and there is nothing in Shakspere's scanty life-record to rule out the possibility that he travelled in Denmark, Italy or anywhere else. He could even have gone with Rutland on his mission to Elsinore in 1603.

THE SHAKESPEARE WHO WENT TO ITALY

Fourteen of Shakespeare's plays or scenes within them are set in Italy. That is partly because he took plots from older works with Italian settings, but in adapting these he added details which indicate that he had personal experience of that country. Shakespeare scholars who know Italy have often concluded that the author of *The Merchant of Venice*, *Othello*, *The Winter's Tale*, *Two Gentlemen of Verona*, and so on, must himself have been there, for his knowledge of Italian speech, manners and topography is, they say, faultless. There were no guidebooks where he could have learnt such things, so if Shakespeare did not travel in Italy, he must have been informed by someone who knew it well.

Dr Karl Elze, editor of the German Shakespeare Society's *Jahrbuch*, is a much-quoted authority on Shakespeare's supposed travels, as deduced from the plays. In one of his *Essays on Shakespeare* (1874) he points out how true to life are the Italian scenes. There is nothing in the plays to indicate that the author knew Stratford, whereas in northern Italy – in Verona, Padua, Bologna, Florence, Pisa and especially Venice – he seems to have been on familiar ground. Elze was too cautious to state outright that Shakespeare had travelled in Italy, but he gave the reasons why other scholars had formed that conclusion, and supported them with his own impressions.

In *The Merchant of Venice*, for example,

> [Shakespeare] has carefully observed and wonderfully hit the local colouring. There lies over this drama an inimitable and decidedly Italian atmosphere and fragrance, which certainly can be more readily felt than explained and analysed. Everything in it is so faithful, so fresh, so true to nature, that the play cannot possibly be excelled in this respect. . . . The moonlight scene at Belmont is a masterpiece that defies all rivalry, and is far above anything that has proceeded from an Italian pen.

The busy scene at the Exchange on the Rialto with gondolas in the background; the villas along the Brenta; the 'traject' or *traghetto* ferry; the names of places and local families; these and other details create a wonderfully true picture of old Venice as an English traveller might have seen it.

The English traveller who knew Venice, who wrote *The Merchant of Venice* and *Othello*, was possibly William Shakspere. There is nothing to show what he was doing up to his late twenties, so there is nothing to say that he did not spend time in Italy, as an actor, trader, secret service agent, nobleman's retainer or whatever. His biographers, however, make no such claim, and Sir Sidney Lee saw no necessity for it. He admitted that Shakespeare's references to cities in northern Italy were 'frequent and familiar' and that he 'supplied many a realistic portrayal of Italian life and sentiment'. Yet, in his judgment, Shakespeare's Italian scenes 'lack the intimate detail which would attest a first-hand experience of the country. . . . He doubtless owed all to the verbal reports of travelled friends or to books, the contents of which he had a rare power of assimilating and vitalising.'

In the enlarged, rewritten, 1915 edition of his *Life of Shakespeare*, Lee acknowledged the strength of evidence that Shakespeare had been to Italy. He had read Elze's article and others by his colleague, Dr Sarrazin, in the *Jahrbuch*; also Sir Edward Sullivan's 'Shakespeare and the Waterways of North Italy' in *The Nineteenth Century* journal of 1908. These gave all the evidence in the case for Shakespeare in Italy and answered every objection that had been raised against it. But there was just one problem. The life of William Shakspere gives no indication that he went abroad, and Lee believed that he never did so. That, he said, 'leaves Dr Sarrazin's and Sir Edward's arguments very shadowy'.

Lee, of course, did not acknowledge the existence of an Authorship question; his primary assumption was that Shakspere of Stratford and Shakespeare the dramatist were the same person. Since Shakspere never travelled, Shakespeare could not have gone to Italy. That was why Lee found the contrary evidence 'shadowy'. Overshadowing it is the Stratfordian assumption. Were it not for that, the picture given by Shakespeare's plays, of an author who knew and loved Italy, would stand unchallenged. This clears the way to the most simple and obvious conclusion, that the experts are right, and whoever wrote Shakespeare's Italian scenes was someone who had lived and travelled in the north of Italy.

This conclusion leaves open the case for Shakspere while emphasizing claims for the three earls, Oxford, Derby and Rutland, who all travelled in Italy. Oxford was there in 1575 at the age of twenty-five; Derby was two or three years younger when he passed through Italy in about 1584, and Rutland entered Padua University in 1596 when he was nineteen. Neither Francis Bacon nor his brother Anthony were ever in Italy, as far as is known, but many of Shakespeare's literary contemporaries, including several Authorship candidates, went there and knew the country. Among them were Nashe, Greene, Munday, Lyly, Rich, Kempe, Daniel and Sir Anthony Sherley. The field is thus only slightly narrowed by the Italian qualification.

As a clue to the Authorship, one feature of Shakespeare's experience in Italy seems particularly relevant. In *The Winter's Tale* (v. 2) the life-like statue of Hermione is said to be the work of Giulio Romano (*c.*1492–1546), who became head of the Roman school of painting in succession to Raphael. The statue is described in the play as, 'a piece many years in doing and now newly performed by that rare Italian master, Julio Romano, who, had he himself eternity and could put breath into his work, would beguile Nature of her custom, so perfectly he is her ape'.

This passage was once used by commentators to prove Shakespeare's essential ignorance of Italy and Italian art, because Giulio was known as a painter and architect, not as a sculptor. Yet Shakespeare was right. Giulio's tombstone in the church of San Barnaba at Mantua has long disappeared, but epitaphs on it were recorded by Vasari in his famous work on Italian artists, and these stated that Giulio was a master of three arts, painting, architecture and sculpture. Vasari was published in 1550 in Italian and not translated until modern times. It seems, therefore, that the author of *The Winter's Tale* learnt that Giulio was a sculptor by reading the original Latin epitaphs on the tombstone at Mantua.

A traveller who was so interested in Giulio Romano that he went to see his tomb and noted the inscriptions on it would certainly, while in Mantua, have gone to the famous Palazzo del Te, built by the artist himself and filled with his paintings and drawings. Exhibited there were

A detail from one of Giulio Romano's murals of the Trojan War in the Palazzo del Te, which were evidently known to the author of Lucrece.

Giulio's great pictures of the Trojan War (above). This work has been identified (by Lionel Cust in his contribution to *Shakespeare's England*) as the original of the Trojan War painting which Shakespeare wrote about in *The*

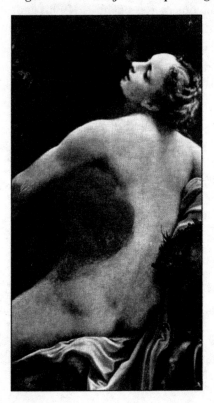

Rape of Lucrece (lines 1366–1456). Cust was prevented by Orthodoxy from concluding that Shakspere had been to Mantua and seen Giulio's work for himself, so he suggested that someone else had told him about it. That is always a possibility, but the picture in *Lucrece* is described at such length and with so much spirited detail, that it seems far more natural to suppose that the poet saw the original with his own eyes. It is difficult to work up such enthusiasm at second hand.

Another Shakespearian allusion to an Italian painting is in *The Taming of the Shrew*, as quoted on page 215. The only copy in England of Correggio's *Io and Jupiter* was the fresco at the

Correggio's Io and Jupiter *(detail), a painting referred to by Shakespeare.*

Earl of Rutland's Belvoir Castle, so, unless Shakespeare was Rutland, he is most likely to have seen the original in Milan (detail shown on page 225). It was on view in the palace of the sculptors Leoni between 1585 and 1600 – too late for Oxford to have seen it but within the period when both Derby and Rutland were in Italy.

The Oxfordian, Looney, ignored this small setback and made a good case for his candidate as the author of Shakespeare's Italian plays. One of Oxford's protégés was Anthony Munday, a prolific writer who went to Italy in 1578. He was there ostensibly as a student, but his covert mission was to spy on the English Catholics in Rome. A product of his Italian experience was *A Comedy of Two Italian Gentlemen*, which was possibly the basis of *The Two Gentlemen of Verona*. That play, supposedly written about 1590–92, was one of Shakespeare's first, and Looney believed that Oxford wrote it even earlier, after his return from Italy, when Rutland was a young boy.

There is such confusion about the dates of Shakespeare's Italian plays, and who was best qualified to write them, that the Stratfordian case seems no less satisfactory than any other. Shakspere's supporters have, perhaps, been too modest in denying him a trip to Italy. That is suggested by the career of Anthony Munday. Like Shakspere, he was the son of a trades-man, a London draper, and his place of education is unknown. In his early twenties he became an actor and engaged himself in all kinds of other activities, writing plays, romances, ballads and pamphlets, putting on pageants and, above all, working for the Secret Service as an anti-Catholic propagandist and security agent. He played a large part in the entrapment and execution of the Jesuit leader, Edmund Campion.

Munday is supposed to have been a collaborator with Shakspere in plays and theatre business. Their close colleague was Christopher Marlowe, another agent in Walsingham's Secret Service. In their book of 1994, *The Shakespeare Conspiracy*, Phillips and Keatman draw attention to Shakspere's associations with spies and agents, who were often, like Anthony Munday, people of his own kind and profession. Since Munday at the age of twenty-five was sent to Italy as a spy, and later toured the conti-nent with a company of actors, it is not impossible that Shakspere at the same age did much the same thing. In that case, it could have been William Shakspere who travelled in Italy and acquired there the local knowledge displayed in his plays.

VIII

THE PROFESSIONAL CANDIDATE

THE MARLOWE–SHAKESPEARE COLLABORATION

Christopher Marlowe wrote wholly or in part several of the Shakespeare plays. This is not just an assertion by Marlovian theorists, but a statement made in various ways by many of the most eminent and orthodox Shakespearian scholars. Yet the official record is that Marlowe was killed in 1593, before a single Shakespeare play had been published. This is a confusing state of affairs, and no one denies that there is a mystery about the Marlowe-Shakespeare relationship. There is no record that the two of them ever met, but the authorities agree that they must have known each other well enough. Shakspere and Marlowe were born in the same year, into the same class of provincial tradesman family, and they were both at the same time following the same profession in the small, intimate world of the London theatre. There is strong evidence that they collaborated in producing plays, and no doubt at all that Shakespeare's writing was heavily influenced by Marlowe.

The debate about Marlowe's hand in Shakespeare has been going on since the eighteenth century, when Edmond Malone acknowledged him as the author of *Titus Andronicus*. This was widely accepted, and for many years it was the fashion among critics to ascribe much or most of Shakespeare's early writings to Christopher Marlowe. Great Shakespearians, Hazlitt, Fleay, Chalmers, Dyce, Verity, Thorndike, Jane Lee, Algernon Swinburne and many others, down to the supremely orthodox Sir Sidney Lee, identified Marlowe as solely, principally or partly responsible for *Titus Andronicus*, *Richard II*, *Richard III* and the three parts of *Henry VI*. 'All the blank verse in Shakespeare's early plays bears the stamp of Marlowe's inspiration', wrote Lee in his essay on Marlowe for the *Dictionary of National Biography*. He believed that the two dramatists worked together; and that Marlowe was a major contributor to several Shakespearian plays.

The most extreme of the 'disintegrators' (those who ascribe parts of the Shakespeare canon to other writers) was J.M. Robertson MP. To balance this tendency he was also a polemical Stratfordian, an arch-defender of Orthodoxy. Throughout the early part of the twentieth century, he and his good friend, Sir George Greenwood, the anti-Stratfordian agnostic, engaged in a weighty battle of books. Robertson denounced his friend and other theorists in *The Baconian Heresy*, Greenwood replied at equal length with *Is There a Shakespeare Problem?*, and so it went on. The odd thing was that, while arguing bitterly over every small point, the two rivals were not so far apart in principle. Greenwood was prepared to allow that Shakspere may have had something to do with the writing of plays, while Robertson was generous with Shakespearian drama and allotted great parts of it to Greene, Peele, Chapman, Marlowe and others – though with nothing for Bacon. Marlowe was his favourite alternative Shakespeare. According to Robertson, Marlowe wrote *Titus Andronicus*, *Richard III*, *The Comedy of Errors*, the first act of *Richard II*, most of *Henry V*, much of *Julius Caesar*, some of *Romeo and Juliet* and passages in other Shakespeare plays.

Modern Stratfordians see the dangers in disintegrationism, and the fashion now is to claim for Shakespeare as much as possible of the writing that appeared under his name. This is not because new evidence has been found to refute the disintegrators, but largely as a response to pressure from the Heretics. Nothing has changed except opinions, and there is just as much reason as ever to respect the judgments of older experts who concluded that at least some of Shakespeare's plays should be credited to Christopher Marlowe.

DR MENDENHALL'S DISCOVERY

The Marlovian theory develops from a firm foundation. Its great advantage over every other heresy is that Christopher Marlowe was a brilliant and prolific writer, a seasoned professional rather than a noble dilettante. The claim that his writing is indistinguishable from Shakespeare's is also firmly based. It is not only a literary opinion but is supported by findings using a statistical method which has never been refuted.

The proof that both Marlowe's and Shakespeare's works were written by the same author was discovered by chance early this century by Dr Thomas Mendenhall, a distinguished physicist who became President of the American Association for the Advancement of Science. He had worked out a method, particularly useful in cases of disputed authorship, of 'fingerprinting' any author by frequency of word-lengths. Every writer, he found, consistently and unconsciously follows a certain pattern in this respect. In any two substantial samples of anyone's writing the same pattern of relative word-lengths occurs – so many two-letter, three-letter, four-letter words per thousand in each sample. Dr Mendenhall did his counting, proved his point, wrote a scientific paper on his discovery and turned to other things.

He was recalled to letter-counting by an enthusiastic Baconian, who commissioned him to use his method on the Bacon–Shakespeare controversy.

To do this properly meant comparing Shakespeare's pattern of word-lengths not only with Bacon's but with those of other contemporary writers. Secretaries were hired, over a million word-lengths were counted, and the result of these long, expensive proceedings was that the client was disappointed. A sample of almost 200,000 words from the works of Bacon, including his *Advancement of Learning* and *Henry VII*, compared poorly with the sample from Shakespeare. Bacon used more two-letter and three-letter words than Shakespeare, and more long words of from seven to thirteen letters, but less words of four, five and six letters.

To round off his work Mendenhall turned to Christopher Marlowe, and what he found astonished him. He had never seen anything like it before. It caused, he reported, 'something akin to a sensation' among the research assistants. Marlowe's word-length frequencies were an exact match with Shakespeare's. It was as rare a coincidence as finding two people with identical fingerprints. Mendenhall published his graphs with an article in *The Popular Science Monthly* (December, 1901). 'A Mechanical Solution to a Literary Problem', he called it.

H.N. Gibson argued against Mendenhall's method and conclusion over eight pages in *The Shakespeare Claimants*. As a mere scientist, Mendenhall did not understand the conditions of Elizabethan literature; how old copyists and modern editors have tinkered with the lengths and spellings of words; how authors collaborated to such an extent that it is impossible to be sure of selecting pure samples of anyone's work; how often revisions were made by other hands. Mendenhall's samples were not large enough to be significant, nor did he test enough authors to be sure that the Marlowe–Shakespeare correspondence was really unique. It is unfair to compare Bacon's prose with Shakespeare's verse. Finally, Mendenhall did not double-check his results, so he and his tired assistants probably made mistakes in their counting.

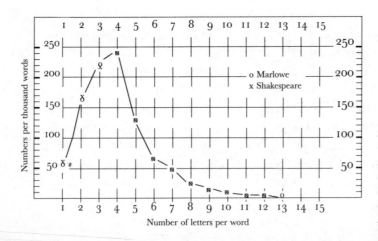

Mendenhall's graph of 1901 shows an exact match between the comparative word-lengths in the writings of Shakespeare and Marlowe.

One of Gibson's objections seems to have arisen from a misunderstanding of the Mechanical Solution. Words of, say, seven letters, he pointed out, come from different vocabularies, relate to different subjects and do not necessarily have anything in common. Thus writers with quite different styles, dealing with subjects which have nothing to do with each other, may be using words of the same length. This ignores the virtue of Mendenhall's method: that a writer's word-length pattern is unconscious and does not significantly vary, whatever the subject or style adopted. Yet no system is perfect. When Mendenhall analysed *a Christmas Carol* he found that the number of seven-letter words in it was unusually high for a Dickens sample. That was because of the repetition of the name, Scrooge.

Modern statisticians have not disputed, other than in a few details, the validity of Mendenhall's method. A paper on the subject by C.B. Williams, in *Studies in the History of Statistics and Probability*, is reprinted in A.D. Wraight's Marlovian book of 1994, *The Story that the Sonnets Tell*. Mendenhall worked long before the age of computers, assembling his data by laborious handcraft. It would be easy enough today to repeat and extend his researches, but no one has yet done so. There is now a flourishing school of Shakespearian 'stylometrists'. Eric Sams has a deprecatory chapter on them in *The Real Shakespeare*. They analyse Shakespeare's plays by sentence-length, numbers of words and syllables in sentences, incidences of common words or rare words, the clustering of images and other criteria, and they apply their data to determining which parts of Shakespeare's plays are by him or somebody else, and to what extent the 'disputed' plays, such as *Edmund Ironside, Pericles, Edward III* and *Sir Thomas More*, should be regarded as Shakespearian.

The result, says Sams, is chaotic. Every stylometrist has a different approach and rejects everyone else's method. Every discovery that has ever been proclaimed by one stylometrist had been disputed by another, equally qualified. In the case of *Edward III* the situation is exactly as it was before computers were invented. Some analysts find that the play is by Shakespeare under the influence of Marlowe, some by Marlowe influenced by Shakespeare, and other findings are in-between or different altogether.

One of Sams's criticisms is that the stylometrists are so eager for respectability that they accept the official dates and attributions of plays rather than questioning and testing them. For the same reason they have been inhibited from using their computers for Authorship studies. It would be interesting to see the respective word-lengths of Marlowe and Shakespeare compared more fully than Mendenhall was able to do it, and then to see whether he and the literary critics are justified in claiming that Marlowe's writing is indistinguishable from Shakespeare's.

One can reasonably accept that Christopher Marlowe was the principal author of the Shakespeare plays, about ten of them, which are supposed to have been written before 30 May 1593, when Marlowe was murdered. Yet it was not just in the early plays that Mendenhall found Marlowe's characteristic fingerprinting. Shakespeare did not change his style after Marlowe's death, but continued in the same vein.

Explanations for that are that Marlowe wrote from beyond the grave, or that he did not really die in 1593. The second is a clear possibility, and the evidence for it is given in the following pages.

MARLOWE'S SHORT LIFE

1564 26 February. Christopher, the eldest son and second child in a family of four boys and five girls, was christened in the church of St George the Martyr, Canterbury.
Parents: John Marlowe, a shoemaker, and his wife Katherine.

1578 Won a scholarship to the King's School, Canterbury.

1581 Entered with a six-year scholarship Corpus Christi College, Cambridge, to study divinity.

1587 Awarded his degree despite having been absent and out of the country on government service. Worked in London as a dramatist for a theatre company, and continued as a secret agent under Sir Francis Walsingham and Lord Burghley. Mission to Utrecht. Thomas Walsingham of Scadbury Manor, Chislehurst, Kent, first cousin of Sir Francis, became his patron. Admitted to Sir Walter Ralegh's philosophical group, the School of Night.

1589 Arrested with Thomas Watson for involvement in a street fight in which Watson killed William Bradley, an innkeeper's son. Bound over to keep the peace.

1592 Fought a bloodless duel with William Corkine, musician of Canterbury Cathedral.

1593 20 May. Arrested at the house of Thomas Walsingham, brought before the Court of Star Chamber, released on bail pending further enquiries. Denounced for blasphemy and atheism.
30 May. Murdered in Deptford by Ingram Friser, who was pardoned on the grounds of self-defence.

THE MYSTERY OF MARLOWE'S MURDER

Marlowe's character is enigmatic, and so are his adult life and the circumstances of his death. As seen by Charles Nicholl in *The Reckoning*, he was 'an atheist and blasphemer, a dissolute homosexual', a treacherous spy, scoundrel and swindler. This judgment is regardless of his scholarship and poetic genius, and Marlowe's biographer, A.D. Wraight, has issued a pamphlet against Nicholl, pointing out that all the detractors of Marlowe were his professional enemies with special reasons for defaming him. Almost everything recorded about his career is disputable, including his alleged murder.

At some time during his six and a half years at Cambridge, Marlowe attracted the attention of the Secret Service and was enrolled as an agent. It was not unusual then, nor is it today, for promising students, particularly those with no definite plans or prospects, to be pressed into serving their country in that capacity. Marlowe's career in espionage began actively while he was still at university. Against all the rules, he left his college during the term, and it became known that he had gone abroad to Reims and entered the Jesuit seminary there. This was a well-known centre of Catholic intrigue against the queen and Protestant England, and it was assumed that Marlowe had gone over to the enemy. The university authorities therefore withheld his degree, but changed their minds upon receiving a letter from the Privy Council. This indicated what Marlowe had really been up to.

> Whereas it was reported that Christopher Morley was determined to have
> gone beyond the seas to Reames and there to remaine, Their Lordships
> thought good to certefie that he had no such intent, but that in all his
> actions he had behaved him selfe orderlie and discreetlie wherebie he had
> done her Majestie good service & deserved to be rewarded for his faithful
> dealinge: Their Lordships request was that the rumor thereof should be
> allaied by all possible meanes, and that he should be furthered in the
> degree he was to take this next Commencement: Because it was not her
> Majesties pleasure that anie one emploied as he had been in matters
> touching the benefitt of his Countrie should be defamed by those that are
> ignorant in th' affaires he went about.

Marlowe had evidently been sent to spy on the English Catholics at Reims. This was the first but not the only time he acted as a double agent. His associates thereafter were the leading, most ruthless spies and spy-catchers of the State Security organization, including Robert Poley, the charming, treacherous betrayer of the Babington plot which led to the execution of

In 1953 a broken panel with a portrait of a young man was found by a Cambridge undergraduate among builders' rubble outside the Master's Lodge at Corpus Christi College. It bore the date 1585 and the age of the subject, twenty-one years. In that year Marlowe, aged twenty-one, was at Corpus Christi, and it is thought very likely that he was the subject of the portrait, which was probably hidden after his disgrace. Restored and repainted, it is now displayed among the College portraits.

Mary Queen of Scots. It was an ugly profession, attracting opportunists and underworld characters of no fixed allegiance. Yet, as always in the history of espionage, motives were mixed. Some of Walsingham's agents were patriotic idealists, dutifully serving the realm against the many dangers, both internal and from abroad, that were active throughout Elizabeth's reign. Others were plain scoundrels.

The details of Marlowe's involvement in this business are too little known either to justify or condemn him. It is a matter of personal judgment, and so is the character of Marlowe as interpreted from his supposed portrait (above). Charles Nicholl sees the young man as sinister, treacherous, 'a bit unhealthy', while to A.D. Wraight he is boyish, intelligent, observant and 'a child of the English renaissance'.

His other associates were of a different kind. Sir Walter Ralegh's School of Night was a group of intellectual free-thinkers who met, necessarily in secret, to discuss openly among themselves such basic questions as the nature of truth and reality and the ideals of philosophy and government. It included scientists, occultists, mathematicians, courtiers and poets. Marlowe and the poet Chapman were members, along with the great astronomer, Hariot, and the 'Wizard' Earl of Northumberland. The subjects raised at their meetings were those on which religion and the state had officially pronounced, and which were therefore forbidden. Those who dared speak freely about them were stigmatized as 'atheists'. That was the charge on which Ralegh and others were later condemned, and which was finally brought against Marlowe.

Marlowe in his short career made many enemies, in the theatre and the world of espionage, among Catholics, Puritans and the opponents of Ralegh. He also had powerful friends, including his patron Thomas Walsingham. At the end of May 1593 he was living with Walsingham at his bachelor establishment at Chislehurst, when he was summoned to appear immediately before the Court of Star Chamber in London. It was a terrifying summons, because the court was well known for sentencing those it found guilty of subversion to the nastiest tortures that experts could devise.

Blasphemy and atheism were the crimes that Marlowe had to answer for. His enemies had acted, striking at Marlowe through one of the most disreputable of the secret agents with whom he had been working, Richard Baines or Bame. Thomas Kyd, Marlowe's former room-mate, had been arrested after a raid in which certain atheistic writings were discovered among his papers. These, he alleged under torture, belonged to Christopher Marlowe. After Marlowe had been brought to court and released on bail, Baines drew up an indictment. These are some of the things he accused Marlowe of saying:

> That Moses was but a juggler, and that one Heriots, being W. Raleigh's man can do more than he.
>
> That the first beginning of religion was to keep men in awe.
>
> That Christ was a bastard and his mother dishonest.
>
> That he was the son of a carpenter, and that if the Jews among whom he was born did crucify him, they best knew him and whence he came.
>
> That Christ deserved better to die than Barabbas, and that the Jews made a good choice, though Barabbas were both a thief and a murderer.
>
> That all Protestants are hypocritical asses.
>
> That St John the Evangelist was bedfellow to Christ and leaned always in his bosom, that he used him as the sinners of Sodom.
>
> That all they that love not tobacco and boys were fools.
>
> That the Sacrament . . . would have been much better being administered in a tobacco pipe.

If Marlowe said any of these things, it could only have been in drink or sport among student friends. They are travesties, not serious expressions of heresy, and clearly they were just meant to be shocking. Baines could well have made them up, imagining how 'atheists' would talk. He was, however, a professional informer, and his evidence carried enough weight to land his victim in serious trouble.

It is not known what happened at Marlowe's appearance before the court, but he was temporarily released on bail and ordered to report daily.

A few days later, 30 May, he attended a meeting at Deptford, only a few miles from the house of Thomas Walsingham, with three other secret agents, Ingram Friser, Nicholas Skeres and the notorious Robert Poley. During that meeting he was murdered.

The official story of Marlowe's death was not known until 1925, when Dr J. Leslie Hotson, the most successful of modern Shakespearian sleuths, published *The Death of Christopher Marlowe*. He had discovered in the Public Record Office the report on the inquest, which the coroner submitted to the Privy Council. Before that time, even among Marlowe's contemporaries, different versions of how he died were in circulation. Meres in 1598 wrote that he had been 'stabbed to death by a bawdy serving man, a rival of his in lewde love'. Another account was that, by the judgment of God, he had stabbed himself through the head while trying to kill another man in a London street. It was also written that he was struck down by the plague as a warning to sinners. The nearest to the official version was that Ingram Friser had invited Marlowe to a feast, and that while they were playing backgammon Marlowe tried to stab Friser, who retaliated by stabbing him through the brain. Sidney Lee in his 1917 *Dictionary of National Biography* entry said that Marlowe was killed in a drunken brawl.

The inquest was held within thirty-six hours of the killing. It was conducted by a coroner with a jury of sixteen local citizens, and the witnesses were Poley, Friser and Skeres. Marlowe's three companions were the only people who knew at first hand what had happened, and their story was accepted by the court, apparently without question.

They had met at ten in the morning at the house of Mrs Bull, a Deptford widow. After about two hours spent together in a room, they were served dinner, and passed the afternoon walking quietly about the garden. At 6 o'clock they went back to the room for supper, and after they had finished Marlowe and Friser began quarrelling about the bill ('le recknynge'). Marlowe was lying on a bed, while the other three sat together alongside it, with their backs to the bed and a table in front of them. Marlowe suddenly seized Friser's dagger and attacked him with it, inflicting two wounds, about a quarter of an inch deep, to his head. Unable to get away because of the table in front and the two people on either side of him, Friser fought Marlowe for the dagger, secured it and thrust the point into Marlowe's skull above his right eye to the depth of two inches, killing him.

The court found nothing suspicious about this story. Friser was detained for breaching the peace, but within a month was set free with a Royal Pardon. He returned to the service of his master, who was none other than

Thomas Walsingham. Poley and Skeres were also employed as Walsingham's agents. After the case was closed, all three of those involved in the death of Marlowe went back to their underworld professions, swindling, informing and blackmailing.

Almost every writer who has commented on this story, not just Marlovians but Hotson and other orthodox professors, has been dissatisfied with it. It conceals far more than it tells. Nothing is said about the important questions: the circumstances of the meeting between these four men of sinister professions; what was the subject they spent all day discussing; what sort of establishment was kept by Widow Bull; how it was that Poley and Skeres did not intervene in the knife-fight. The incident has all the hallmarks of a gangland killing, an execution that someone had ordered, a day-long grilling of a suspected double-agent, followed by his liquidation. There were many people who might have had good reasons for needing the death of Marlowe. Almost any of his associates, Thomas Walsingham, members of the School of Night, literary or Secret Service colleagues, might well have feared that Marlowe, on his next appearance in the Star Chamber, would implicate them in whatever he was accused of. Marlowe was so deeply involved in the Elizabethan world of conspiracy that it is not surprising that he was executed by someone's agents. Nor, if powerful people were involved, is it surprising that the inquest was an incurious, inconclusive formality. One does not have to be 'behind the scenes' to realize that official cover-ups have always been, and still are, readily organized.

The evidence, however, allows for another interpretation. The theory, on which the further theory of Marlowe's authorship of Shakespeare depends, is that Marlowe did not really die in the house of Mrs Bull at Deptford, but that the whole thing was a deception. It was a typical Secret Service manoeuvre, to feign an agent's death as a preliminary to resurrecting him in a new character. Alternatively, it was a way in which Walsingham could have saved his friend, and also himself and others, by smuggling him out of the country. The details can easily be imagined. A corpse was procured, perhaps of a foreign seaman killed in a Deptford waterside brawl; it was brought into Mrs Bull's house, with or without her connivance; the four conspirators then dressed it in Marlowe's clothes, and at nightfall Christopher Marlowe went down to the harbour and took ship for the Continent. There is nothing to disprove this version of events. None of Marlowe's nearby friends or relations were called to identify his body. It is not known where they buried it.

The theory of Marlowe's bloodless disappearance was proposed as early as 1895 by an American lawyer, Wilbur Ziegler, in the preface to his novel,

It Was Marlowe: A Story of the Secret of Three Centuries. His idea was that Marlowe survived his supposed death to become joint author, together with Ralegh and the Earl of Rutland, of the better part of Shakespeare's plays. After the discovery of the inquest report in 1925, a similar view was taken by a succession of writers, including Gilbert Slater in *Seven Shakespeares*. He could not believe that Walsingham would have ordered or allowed the murder of his dear friend. It was more likely that he used his own agents to fake the murder, and sent Marlowe to a refuge in Italy, from which he later returned in a new personality. That is how he contributed to the group that wrote Shakespeare.

In 1955 this theory was assimilated and reformulated by a New York publicist, Calvin Hoffman. His book, *The Murder of the Man who was Shakespeare*, left no room for doubt that Christopher Marlowe had survived his murder to become the sole, supreme author of Shakespeare. Hoffman re-invigorated the Marlovian cause and made it a rival to Oxfordism as the most popular Authorship theory. His ambition, which he achieved in 1956, was to open the Walsingham family vault in Chislehurst church, in the hope of finding Marlowe–Shakespeare manuscripts. The tomb was filled only with sand, but below it were some coffins, and these he was not allowed to open.

It is by no means impossible that Marlowe survived his reported murder, went abroad and later returned in disguise to write under the name of Shakespeare. There is no firm evidence for this, but Marlovians have detected a few possible hints. Most suggestive are some lines in the prologue to Marlowe's play, *The Jew of Malta*. It was a popular play in his lifetime, but was not published until forty years after his death, and the prologue is thought to have been a later addition. It is spoken in the name of Machevil, probably meaning the author himself, for Marlowe in his time was called Machiavellian, and the first four letters of the name, MACH, produce Ch. Ma. This is almost Ch. Marl. which is the name under which Marlowe's *Dr Faustus* was published in 1604.

> Albeit the world thinks Machevil is dead,
> Yet was his soul but flown beyond the Alps,
> And now the Guise is dead, is come from France
> To view this land and frolic with his friends.
> To some, perhaps my name is odious,
> But such as love me guard me from their tongues,
> And let them know that I am Machevil,
> And weigh not men and therefore not men's words;

Admired I am of those who hate me most.
Though some speak openly against my books
Yet will they read me, and thereby attain
To Peter's Chair: and when they cast me off,
Are poisoned by my climbing followers.
I count religion but a childish toy,
And hold there is no sin but Ignorance,
Birds of the air will tell of murders past;
I am ashamed to hear such fooleries ...

These lines apply well enough to Marlowe. The world thinks that he died in 1593, but in fact he went across the Alps to Italy. Now he has come back to England to 'frolic with his friends'. The Duke of Guise who prevented his return was an anti-Protestant campaigner and a character in Marlowe's *Massacre of Paris*. He could well stand for Richard Baines, Marlowe's prosecutor, who died soon after the affair. References to friends who 'guard me from their tongues' and to foolish talk of past murders also fit the case of Marlowe.

Certain enigmatic lines in *As You Like It*, written about 1599, have possible bearing on the Marlowe mystery. The author certainly had him in mind when he quoted a line from the 'dead shepherd's' *Hero and Leander* (v. 1):

Dead shepherd, now I find thy saw of might,
Who ever lov'd that lov'd not at first sight?

A sentence spoken by Touchstone during his conversation with Audrey (iii. 3) has no apparent meaning except as an allusion to the murder scene at Deptford. 'When a man's verses cannot be understood, nor a man's good wit seconded with the forward child Understanding, it strikes a man more dead than a great reckoning in a little room.'

In the inquest on Marlowe's death the key word was 'le recknynge', which was given as the cause of the quarrel. Touchstone says that for a man to be misunderstood makes him *more dead* than the affair of the reckoning, implying that that affair was not in fact so deadly. The reckoning was not mentioned in contemporary accounts of Marlowe's death and this detail was not discovered until 1925, so the author of *As You Like It* must have had more than common knowledge about the Deptford incident.

Marlovians identify Touchstone as the true author of the play, Christopher Marlowe. Audrey, the country girl whom he deceives with a promise of marriage, is the Elizabethan play-audience, and William, the honest rustic from the Forest of Arden, is of course William Shakspere.

The last point is agreed on by Authorship theorists of all schools. A touch-stone is a stone of no worth itself, which has the property of detecting the worth of metals when it touches them. In a scene with William and Audrey (v. 1), Touchstone touches William and then confuses him with strange talk.

> *Touchstone.* Give me your hand. Art thou learned?
> *William.* No, sir.
> *Touchstone.* Then learn this of me: to have is to have; for it is a figure in rhetoric that drink, being poured out of a cup into a glass, by filling the one doth empty the other; for all your writers do consent that ipse is he: now you are not ipse, for I am he.
> *William.* Which he, sir?
> *Touchstone.* He, sir, that must marry this woman.

The country vicar who is summoned to marry Touchstone and Audrey is Sir Oliver Mar-text. The first letters of his names are OL MAR, making MARLO, a common spelling of Marlowe. Hoffman sees Mar-text as meaning Marlowe's text. Thus Marlowe's text is marrying Marlowe (Touchstone) to Audrey, the theatre audience, while William Shakspere is dismissed. By this interpretation it appears that only Christopher Marlowe could have written the play.

Throughout *As You Like It* there are passages which seem obscurely meaningful, and the play has attracted many theorists. Oxfordians believe Edward de Vere to be Touchstone; Lefranc thought that William Stanley, the real author of the play, was represented in it by the melancholy Jaques. With so many different interpretations of the same material, each about as convincing as the other, it seems there is no good reason to believe any of them, absolutely.

Were it not for the record of his early death, Christopher Marlowe would be the strongest of Shakespeare candidates. It is not disputed that he contributed in some way to the early plays of Shakespeare, and critics would be more willing to admit his influence throughout the works if they were not inhibited from attributing to Marlowe anything written after 1593. Mendenhall in his word-length analysis found the same pattern in Marlowe's works and in the whole of Shakespeare, not just the early plays.

Signature of Christopher Marley (Marlowe).

239

Marlowe was a divinity student and a classicist, a translator of Ovid. His learning was of the kind and quality that scholars find in Shakespeare, and there is nothing much within Shakespeare's range of knowledge that he could not have mastered. Nevertheless, there is something lacking in his case. Marlowe's own writings are youthful, vigorous, lyrical, but critics do not find in them the same great qualities of nobility and humanity that distinguish the works of Shakespeare's maturity. Some of the claims made for Shakespeare's innate culture and aristocratic expressions have no doubt been exaggerated, but, to the extent that they are justified, they are as unfavourable to Marlowe as they are to William Shakspere. The most telling objection is that Marlowe was no lawyer. Shakespeare, is said to have used legal terms and metaphors throughout his writings in a way that would only come naturally to a professional, but there is no reason why Marlowe should have done so. If the author of Shakespeare was a well-practised lawyer, he was not Christopher Marlowe.

To these and other objections the Marlovians have only one answer, but, if it is correct, it gives them a very formidable case. Those who believe that Marlowe was the main author of all Shakespeare's works must also believe that he lived on for many years after the 1593 affair at Deptford. This is clearly a possibility. The Marlovians have opened a new department in Shakespeare Authorship studies, bringing in the Elizabethan underworld of spies, criminals and traitors that merged into the worlds of propaganda, literature and high culture. It is impossible to separate Marlowe and his mysterious, often sinister associates from Shakspere and the circumstances in which Shakespeare's plays were produced. Marlowe undoubtedly had a hand in Shakespeare. If he really did survive his own murder there is no limit to what he can be supposed to have done later.

IX

A Last Look Round

The Confusions of Group Theory

People who know about computers and nothing much else can often be heard fantasizing about a database, compiled from all books and everything that has ever been published in the world. From that, they suppose, could be distilled 'information'.

Even a small sampling of Authorship literature shows the fallacy in that. A deafening pandemonium would be the only result, with thousands of writers of various mental balances shouting opinions and abuse at each other. Properly directed, computers have a useful function in stylistic analyses of Shakespeare and other authors, but so far they have contributed almost nothing to the present subject.

Given access to the full range of literature, a computer that survived the test would probably come up with the message that Shakespeare was written by a consortium of about fifty authors, all those for whom any reasonable claim has been put forward. And that might well be somewhere near the right answer.

Among theorists of every persuasion there are some who admit that their candidate was not the only Shakespeare but the leader of a group. These seem at first very reasonable people, open-minded and tolerant, but the real reason for their liberal views is soon apparent. They are confused. If Shakspere is a dubious candidate for Authorship, so in different ways are all the others. Each of them has weak points and inadequacies. Yet each of them uniquely has certain attributes of Shakespeare. Bacon was a match for Shakespeare in his knowledge of law and lawyers' talk; Oxford makes an excellent Hamlet; Derby must have known the Court of Navarre; Rutland went to Denmark and other places at the right times; Marlowe was a professional writer in the style of Shakespeare; Ralegh knew the Americas as Shakespeare seems to have done. Nor, having gone so far, can one fail to see the hands or influence in the plays and poems of Edward Dyer ('the Dyer's hand' – Sonnet 111), the Countess of Pembroke (Swan of the Wiltshire Avon) and many others.

One way out of the confusion is by the pick-and-mix method. Take all the candidates who have claims to some part of Shakespeare, and make them into a group with whoever you like as leader. Given below are the components of just a few of the group theories published in the course of a century. Group leaders, if any, are in capitals.

BACON, RALEGH, Spenser, Sidney, Sackville, Paget, Oxford
(Delia Bacon, *The Philosophy of Shakespeare Unfolded*, 1857)

Southampton, Ralegh, Essex, Rutland, Montgomery, Bacon,
Shakspere (copyist)
(Appleton Morgan, *The Shakespeare Myth*, 1881)

Greene, Peele, Daniel, Marlowe, Shakspere, Nashe, Lodge,
Bacon (editor)
(T.W. White, *Our English Homer*, 1892)

MARLOWE, Ralegh, Rutland and others
(W.G. Ziegler, *It Was Marlowe*, 1895)

Shakspere, Bartholomew Griffin, Ferrers, Derby, Southampton, Pembroke
(J.P. Yeatman, *The Gentle Shakespeare*, 1896)

Bacon (*Venus and Adonis, Lucrece*, play editor), Sidney (Sonnets), Drayton,
Dekker, Munday, Chettle, Smythe, Haywood, Webster, Middleton,
Porter, Wilson
(J.H. Stotsenburg, *The Shakespeare Title*, 1904)

SHAKSPERE, Peele, Greene, Chapman, Marlowe and others
(J.M. Robertson, *The Shakespeare Canon*, 1924)

Shakspere, Barnes, Warner, Donne, Daniel
(H.T.S. Forrest, *The Five Authors of 'Shakespeare's Sonnets'*, 1923)

Bacon, Ralegh, Derby, Rutland, Oxford, Marlowe, Countess of
Pembroke
(Gilbert Slater, *Seven Shakespeares*, 1931)

RUTLAND, Bacon (*Venus and Adonis, Lucrece, Love's Labour's Lost*),
Oxford (Sonnets)
(Pierre Porohovshikov, *Shakespeare Unmasked*, 1940)

DYER, Nashe, Daniel, Barnes, Southampton and others
(Alden Brooks, *Will Shakespeare and the Dyer's Hand*, 1943)

OXFORD, Shakspere, Bacon, Beaumont, Fletcher, Ralegh and others – by
spirit communication
(Percy Allen, *Talks with Elizabethans*, 1945)

DERBY, Oxford, Rutland, Ralegh, Bacon, Countess of Pembroke,
   Countess of Rutland
   (A.J. Evans, *Shakespeare's Magic Circle*, 1956)

John Williams, Richard Vaughan, Countess of Pembroke, Marlowe,
   Sidney, Spenser, Daniel
   (George and Bernard Winchcombe, *Shakespeare's Ghost Writer*, 1968)

Between them, the thirteen authors name thirty-seven different people as
contributors to Shakespeare, and several of them imply that yet others
were involved. The number of times they are each mentioned is:

8   Bacon
6   Ralegh
5   Marlowe, Rutland
4   Oxford, Shakspere
3   Daniel, Derby, Countess of Pembroke, Sidney,
    Southampton
2   Barnes, Greene, Nashe, Peele, Spenser
21 others

For all its inadequacies, this ordering of group-candidates is of some value
as an illustration of the Groupist viewpoint. The consensus, composite
Shakespeare is made from two classes of writers, the professionals and
the aristocrats; and standing alone, detached and above them all, is
Francis Bacon. It is difficult to exclude Bacon from any Group theory. Not
only was he the most idealistic philosopher of the age, but he knew everything that was going on. According to some estimates he was a cold,
sly, calculating lawyer, while to other eyes he was a god-like genius who
sacrificed himself for humanity. That sounds like a very remarkable
person, as Bacon no doubt was. He must certainly have known the
truth about Shakespeare's authorship. It was his business to do so. And if
there was a conspiracy behind it, Bacon would have been involved, and
probably controlled it.

   Among the professional writers and theatre people, some of whom must
be included in any plausible group, Shakspere and Marlowe are obvious
candidates. To them can be added writers such as Greene, Peele and
Nashe, whom even the most orthodox critics have sometimes credited
with parts of Shakespeare's work.

Queen Elizabeth borne by nobles in 1600. One of her bearers was probably the Earl of Oxford, which possibly explains the 'canopy' reference in Sonnet 125.

Then there are the aristocrats, three of whom – Oxford, Derby, Rutland – have already been shown to have Authorship claims. The case for Oxford is today the best supported, and it is particularly strong if he is regarded as the head of a group. The other two are well qualified for group membership, but if that is allowed, it brings up one of the main objections to group theory and exposes a weakness. The courtier candidates were all so closely linked by kinship and marriage, and so aware of each other's affairs, either directly or through mutual relations, that if there was a Shakespeare group among them, any of them could have been part of it. Southampton, Sidney, the Pembrokes, even Queen Elizabeth herself, might have contributed to it, and so might any of their poets, protégés and literary friends – Ralegh, Dyer, Spenser, Daniel . . . until the group becomes an army.

This problem has been met before, in the wider context. Theorists find cryptic references to Bacon, Oxford and other candidates in the writings of so many contemporaries, that the Orthodox are entitled to be sceptical.

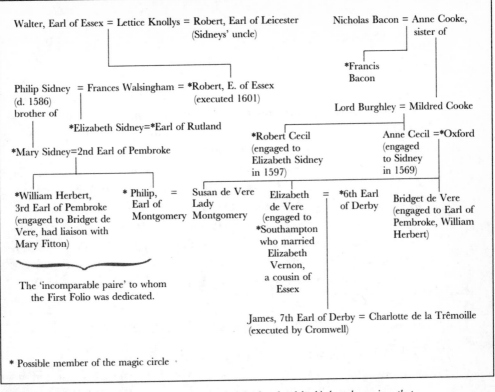

Walter, Earl of Essex = Lettice Knollys = Robert, Earl of Leicester
(Sidneys' uncle)

Nicholas Bacon = Anne Cooke, sister of

*Francis Bacon

Philip Sidney = Frances Walsingham = *Robert, E. of Essex
(d. 1586) (executed 1601)
brother of

Lord Burghley = Mildred Cooke

*Elizabeth Sidney=*Earl of Rutland

*Robert Cecil
(engaged to
Elizabeth Sidney
in 1597)

Anne Cecil =*Oxford
(engaged
to Sidney
in 1569)

*Mary Sidney=2nd Earl of Pembroke

*William Herbert,
3rd Earl of Pembroke
(engaged to Bridget de
Vere, had liaison with
Mary Fitton)

* Philip,
Earl of
Montgomery

= Susan de Vere
Lady
Montgomery

Elizabeth
de Vere
(engaged to
*Southampton
who married
Elizabeth
Vernon,
a cousin of
Essex

= *6th Earl
of Derby

Bridget de Vere
(engaged to Earl of
Pembroke, William
Herbert)

The 'incomparable paire' to whom
the First Folio was dedicated.

James, 7th Earl of Derby = Charlotte de la Trêmoille
(executed by Cromwell)

* Possible member of the magic circle

Many of the leading Shakespeare candidates were so closely related by birth and marriage that they could have formed a 'magic circle' guarding the secret of their literary activities from outsiders. Most likely to have been 'in the know' was Francis Bacon who moved among them and generally organized their affairs. Chart after A.J. Evans, Shakespeare's Magic Circle, *1956.*

If so many writers knew the secret of Shakespeare's authorship, their close friends would also have known it, and so eventually would the whole of London. Yet, incredibly, no one spoke out about it. Long after Elizabeth's reign, when reasons for secrecy no longer applied, no one whispered to their children or passed down any family tradition that they were descended from someone who was partly responsible for the works of Shakespeare. Not even Shakspere's family ever gave the slightest hint that their kinsman William was the great poet.

Group theory seems at first sight to be a promising solution, the ideal refuge for doubters. Those who cannot decide between the various Shakespeare candidates may comfortably conclude that they all worked together as a secret Shakespeare Society. That is all right, in principle, but when it comes to specifying the group members, and rejecting other claimants, confusion sets in. Everyone has their own ideas about who should be allowed in or excluded, and no one has shown how even a small, dedicated group could have maintained such long-lasting secrecy.

All the same, group theory still maintains its basic attractions. It was the original anti-Stratfordian theory of Delia Bacon, and its seems again to be making headway among Heretics generally. The phenomenon of Shakespeare's vocabulary, equal to that of two or three other writers combined, has never been explained under the assumption that he was the man from Stratford with no known education. The natural inference is that two or three writers, most likely more, combined their stocks of words to compile a richer vocabulary than any single individual has ever commanded. These writers cannot all have been of the same backgrounds and ways of life, for in that case they would all have used a similar range of words.

'There were many pens in Shakespeare' is the conclusion on which many baffled investigators have rested. But, they usually admit, there was one Master-Mind. Shakespeare cannot entirely hide himself behind a group. Even if he was a composite figure, he must have had a head.

WHO WAS WILL SHAKSPERE?

If there was a secret about Shakespeare's authorship, one man who would have known it was William Shakspere. Whether or not he wrote the plays and poems himself, he must have been involved in any arrangement which allowed them to be published under a theatrical form of his name. If it were known what sort of man he was, and what he actually did during his years away from Stratford, it would be easier to form some conclusion about the part he played in the creation of Shakespeare.

In the world of scholarship, the Shakspere biography industry is unique. No other life has been so deeply, keenly, lengthily researched by so many qualified investigators. Schoenbaum gives a wonderful account in *Shakespeare's Lives* of the labours and obsessions with which the quest for Shakspere has been pursued over three centuries.

The object of all these efforts has been to shed light upon the works of Shakespeare by comparing them with the author's life. To that extent the whole thing has been a failure. Many scraps of records have been turned up by the investigators, but every one of them is a disappointment. They tell about Shakspere's business dealings, his minor debts and brushes with the law, his shares in a theatre and the bare fact that he acted in plays. Yet they say nothing about his literary attainments, and they are of no real help to readers of Shakespeare.

This brings the subject back to its starting-point, the gap between Shakespeare and Shakspere. Even the most orthodox Shakespearians are dismayed by this. In his recent book, *Shakespeare: the Evidence*, Ian Wilson notices 'the most extraordinary gulf between the Shakespeare of Literature and the Shakespeare of History'. He quotes the puzzled comment on Shakespeare by the Oxford scholar, Dr Blair Worden:

> The relationship between an artist's biography and his writing is always a difficult subject, but there can be no other important writer since the invention of printing for whom we are unable to demonstrate any relationship at all.

It was that very point that started Abel Lefranc on his Authorship researches. In all his experience as a professor of literature he had never known a case where there was no apparent connection between an author's life and his writings. In the study of literature it is standard, invariable practice to peruse an author's texts in conjunction with his life-experiences. Only in Shakespeare's case is this impossible or fruitless.

If this evidence from literary specialists is squarely faced, it means beyond doubt that someone other than Shakspere was the main author. Yet Shakspere must have been involved in some capacity. Only a few items in his life-record are of much use in imagining what his function might have been, but together with hints, legends and personal impressions they suggest the following.

Will Shakspere was a high-spirited young man, who got into various kinds of trouble in Stratford and left early to make his way in the world. According to Jonson he was an amusing fellow, good company and a great talker. This was repeated by others who knew or had heard about him. Drayton, Shakspere's Warwickshire neighbour, said that he had 'as smooth a comic vein' as anyone who dealt in the theatre. Ward in 1662 was told that he was a 'natural wit', and Aubrey heard that Will Shakspere was 'very good company, and of a very readie and pleasant smoothe wit'.

Wit, meaning lively intelligence and good humour, was evidently a characteristic of the Shakspere family. Susanna, William's daughter, was said on her gravestone to have been 'witty above her sex' and to have inherited that quality from her father. Her grandfather, John Shakspere, was also witty. He was described (though on dubious hearsay evidence) as a 'merry cheeked old man' who liked a joke. By the same account young William did not enjoy his father's humour, but likely enough he inherited it.

It was easy enough for this energetic, quick-witted young man to find work in the bohemian underworld of London. As a newcomer, with nothing to help him but his personality, he had to take whatever jobs were offered, so he began on the lowest rung of the ladder, working for the disreputable theatre people.

Working in the theatre in those days was on the same level as working in a whorehouse, and the two were closely connected. A theatre was not just a playhouse but a social exchange of many kinds. Crooks and conmen, pimps and prostitutes of both sexes made it their cruising-ground. Young gentlemen went to the play for adventures and assignations as well as to see the actors. That is why the Puritans were so extremely against theatres and eventually had them shut down.

Shakspere's early employment, at the rough end of theatre work, brought him inevitably into the world of criminals and prostitutes. Biographers suppose that his first employer was Philip Henslowe, who made his money not only from theatre productions but from the property he let as brothels. The only known anecdote about Shakspere in his time, Manningham's story of 1602 about his exploit with the woman who slept with actors, may not be true, but says something about his reputation.

The most revealing document about Shakspere's London life was unknown to his Victorian biographers, who would have been horrified by it. It was unknown until 1931, when the indefatigable Leslie Hotson

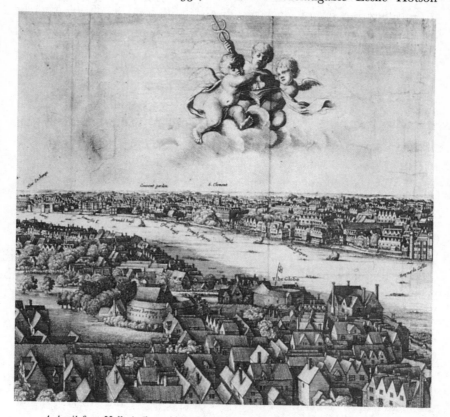

A detail from Hollar's 'long view' of London in 1647 from theatreland on Bankside.

unearthed it from the great paper mine in the Public Record Office. Dated 29 November 1596, it recorded a writ for Shakspere's arrest, along with three others, following a petition against them. The entry, originally in Latin, said:

> Be it known that William Wayte craves sureties of the peace against
> William Shakspere, Francis Langley, Dorothy Soer wife of John Soer,
> and Anne Lee, for fear of death, and so forth. Writ of attachment issued
> to the sheriff of Surrey, returnable on the eighteenth of St Martin
> [i.e. 29 November 1596].

Hotson probed further into the records and uncovered a squalid tale of rivalry among villains. The other men in the case were gangsters and racketeers, and the quarrel between them had been going on for some time. Shakspere's ally, Francis Langley, was an older man who had made his money by crooked means and had previously been charged with violence and extortion. The year before the incident he had built the Swan Theatre and other property on land he had acquired south of the Thames. The Lord Mayor of London did all he could to prevent the building of the theatre, foreseeing it as a meeting-place for 'thieves, horse-stealers, whore-mongers, cozeners, connycatching persons, practisers of treason, and such other like'. But the City authorities had no jurisdiction on the south, Surrey side of the Thames, where theatres and brothels flourished under the protection of gangsters.

Shakspere's adversary, William Wayte was the henchman of his step-father, William Gardiner, a corrupt and vicious magistrate of Surrey. Previous to the petition for sureties against Shakspere and Langley, Langley had similarly petitioned against Wayte and Gardiner for fear of his life. The two sides were in open warfare, with Gardiner doing his best to ruin Langley's business, and the other side retaliating with threats of violence.

William Gardiner, a Bermondsey leather-merchant, was the biggest racketeer in his manor. He had enriched himself by criminal dealings, swindling even his own family and oppressing the tenants in his slum properties. He and Langley were in the same kind of business and among the same kind of people as the Lord Mayor described. Naturally they were enemies. Hotson could find out nothing definite about the two women in the case, Dorothy Soer and Anne Lee, from whom Wayte feared violence. Being associates of Langley, perhaps helping in the management of his houses around the theatre, they too would have been involved in entertainment or prostitution. It is most likely that the real cause of the trouble between Gardiner's men and the supporters of Langley was the usual one between urban gangsters, that is, control of the local vice trade and organized crime.

Such people were Shakspere's associates in London. He was a principal in their quarrel, so presumably he was involved in their rackets. This aspect of Shakspere has not properly been assimilated, even by his modern biographers. It contributes nothing to the wished-for picture of a gentle, studious poet, but it is entirely in keeping with the Shakspere of biographical fact, the shady businessman of Stratford.

Shakspere did well in theatre business, but he had no great reputation among colleagues. If he had written and sold plays or been prominent on the stage, he would have been mentioned often in Henslowe's diary, Alleyne's records or the notes and letters that people wrote about the theatre. He was never mentioned and left no record or memory of any part he acted. The only legend, given by Rowe in 1709, is that he played the Ghost in Hamlet, and that was 'the top of his performance'. The received impression is that he took minor or comical parts, such as the rustic William in *As You Like It*.

Shakspere's main business in the theatre is indicated well enough by the allusions of his contemporaries. Robert Greene on his deathbed portrayed him as a ruthless exploiter of authors, and warned other writers against falling into his evil clutches, as he himself had done. Shakspere had cheated him out of his literary properties or, as someone later put it, 'purloined his plumes', and Greene was a ruined man. He denounced his exploiter as an 'upstart crow', meaning that he was a thief and plagiarist who passed off other writers' work as his own.

Greene was in a desperate state when he wrote his diatribe, but there must have been truth in it because Ben Jonson coolly and carefully said much the same thing about Shakspere's working methods in his Poet-Ape epigram. He began, said Jonson, by acquiring old plays and adapting them for new productions. Then he went on to steal from living writers, linking extracts from their works with strands of his own writing, and thus making up plays from which he alone profited. When writers complained, Shakspere said it did not much matter whose name appeared as author. In that he was to some extent right, since the theatre records prove that the writers who were paid for plays, and who presumably wrote them, were often not the same as those in whose names they were acted and published.

The nature of Shakspere's theatre work is further indicated by the case of *Titus Andronicus*. Sidney Lee accepted as reliable the story heard by

Ravenscroft in 1678, that Shakspere had not written the play but merely added a few touches to someone else's composition.

The picture so far is of an unscrupulous young man in the theatre business. He provides plays for the company he is working with, using mostly old or borrowed material, and these are put out under a version of his name, or sometimes just the initials W. S. Everyone in the theatre knows what he is up to, but they do not think it a very serious matter, and there is not much the aggrieved writers can do about it. Besides, it is convenient to have a stock name to attach to plays which for some reason the real author does not wish to acknowledge. One such, no doubt, was the 'private author' who, according to Ravenscroft story, brought *Titus Andronicus* to be acted. Shakspere presumably came to some arrangement with this person and edited his play for the stage. It was known as a Shakespeare play and mentioned as such by Meres in 1598, but the original edition of it in 1594 and the second in 1611 were published anonymously, and its first printing under Shakespeare's name was for the First Folio in 1623.

If one private author brought Shakspere a play and arranged for him to produce it under his theatre name, it is likely enough that others did the same. This also would have been known to the actors, but the conventional understanding among them was that Shakespeare's name on a play meant that the real author wanted no questions asked, and it was in their interest to oblige him. The public knew that there was an actor and writer named Shakespeare, but not many knew him personally, and no one at the time fully appreciated the exceptional quality of Shakespearian drama. The gap between the man and the works was not then visible and only later became obvious. All plays were licensed and approved by the censor, so presumably everything was in order, and there was no reason for public suspicion or curiosity about authorship.

If some great man or group of idealists had plays and poems which they wanted to put out incognito, a made-up pseudonym would defeat their purpose – it would proclaim a mystery and attract curious attention. The best thing would be to consult Mr Shakspere. He was known in the profession as a man who gathered plays from old or unknown sources, added to them material from other, sometimes still-living dramatists, and had them staged under his theatre name, Shakespeare. No one knew exactly where he found the writings he produced, and no one was very concerned about it. Shakspere was ideally placed to be agent for the person or group who wanted their writings to be introduced surreptitiously to the public.

Another advantage in using Shakspere was that he was a discreet man. With his dubious theatre occupations and his criminal associates, it was not in his interest to be talked about. He worked, as Pope rightly said, 'for gain, not glory'. It was profitable work; his employers were generous and he soon became a rich man. Shakspere was careful in business and conventional in his ambitions. To improve his status he acquired a coat of arms on behalf of his family, which entitled him to the style of gentleman. For that he was caricatured on stage by Ben Jonson, but back home in Stratford he cut an important figure, purchasing a fine mansion and laying the grounds for his early retirement.

Shakspere's London career was not essentially different from his known life in Stratford. He was an opportunist, no more honest than he could afford to be; but after the Langley affair he avoided scandal, invested his earnings and retired comfortably at the right time.

When Shakspere died the silence continued. No one either in Stratford or London lamented or even noticed the passing of a great poet. Those who might have written did not do so, and their silence is eloquent. It speaks of a literary world in which those who had known the late Mr Will Shakspere personally had nothing much to say about him. Nineteen years later, when Cuthbert Burbage mentioned Shakspere's name in connection with some theatre business, it was merely as a 'deserving man' among other old actors with whom his family had been associated.

Shakspere was the channel through which Somebody, together with several others unknown, infiltrated their writings into the theatre and publishing-house. These were not always finished plays, but speeches, lyrics and dramatic passages in the form, perhaps, of old-style masques. As a finder and broker of plays, Shakspere had access to the best writings of his contemporaries as well as to old works. Taking from here and there he made a modern drama out of the material he had been given, bridging gaps with lines of his own writing. The result was highly successful. Shakspere was a professional and knew how to please both the actors and the theatre audience. At this sort of work he was, perhaps, a genius.

He made his money, went back home and died; and if only the Works of Shakespeare had not become so remarkably famous, no one would ever have heard of him again.

ON REACHING CONCLUSIONS

In 1926 Georges Connes of the Department of Literature at Dijon published a book which covered some of the same ground as this one. In *Le mystère shakespearien* he gave his own version of the cases for Bacon, Oxford, Rutland and Derby as Shakespeare, putting each case positively and quoting the best of the respective advocates. He began with a slight anti-Stratfordian prejudice – just enough to arouse curiosity about the subject – but with no prepared conclusion. He probably assumed that he would identify the most likely Shakespeare in the course of his researches and writing, but the end of his book drew near and he was still thoroughly confused. If you study only the case for Bacon, or Oxford or one of the others, he complained, it looks entirely convincing – until you read the next case, which then in turn seems the strongest.

When he came to the last chapter, where he had promised to state his conclusion, Connes found that he had no firm conclusion to offer. His solution to this was to startle his readers, whom he had prepared for an anti-Stratfordian revelation, by announcing that, of all the cases he had reviewed, the case for the Stratford man seemed the least unsatisfactory of all. This, he said, was not even his opinion, merely his general impression, and he became irritable about readers who expected him, a young man, to solve a problem which had long defeated his elders and betters. His last words were a complaint about the subject as a whole. He regretted that part of his life which he had spent upon it. It was a complete waste of time, and he swore never to devote another minute to studies in Shakespeare authorship. The only virtue in the subject was that it could lead people into reading Shakespeare.

It was a shrewd ploy of Georges Connes to end up joining the Orthodox, however waveringly. Shakspere as Shakespeare supplied a neat solution to readers' demand for an opinion, and it allowed his book to be recommended by literary professors to their students. Connes later broke his resolution to foreswear Authorship studies, returning again to the subject and finally wavering towards the party of his compatriots, the French Derbyites.

It is tempting to adopt the Connes solution, but it cannot honestly be done. The doubts about Shakspere that started this enquiry still stand. It may be a criticism of this book that many of the authors quoted in it are old fashioned, and their opinions have been superseded by others. Even so, many of the points they raised have never been answered, nor have their opinions all finally been refuted. The same doubts have persisted for many years, and new ones have been added. The fact that it has been impossible to establish any alternative theory of Authorship does not vindicate the Orthodox position, merely preserves its respectability.

One of the greatest difficulties in this subject is that it is almost impossible to state any given fact or inference about Shakspere or the Authorship without finding that it has been disputed. As Lefranc put it: 'It is only too often the case, in anything to do with Shakespeare and his biography, that whenever one tries to get to the root of anything one is confronted by totally opposite and contradictory opinions.'

Connes noticed the same thing and wrote laughingly about it. Some critics affirm that *Venus and Adonis* was the work of a very young man, and the Rutlanders, whose candidate was sixteen-and-a-half when the poem appeared, naturally agree. Other critics of equal standing see the mind of a mature person behind it, and that suits the Oxfordians, because de Vere was then forty-three. The Derbyites find that in *Richard III* Shakespeare (William Stanley) is particularly kind to the Stanley family, and above all to Thomas Stanley of the Isle of Man. On the other hand, the critic Gervinus wrote that Shakespeare depicted Thomas as a servile hypocrite. Many authorities are convinced that Shakespeare's works were written by an aristocrat, whereas H.G. Wells met some English villagers who were putting on a Shakespeare play, and heard their impression that its author was an ordinary sort of man, just like themselves.

Even in plain, technical matters it is impossible to find unanimity. From one authority Connes learnt that the First Shakespeare Folio was 'one of the finest known examples of the printer's art', whereas Sidney Lee called it mediocre and complained about numerous errors in its printing and pagination. A third opinion, given by Baconian writers, is that the Folio is the most wonderful book ever, and the apparent mistakes in it were deliberately contrived by Sir Francis Bacon as part of his cipher.

The life of William Shakspere has been scrutinized so often from so many different angles and viewpoints that, unless further evidence turns up, there is nothing new to say about it. It is an exhausted subject. It provides no insights into the circumstances or meaning of Shakespeare's writings, and it has yielded nothing conclusive towards solving the Authorship problem. Its only value to this subject is that it substantiates it. It is the negative aspects of Shakspere's biography – the gaps, the doubts, the silences, the constant, surprising omissions – that demonstrate the existence of a problem. Yet negatives alone, however numerous and meaningful, cannot give rise to a positive thesis. Shakspere's life casts doubt upon his authorship, but the Stratfordians do not feel threatened by its inadequacies, and it does not suggest any better candidate.

Even if William Shakspere is banished from the mind, removing all prejudice that could obstruct perception of the true author, no other candidate comes clearly into perspective. One is left with no Shakespeare at all, which is intolerable. Better Orthodoxy than a complete void. This book must have a conclusion; otherwise it could be likened to a mystery story without its last chapter. Among the leading candidates who have been brought on stage, and those lurking in the wings, there must be someone who has the key to this puzzling business.

The common solution, adopted by many authors when they do not really know the answer to a mystery, is to create a Theory. This cannot be done here, because the firmest conclusion that has been reached and demonstrated in these pages is that Authorship theories of all kinds can all too easily be formed, and become obstructions. Once in the grip of a theory, it is impossible to see beyond it or gain further understanding of the subject. This is made plain by an overview of the battle of the theorists, which has gone on vigorously but quite inconclusively for over a century. Nothing worthwhile has been achieved or settled by the dogmatic, adversarial spirit of the debate so far.

When the cases for each candidate are compared together, it can be seen how subjective they all are. The very same data, the same Shakespearian characters and passages, are interpreted by different theorists as unique, compelling evidence for their respective candidates. Hamlet, for example, was firmly identified by Freud and Looney as a self-portrait of Oxford, complete down to the smallest autobiographical and psychological detail. Equally clearly, Demblon found many points of comparison between the Prince of Denmark and the Earl of Rutland. Stratfordian professors tell their students that Hamlet is very like Will Shakspere, yet Lefranc in a chapter of *Sous le masque* ridiculed the Shakspere-as-Hamlet theory, and demonstrated that William Stanley filled the role far better than anyone else. In *Shakspere and Sir Walter Ralegh* Henry Pemberton gave lengthy proof that, in the figure of Hamlet, the great Elizabethan poet, courtier and navigator accurately pictured his own character and experience. Every major candidate, it seems, can be represented as the original of Hamlet.

It is even worse in the case of Shakespeare's Sonnets. These seem obviously personal, expressing the mind and feelings of the poet himself. Eminent Shakespearians have often denied this, but most authorities, and all the Heretical theorists, accept that there are many self-references in the Sonnets. Quite remarkably, all parties in the argument, Stratfordians included, have no difficulty in seeing their own candidate as the Sonneteer. Many different names have been suggested, and insisted upon. Most remarkable of all, the Sonnets have faithfully provided every theorist with the required evidence, sometimes giving actual names. The Stratfordians rely upon the 'Will' sonnets, but these are also claimed by the Derbyites because their candidate was a William. In Sonnet 20, 'Hews' denotes

William Hughes to whom, by Oscar Wilde's reckoning, the Sonnets were dedicated. Sonnet 111 yields the name of two different candidates, Manners (Earl of Rutland) and Dyer. Sonnet 76 identifies three candidates – two in the same phrase. 'Ever the same' has an anagram of Vere (Oxford), and it is a translation of *Semper eadem*, the motto of Queen Elizabeth, while the word 'strange' in the preceding line could be an allusion to Lord Strange, later Earl of Derby.

In support of their various theories, writers have done wonders with the Sonnets. Alfred Dodd, who was certain that Francis Bacon wrote them, rearranged their order to illustrate the tragedy of that 'Immortal Master'. Canon Rendall made another arrangement to illustrate the life of Oxford. A.D. Wraight has recently regrouped the Sonnets to show how accurately they reflect the life and character of Marlowe.

In response to lines in the Sonnets which imply that the poet was lame, many of the theorists have discovered that their candidate limped or had trouble with his legs. Oxford is said to have been wounded in his fight with Knyvet; Derby perhaps was lamed in one of his duels; Rutland on his expedition to the Azores; Marlowe in battle against the Armada. The last two Sonnets seem to refer to Bath, and Ralegh went to Bath in 1602 when he was ill – lameness perhaps; but Rutland was also in Bath, to cure his swollen legs. It has probably been claimed that Shakspere too walked with a limp.

One thing that is clearly proved by the Shakespeare controversy is that, as Charles Fort put it, 'For every expert there is an equal and opposite expert.' In every case where some problem to do with Shakespeare has been submitted to specialists, the only result has been total disagreement among them. From the analysis and dating of Shakespeare's texts to the question of Shakspere's handwriting there has been no lasting consensus about anything. The latest confusion, among the computer-equipped Shakespearean stylometrists, continues the record of uncertainty.

Shakspere's supposed signatures have been studied and written about by every kind of supposed expert, but their contradictions leave no one the wiser. The decline of graphology, the science of inferring character from handwriting, was partly due to the failure of its Shakespearian practitioners. Frau Kintzel, a famous graphologist in her time, applied her science to Shakspere's will, which she assumed he had written himself. With much technical detail, about the spacing, sloping and other characteristics of its letters, she demonstrated that the writer of the will was a 'literary Titan', a noble genius of the same rank as Beethoven and Goethe. When informed that the writing was actually that of Collins, Shakespeare's lawyer, she stuck to her guns. Whether a famous writer or a humble country clerk, she insisted, the man who wrote that will was a universal genius.

Frau Kintzel was laughed at, but that was not the end of her. No Shakespearian theorist has ever permanently been crushed. If Eric Sams is right, and Shakspere did after all write his own will, Frau Kintzel's testimony is highly relevant.

It is easy, as above, to make the subject of Authorship seem altogether ridiculous. That is not unjustified, because large parts of it make no sense and lead nowhere. Anyone who decides to go further into it should be warned of its dangers, the frustrations and obsessions they will encounter and the derision they will attract from respectable people who disapprove of it. Many of the Shakespeare scholars would like to see the whole subject suppressed. That is not entirely out of self-interest, for most of them genuinely believe that there is no Authorship problem. It pains them that there are still people interested in the topic, and they are kindly concerned to free them from delusion.

Despite their superior airs, the Stratfordians are no less victims of their own beliefs than the Baconians or other dogmatists. They too are 'theorists'. There seems to be a peculiar Stratfordian cast of mind, a straightforward, sensible, rather literal mind, in contrast to the subtle Baconian mind, the refined Oxfordian mind, the romantic, Gallic mind of the Derbyites, the Rutlanders' methodical type of mind and the conspiratorial mind of Marlovians. There will always be people of such varied mentalities, and they can happily co-exist, even in this maddening subject, once they recognize how largely subjective are the theories behind their different viewpoints. The Authorship question is so instructive and fascinating that it is a shame to limit it by prejudices, rather than enjoying the full range of its mysteries. If it were not for the taboos and inhibitions that prevent young scholars from approaching it, this would be a popular and rewarding subject.

A LIKELY STORY

Monsieur Connes was right. It is not enough just to give a general account of the Authorship controversy, and leave it at that. After coming so far through this forest of intricate and contradictory evidence, readers might like to hear the whole thing discussed, as a basis for their own discussions and decisions. Nothing so firm as a theory can be offered. There are plenty of these to be found in other books, and everyone is free to form their own. If any satisfactory theory had been met during this enquiry – a theory based on good evidence, without too many loose ends and not too seriously disputable – it would now be made welcome. Sad to say, nothing of the kind has appeared. All that has been gained are one or two unsteady opinions, a few impressions and a picture of William Shakspere at work.

An overall impression is that the Shakespeare mystery is so elaborate and beguiling, so full of promising clues that lead nowhere, so consistently frustrating and confusing, that it looks like an artefact. Someone set it up, intending that it should not easily be solved. That was partly out of practical necessity, so as not to provoke opposition, but there was another, more lasting reason for secrecy. If it were known by whom and for what purpose the plays were written, that would diminish their effect. They were presented as simple theatrical entertainments. That was the secret of their influence. No one was meant to suspect that the purpose of Shakespeare was to change the world, nor that behind the name was a very determined group of reformers, radical and resourceful.

The Elizabethan age was felt by those living in it to be a time of great changes. The medieval world-order had collapsed, and wider prospects were being opened up. A feeling of revelation was in the air; minds were claiming freedom; explorers were bringing in new worlds, scientists discovering new methods, and the ancient traditions of alchemy and mysticism were rising again into influence. A new world-order, based on an ideally constituted, scientific and philosophical world-view, had become imaginable and could therefore be realized.

The Shakespearian image of an enchanted realm is related to the underlying symbolism of Elizabeth's reign. In the mythology of state, a Virgin Queen, goddess-spirit of the land of England, ruled unblemished over a pure, perfectly ordered kingdom. That, of course, was not the actual state of things, but it expressed the archetypal ideal that entered consciousness during the English Renaissance. Poets and scholars generally were affected by it, and the Shakespeare plays were among its products.

There was one man at the time with the learning, imagination, cunning and position in affairs to create the state myth and organize cultural support for it. Francis Bacon was theatrically inclined and dwelt among mysteries. His loyalty was not only to his period and nation but had a far higher object. His divine mission, as he regarded it, was to create and establish an all-inclusive code of knowledge and wisdom as the guiding standard for an enlightened order of society. This was Bacon's Great Instauration, the work to which his entire life was devoted. Part of that work was the science and philosophy published under his own name, but the greater part of it was on the transformational level. Few people are transformed by reason, but everyone is susceptible to feelings and emotions, and the best way of implanting ideas in the minds of others is to keep them unaware of being consciously influenced. It is not through lectures from great thinkers that things are changed, but through music, drama and popular entertainment.

One of the mysteries of Shakespeare is that, while some parts of the plays are considered poor or mediocre, every generation finds them uniquely powerful. They engage the imagination and minds are affected by them. They are indeed transformational. Displayed in them are the various human types, passions and psychologies, their reactions, irritations and harmonies, and the changes between order and chaos that are paralleled by the processes of alchemy. It is often exclaimed about Shakespeare that he exhibits the whole of human life. No author who creates such an effect can do so quite unconsciously. If there was one mind and purpose behind Shakespeare, surely it was the subtle, devious mind and the practical, idealistic purpose of Francis Bacon.

Bacon was not the only great idealist of his time. Everyone who was affected by the spirit of the age had their own conception of it. Many voices are heard in Shakespeare, giving lyrical, arcadian, romantic, scientific, patriotic and other expressions of an ideal order, established under the spell of religion, royalty, learning, magic, mythology or perfect love. There are minds in Shakespeare which are not the mind of Bacon. There is the mind of a countryman, an adventurer, a passionate poet, and some have discerned the mind of a woman. Constantly heard is an old-world tone, a harking back to days of feudalism and chivalry, when life was simple and principled and the whole of England was the hunting-ground of the nobility. That is not the tone of a crafty, modern-minded London lawyer. It could be Oxford's voice, or it could be Derby's or Rutland's or it could belong to any of the nobly-born candidates for Shakespeare.

The mystery was so well crafted that it is impossible to deconstruct it. There are no firm grounds for deciding who wrote what, or who took whom as the model for any Shakespearian character. The poems are most obviously by individuals and offer the clearest field for speculation. On the balance of evidence it seems reasonable to guess that Bacon wrote *Venus and Adonis*, as was apparently suspected at the time, and that Oxford was the poet of the Sonnets. The anagram in Thorpe's dedication adds conviction to the strong case that Oxfordians have previously made out.

Further impressions are that Oxford is the most convincing of the major candidates as the model for Hamlet; that Rutland lent certain details to that play; that Derby contributed to *Love's Labour's Lost* and, if the identification of Prospero's island as the Calf of Man is correct, to *The Tempest*; that Ralegh was one of the leading idealists behind the enterprise; that Marlowe, before he was mysteriously removed from the scene, wrote much of Shakespeare and was deeply involved in the whole affair.

These writers mostly knew each other and were all influenced by the free-thinking idealism of their period. For reasons already given, it is unlikely that they formed any distinctive Shakespeare group. Many of them at times were political enemies. Revolutionary movements are typically organized in cells, none of which is aware of the others' activities, or even existence. A similar arrangement is necessary for reformers whose ideals are different from those established by Church and State. The contributors to Shakespeare were drawn from various groups and coteries, each with its usual meeting place. Likely sites include Wilton House on the banks of the Wiltshire Avon, where Mary, Countess of Pembroke and 'Swan of Avon', was the presiding genius; Scadbury Manor in Kent, where Thomas Walsingham entertained men of letters; the houses where Ralegh assembled his School of Night; the great country mansions where poets mingled with plotters.

At the centre of all plots and mysteries was Francis Bacon. He was connected by family to several of the leading characters in the Shakespeare business. Through his uncle-by-marriage, Lord Burghley, he was related to Oxford, who married Burghley's daughter. The Earl of Derby married the daughter of Oxford and Bacon acted as lawyer in Derby's affairs. During Rutland's minority Bacon was his effective guardian. He knew everyone's secrets and created secrets of his own. If the confusion of clues in the Authorship puzzle was the work of some ingenious puzzle-maker, Bacon was the expert in that field. At his house in Twickenham he gave private and confidential employment to many writers, and he is known to have commissioned work from others. Literary authorities are certain that much of Shakespeare could not possibly have been written by a person of Bacon's mentality. Yet only he could have dreamed up and set in motion a scheme for universal enlightenment, partly through the Shakespearian drama. Only he could have carried it through in such secrecy.

There was another link between those who created Shakespeare. Everything that was acted or published under that name proceeded through one man, William Shakspere. He too was a man of secrecy, and his line of business has already been imagined. He served his purpose, went back home and quietly died. Bacon and his collaborators instructed agents to arrange for the Stratford memorial, and the First Folio perpetuated the convention that the sole author of Shakespeare's plays was that jovial old theatre character, William Shakspere.

In this final glimpse of the worthy Mr Shakspere he is in the heyday of his London career, sitting in his office by the theatre. He is working on a play, brought to him by a gentleman on behalf of someone else. He thinks he knows who is behind it, but he is not paid to be inquisitive. His commission is to prepare the play for the stage and arrange for it to be acted. The company will put it on under the usual name, Shakespeare.

He sets to work just as Ben Jonson described. The play he has been given has a framework, with certain scenes and speeches that have to be retained, but otherwise he has a fairly free hand. It is magnificent writing, but the author is obviously not a professional dramatist, and the work in its present form is not suited for the modern theatre. Shakspere knows what to do with it. He takes a scene with some witty dialogue from an old, forgotten script. He remembers a play in which he bought a share from Greene (and paid him what seemed a reasonable sum at the time, despite the man's complaints). From these and other pieces he adds comedy and dramatic effects to the material he has been given, and makes skilful adjustments overall to provide continuity. To hide the joins he puts in some boisterous lines of his own, which he knows the actors will enjoy speaking. From 'shreds', as Jonson called them, he has made a 'whole piece'. Then, of course, he has to copy it all out so that it is one hand. It is neatly done, and the players tease him about how he never blots a line. That is the hallmark of a 'Shakespeare' play.

And that is just one story. There are many others, some very attractive, by first-rate scholars and mythmakers, and there is nothing to prove that any one of them is entirely wrong, or absolutely right. The only honest answer that can be given to someone who wants to know who wrote Shakespeare is that it is a perfect mystery, dangerously addictive, but very worthwhile looking into.

BIBLIOGRAPHY

SHAKESPEARIAN BIOGRAPHERS AND POLEMICAL STRATFORDIANS

Aubrey, John *Brief Lives*, ed. Oliver Lawson Dick, London, 1949

Burgess, Anthony *Shakespeare*, London and New York, 1970

Chambers, E.K. *William Shakespeare: A Study of Facts and Problems*, Oxford, 1930

Churchill, R.C. *Shakespeare and his Betters*, London, 1958

Collins, J. Churton *Studies in Shakespeare*, London, 1904

Eccles, Mark *Shakespeare in Warwickshire*, Madison, Wisconsin, 1961

French, George R. *Shakespeareana Genealogica*, London, 1869

Gibson, H.N. *The Shakespeare Claimants*, New York, 1962

Halliwell-Phillipps, James O. *Outlines of the Life of Shakespeare*, 2 vols, London, 1881

Lang, Andrew *Shakespeare, Bacon and the Great Unknown*, London, 1912

Lee, Sir Sidney *A Life of William Shakespeare*, London, 1898; 2nd edn 1916

Neilson, W.A. and A.H. Thorndike *The Facts about Shakespeare*, London, 1923

Robertson, J.M. *The Baconian Heresy: A Confutation*, London and New York, 1913

—*An Introduction to the Study of the Shakespeare Canon*, London and New York, 1924

Rowse, A.L. *William Shakespeare: A Biography*, London and New York, 1963

—*Shakespeare the Man*, London, 1973

Sams, Eric *The Real Shakespeare*, New Haven and London, 1995

Schoenbaum, Samuel *Shakespeare's Lives*, Oxford and New York, 1970

—*William Shakespeare: A Documentary Life*, Oxford, 1975

—*William Shakespeare: Records and Images*, London, 1981

Spurgeon, Caroline F.E. *Shakespeare's Imagery*, Cambridge, 1971

Stopes, Charlotte C. *The Bacon-Shakespeare Question Answered*, 2nd edn, London, 1889

—*The True Story of the Stratford Bust*, London, 1904

—*Shakespeare's Environment*, London, 1914

Wilson, Ian *Shakespeare: The Evidence*, London, 1993

Yates, Frances *A Study of Love's Labour's Lost*, London, 1936

—*Majesty and Magic in Shakespeare's Last Plays*, Boulder, Co., 1978

SHAKESPEARE'S SPECIALITIES

Bucknill, Sir John C. *The Psychology of Shakespeare*, London, 1858

—*The Medical Knowledge of Shakespeare*, London, 1860

Campbell, Lord *Shakespeare's Legal Acquirements Considered*, London, 1859

Coghill, Neville *Shakespeare's Professional Skills*, Cambridge, 1964

Cooper, Alfred Duff *Sergeant Shakespeare*, London, 1949

Dyer, T.F.T. *Folk-lore of Shakespeare*, London, 1884

Ellacombe, Rev. Henry N. *Shakespeare as an Angler*, London, 1883

—*Plant-Lore and Garden-Craft of Shakespeare*, London, 1884

Falconer, A.F. *Shakespeare and the Sea*, London, 1964

Madden, D.H. *Diary of Master William Silence*, London, 1897

Rushton, W.L. *Shakespeare as a Lawyer*, London, 1858

—*Shakespeare an Archer*, London, 1897

Simpson, R.R. *Shakespeare and Medicine*, Melbourne, 1959

Thoms, William J. *Three Notelets* (incl. 'Folk lore of Shakespeare', 'Was Shakespeare ever a Soldier?'), London, 1865

Whall, W.B. *Shakespeare's Sea Terms Explained*, London, 1910

Wordsworth, Bishop C. *Shakespeare's Knowledge and Use of the Bible*, London, 1864

DOUBTERS, GROUPISTS AND AUTHORSHIP INVESTIGATORS

Amphlett, H. *Who was Shakespeare? A New Enquiry*, London, 1955

Bacon, Delia *The Philosophy of Shakspere's Plays Unfolded*, London, 1857

Castle, Edward J. *Shakespeare, Jonson, Bacon and Greene: A Study*, London, 1897

Connes, Georges *Le mystère shakespearien*, Paris, 1926

Cox, Jane 'Shakespeare's Will and Signatures', in *Shakespeare in the Public Records*. ed. David Thomas, London, 1985

Evans, A.J. *Shakespeare's Magic Circle*, London, 1956

Forrest, H.T.S. *The Five Authors of Shakespeare's Sonnets*, London, 1923

Friedman, William and Elizabeth *The Shakespearean Ciphers Examined*, Cambridge, 1957

Greenwood, Sir Granville George *The Shakespeare Problem Restated*, London, 1908

—*Is there a Shakespeare Problem?* London, 1916

—*Shakespeare's Law*, London, 1920

Hookham, George *Will o' the Wisp or the Elusive Shakespeare*, Oxford, 1922

McMichael, George, and Edgar M. Glenn *Shakespeare and his Rivals*, New York, 1962

Morgan, Appleton *The Shakespeare Myth*, Cincinnati, 1881

Phillips, Graham, and Martin Keatman *The Shakespeare Conspiracy*, London, 1994

Slater, Gilbert *Seven Shakespeares*, London, 1931

Standen, Gilbert *Shakespeare Authorship: A Summary of Evidence*, London, 1930

BACONIANS

Bayley, Harold *The Tragedy of Sir Francis Bacon*, London, 1902

—*The Shakespeare Symphony*, London, 1906

Beaumont, W. Comyns *The Private Life of the Virgin Queen*, London, 1947

Begley, Rev. Walter (A Cambridge Graduate) *Is it Shakespeare?* London, 1903

Dodd, Alfred *The Marriage of Elizabeth Tudor*, London, 1940

—*The Secret History of Francis Bacon*, London, 1941

—*The Secret Shake-speare*, London, 1941

—*The Immortal Master*, London, [1943]

—*The Martyrdom of Francis Bacon*, London, [1946]

Donnelly, Ignatius *The Great Cryptogram*, 2 vols, London, 1888

Driver, Olive W. *The Bacon-Shakespeare Mystery*, Massachusetts, 1960

Durning-Lawrence, Sir Edwin *Bacon is Shake-speare*, London, 1910

Eagle, Roderick *Shakespeare: New Views for Old*, London and New York, 2nd edn, [1943]

Gallup, Elizabeth W. *The Biliteral Cypher of Francis Bacon*, 2 vols, Detroit, 1899

Holmes, Nathaniel *The Authorship of Shakespeare*, 2 vols, New York, 1866

Johnson, Edward D. *Shakespearean Acrostics*, London, 1947

—*The Shakespeare Illusion*, London, 1965

Leary, Penn *The Second Cryptographic Shakespeare*, Omaha, Nebr., 1990

Melsome, W.S. *The Bacon-Shakespeare Anatomy*, London, 1945

Mudie, Alfred *The Self-Named William Shakespeare*, London, 1925

Owen, Dr Orville *Francis Bacon's Cipher Story*, 5 vols, Detroit and New York, 1893–95

Penzance, Lord *A Judicial Summing-up on the Bacon-Shakespeare Controversy*, London, 1902

Pott, Constance W. (Mrs Henry) *Bacon's Promus of Forms and Elegancies*, New York, 1883

—*Francis Bacon and his Secret Society*, New York, 1891

Reed, Edwin *Francis Bacon, our Shake-speare*, London, 1902

Theobald, Bertram G. *Shake-speare's Sonnets Unmasked*, London, 1929

—*Exit Shakspere*, London, 1931

—*Enter Francis Bacon*, London, 1932

Theobald, R.M. *Shakespeare Studies in Baconian Light*, London, 1904

Twain, Mark *Is Shakespeare Dead?* New York and London, 1909

Wigston, W.F.C. *The Columbus of Literature*, London, 1892

—*Bacon and the Rosicrucians*, London, 1899

Woodward, Frank *Francis Bacon's Cipher Signatures*, London, 1925

Woodward, Parker *The Strange Case of Francis Tidir*, London, 1901

OXFORDIANS

Allen, Percy *The Case for Edward de Vere as 'William Shakespeare'*, London, 1930

—*The Oxford–Shakespeare Case Examined*, London, 1931

Barrell, Charles W. *Elizabethan Mystery Man*, New York, 1940

Clark, Mrs Eva Turner *The Man who was Shakespeare*, New York, 1937

Douglas, Col. Montagu W. *Lord Oxford and the Shakespeare Group*, Oxford, 1952

Freud, Sigmund *An Outline of Psychoanalysis*, London, 1940

Frisbee, George *Edward de Vere: A Great Elizabethan*, London, 1932

Holland, Capt. H.H. *Shakespeare through Oxford Glasses*, London, 1923

Looney, J. Thomas *'Shakespeare' Identified*, London, 1920

Ogburn, Charlton, Jr. *The Mysterious William Shakespeare*, New York, 1984

Ogburn, Dorothy and Charlton *This Star of England*, New York, 1952

Ogburn, Dorothy, and Charlton Ogburn, Jr. *Shake-speare: The Man behind the Name*, New York, 1962

Rendall, Canon G.H. *Shakespeare's Sonnets and Edward de Vere*, London, 1930

Ward, Capt. B.M. *The Seventeenth Earl of Oxford*, London, 1923

Ward, Col. B.R. *The Mystery of 'Mr. W. H.'* London, 1923

DERBYITES

Boulanger, Jacques *L'affaire Shakespeare*, Paris, 1919

Evans, A. J. See under *Doubters, etc.*

Lefranc, Abel *Sous le masque de 'William Shakespeare'*, 2 vols, Paris, 1919

—*A la découverte de Shakespeare*, 2 vols, Paris, 1945, 1950

—*Under the Mask of William Shakespeare*, transl. and intro. by Cecil Cragg. Braunton, Devon, 1988

Lucas, Richard M. *Shakespeare's Vital Secret*, London, 1938

Morhardt, Mathias *A la rencontre de William Shakespeare*, Paris, 1938

Titherley, A.W. *Shakespeare's Identity*, Winchester, 1952

RUTLANDERS

Alvor, Peter *Das neue Shakespeare-Evangelium*, Munich, 1906

—*Die Lösung der Shakespeare-Frage*, Leipzig, 1909

Bleibtreu, Carl *Der wahre Shakespeare*, Munich, 1907

—*Shakespeares Geheimnis*, Berne, 1923

Demblon, Célestin *Lord Rutland est Shakespeare*, Paris, 1912

—*L'auteur d' 'Hamlet' et son monde*, Paris, 1914

Dessart, A. *Lord Rutland est-il Shakespeare?* Liege, 1913

Porohovshikov, Pierre S. *Shakespeare Unmasked*, New York, 1940; London, 1955

Sykes, Claud W. *Alias William Shakespeare?* London, 1947

MARLOVIANS

Hoffman, Calvin *The Murder of the Man who was Shakespeare*, London, 1955

Honey, William *The Shakespeare Epitaph Deciphered*, London, 1969

Rhys Williams, David *Shakespeare thy Name is Marlowe*, London, 1966

Wraight, Mrs A.D. *The Story that the Sonnets Tell*, London, 1994

—(with Virginia F. Stern) *In Search of Christopher Marlowe*, London, 1965

Zeigler, Wilbur G. *It was Marlowe: A Story of the Secret of Three Centuries*, Chicago, 1895

SOME OTHER THEORISTS

Brooks, Alden *Will Shakspere: Factotum and Agent* (Dyer and others), New York, 1937

—*Will Shakspere and the Dyer's Hand*, New York, 1943

Brownlee, A. *William Shakespeare and Robert Burton*, Newbury, Berks., 1960

Caldwell, G.S. *Is Sir Walter Ralegh the Author of Shakespeare's Plays?* Melbourne, 1877

Nicol, J. C. *The Real Shakespeare* (Southampton), London, 1905

Pemberton, Henry, Jr. *Shakspere and Sir Walter Ralegh*, Philadelphia and London, 1914

Sweet, George E. *Shake-speare the Mystery* (Queen Elizabeth), Stanford, Ca., 1956

Winchcombe, George and Bernard *Shakespeare's Ghost Writers*, Esher, Surrey, 1968

SOURCES OF ILLUSTRATIONS

9: *William Shakespeare, His Method of Work.* Lithograph by Max Beerbohm. Courtesy of Mrs E. Reichmann. The author's collection. **12**: Psalm XLVI from the Bible, 1611. **15**: The name 'Shaxberd' on *The Revels Accounts.* Manuscript, 1604-5. Public Record Office, London. **17**: The Flower Portrait of Shakespeare. Oil painting by an unknown artist. From the RSC Collection with the permission of the Governors of the Royal Shakespeare Theatre. Photo History of Art Photographic Collection, University of Warwick. **21 left**: Lord Penzance. Photograph from *A Judicial Summing-Up. The Bacon-Shakespeare Controversy* by Sir James Plaisted Wilde, Baron Penzance, 1902. **21 right**: Nathaniel Holmes. Photo Electrotype from *The Great Cryptogram* by Ignatius Donnelly, vol. II, 1888. **22**: George Greenwood. Photograph by Walter Stoneman, 1917. By courtesy of the National Portrait Gallery, London. **25**: Master and pupils in school. Woodcut, 16th century. **28**: Detail of a ship from the title-page of *General and Rare Memorials pertayning to the Perfect Art of Navigation* by John Dee, 1577. Bodleian Library, Oxford. **35**: Queen Elizabeth and her courtiers hawking. Woodcut from *The Booke of Falconerie* by George Turbervile, 1575. **43**: *The Dreams of the Youthful Shakespeare.* Engraving by Augustus Fox after Richard Westall, 1827. **46**: Mark of John Shakspere on a Deed of Conveyance, January 1596-97, from *Outlines of the Life of Shakespeare* by James O. Halliwell-Phillips, 1886. **48**: Shakespeare with his Family at Stratford. Lithograph published by F. Sala & Co, Berlin. 19th century. **52**: Shakespeare's dedication to the Earl of Southampton from *Venus and Adonis*, 1593. **53**: Title-page of *The London Prodigall* supposedly by Shakespeare, 1605. **56**: William Shakespeare. Statue by Peter Scheemakers, erected 1740. Westminster Abbey, London. Photo Warburg Institute. **57**: Verse on Shakespeare's tomb in Stratford-upon-Avon church from *The Home of Shakespeare* by Frederick W. Fairholt, 1847. **58**: A performance of *Titus Andronicus.* Drawing possibly by Henry Peacham, c.1594. Reproduced by permission of the Marquess

of Bath, Longleat House, Warminster, Wiltshire. Photo Courtauld Institute of Art. **60**: Coat-of arms of the Lucy family. **63**: 'View of the Brook House, in which Shakespare was really born, April 23, 1564'. Engraving after John Jordan, 1799 from *The Gentleman's Magazine*, April 1808. **64 top**: 'The House in Stratford upon Avon in which Shakspeare was born'. Engraving after R. Greene, 1769. **64 below**: 'Exterior of Shakespere's House in…1824'. Engraving. **64 left**: Cup carved from the mulberry tree said to have been planted by Shakespeare. It was presented to David Garrick in 1769. Engraving, c.1825. **65**: James Orchard Halliwell-Phillipps. Photograph, mid-19th century. Shakespeare Birthplace Trust. **66**: Anne Hathaway's cottage. Aquatint after Samuel Ireland, 18th century. **67**: Robert Greene writing in his shroud. Woodcut, 1598. **68**: Title-page of *Greenes, Groats-worth of Witte* by Robert Greene, 1592. **70**: Ben Jonson. Oil painting after Abraham van Blyenberch, early 17th century. By courtesy of the National Portrait Gallery, London. **73**: Draft grant of arms to John Shakspere. Manuscript, 1596. College of Arms, London. **75**: 'To the Memory of my beloued, the Avthor, Mr. William Shakespeare' by Ben Jonson from the First Folio edition of *Mr. William Shakespeares Comedies, Histories, and Tragedies*, 1623. **77**: Mary Pembroke. Engraving by Simon van de Passe, 1618. By courtesy of the National Portrait Gallery, London. **79**: Verse 'To the Reader' by Ben Jonson from the First Folio edition of *Mr. William Shakespeares Comedies, Histories, and Tragedies*, 1623. **82**: The Globe Theatre. Drawing after Jan Claesz Visscher's view of London of c.1616. Copyright British Museum. **84**: Martin Droeshout's portrait of Shakespeare on the title-page of the First Folio edition of *Mr. William Shakespeares Comedies, Histories, and Tragedies*, 1623. **85**: William Shakespeare. Engraving by Martin Droeshout from the Fourth Folio edition of *Mr. William Shakespeares Comedies, Histories, and Tragedies*, 1685. **87**: William Shakespeare. Engraving by William Marshall from *Poems: written by Wil. Shake-speare, Gent.*, 1640. **89 left**: Shakespeare's monument from *Antiquities of Warwickshire* by William Dugdale, 1656. **89 righ**t: Detail of Shakespeare's monument in Stratford-upon-Avon church by Gerard Johnson, originally 17th century. From *Bacon is Shake-speare* by Edwin Durning-Lawrence, 1910. **90**: Shakespeare's monument. Drawing by George Vertue, 1737. By permission of The British Library. **91**: Shakespeare's monument from *The Life of Shakespeare* by Nicholas Rowe, 1709. **94**: Poem under Shakespeare's monument in Stratford-upon-Avon church. From *Outlines of the Life of Shakespeare* by James O. Halliwell-Phillips, 1886. **95 top left**: The Chandos Portrait of Shakespeare. Oil painting by an unknown artist. By courtesy of the National Portrait Gallery, London. **95 below left**: William Shakespeare. Oil painting attributed to Cornelius Janssen (born 1593). The Folger Shakespeare Library, Washington, DC. **95 top right**: The Grafton Portrait of Shakespeare. Oil painting dated 1588. The John Rylands Library, Manchester. **95 below right**: The Felton Portrait of Shakespeare. Oil painting inscribed 1597. The Folger Shakespeare Library, Washington, DC. **97**: Mark of Judith Shakespeare as a witness on a document, 1611. From *Outlines of the Life of Shakespeare* by James O. Halliwell-Phillips, 1886. **99**: Shakespeare's signatures on four documents: a deposition given to the Court of Requests, 1612, Public Record Office, London; vendor's copy of a deed of purchase for a property in Blackfriars, 1613, reproduced by permission of the Guildhall Library, London; mortgage deed for the Blackfriars property, 11 March 1613, by permission of the British Library; second and third pages of his will, 1616, Public Record Office, London. **101**: Last page of Shakespeare's will. Manuscript, 1616. Public Record Office, London. **103**: James Wilmot (1726–1808). Engraving. **104**: Shakespeare's signature (original in reverse) on *Archaionomia* by William Lambarde, 1568. The Folger Shakespeare Library, Washington, DC. **110**: Edward Alleyn (detail). Oil painting by an unknown artist. By kind permission of the Governors of Dulwich College. **111**: Michael Drayton (putative). Oil painting by an unknown artist, inscribed 1599. By courtesy of the National Portrait Gallery, London. **114**: Francis Bacon. Oil painting after Paul van Somer, after 1731. By courtesy of the National Portrait Gallery, London. **119**: Sonnet 20 from *Shake-speares Sonnets*, 1609. **120**: Delia Bacon. Photograph by Theodora

Bacon, 1888. From *Delia Bacon: A Bibliographical Sketch* by Theodora Bacon, 1888. **122**: Title-page and list of characters from *The Great Assises*, 1645. **124**: *Venus and Adonis*. Two details from a mural by an unknown artist in the White Hart Inn, St Albans, *c.*1600. Photo St Albans Museum, and **below** photo Francis Carr. **125**: The crest of Sir Francis Bacon from a presentation copy of *Novum Organum*, 1620. From *Bacon is Shake-speare* by Edwin Durning-Lawrence, 1910.

130: Henry Wriothesley, 3rd Earl of Southampton. Oil painting after John de Critz the Elder, *c.*1601–3. From the Duke of Buccleuch's Collection at Boughton House, Northamptonshire. **132**: Line drawing and transcript of the first page of the Northumberland Manuscript from *Collotype Facsimile & Typescript of an Elizabethan Manuscript preserved at Alnwick Castle, Northumberland* by Frank J. Burgoyne, 1904. **137**: Verses from *The Rape of Lucrece* by William Shakespeare, 1594. **139**: Annotated page of *Loves Labors Lost* from Durning-Lawrence's copy of the First Folio edition of *Mr William Shakespears Comedies, Histories, and Tragedies*, 1623. From *Bacon is Shake-speare* by Edwin Durning-Lawrence, 1910. **145**: Elizabeth Wells Gallup. Photograph, *c.*1915. **146**: Statue of Sir Francis Bacon in St Michael's Church, St Albans. Photo St Albans Museum. **146 below**: Dr Owen's wheel created to decipher texts. Photograph from *Sir Francis Bacon's Cipher Story* by Orville W. Owen, 1894. **147**: Digging in the bed of the River Wye for Sir Francis Bacon's lost manuscripts. Illustration by Cyrus Cuneo from *Illustrated London News*, 11 March 1911. **148**: Ignatius Donnelly. Photograph. **149**: Page of *Henry IV* with decoding annotations by Ignatius Donnelly. Illustration from *The Great Cryptogram* by Ignatius Donnelly, vol. II, 1888. **151**: Robert Dudley, Earl of Leicester. Drawing by Federigo Zuccaro, 1575. Copyright British Museum. **154**: Constance M. Pott. Photo Electrotype from *The Great Cryptogram* by Ignatius Donnelly, vol. II, 1888. **158**: Title-page of *Cryptomenytices* by Gustavus Selenus, 1624. **160**: Title-page of *Avgmentis Scientiarum* by Sir Francis Bacon, vol. IX, 1645. **163**: Sigmund Freud. Photograph, 1912. **163 below**: Edward de Vere, 17th Earl of Oxford. Oil painting by Marcus Gheeraedts the Younger. © Christie's. **166**: Falconer. Woodcut from *The Booke of Falconerie* by George Turbervile, 1575. **172**: Bolebec's coat-of-arms. **173**: The Earl of Oxford bearing the Sword of

State before Elizabeth I, 1572. Etching after Marcus Gheeraedts the Younger by Wenceslaus Hollar, 1688. **176**: Anne Vavasor. Oil painting possibly by Marcus Gheeraedts the Younger. Private Collection. **178**: Title-page from *Shake-speares Sonnets*, 1609.
179: Dedication from *Shake-speares Sonnets*, 1609. **182**: John Benson's preliminary address for *Poems: written by Wil. Shakespeare, Gent.*, 1640. **184**: Title-page emblem from *Minerva Britanna* by Henry Peacham, 1612. **186**: Annotated pages from the Bible which belonged to the Earl of Oxford. The Folger Shakespeare Library, Washington, DC. **187**: Ashbourne portrait of Shakespeare (detail). Oil painting by an unknown artist, 1612. The Folger Shakespeare Library, Washington, DC.
188: Preface from *Troylus and Cresseid* by William Shakespeare, 1609. **192**: Title-page from *Loues Labors Lost* by William Shakespeare, 1598. **193**: Lines from *Colin Clouts come home againe* by Edmund Spenser, 1595. **194**: Coat-of-arms of the Derbys. **194 below**: The Gatehouse and Eagle Tower, Lathom House, *c.*1640. Drawing by Gerard Swarbrick, 1992. **195**: Ferdinando, 5th Earl of Derby. Oil painting by Marcus Gheeraedts the Younger. Private collection. Copyright reserved.
198: Marguerite de Valois. Oil painting by François Clouet. Musée Condé, Chantilly. **199**: Troupe of Commedia dell'Arte actors at the Court of Navarre. Oil painting by François Bunel the Younger, *c.*1578–90. Musée de Béziers. **204**: William, 6th Earl of Derby. Oil painting by Marcus Gheeraedts the Younger. Private collection. Copyright reserved. **205**: John Dee. Oil painting by an unknown artist.

Ashmolean Museum, Oxford. **208**: View of the Calf of Man. Manx National Heritage. **214**: Executions after the Gunpowder Plot. Engraving. **216**: Sonnet 111 from *Shake-speares Sonnets*, 1609. **218**: Robert Devereux, 2nd Earl of Essex. Oil painting after Marcus Gheeraedts the Younger, *c.*1596. By courtesy of the National Portrait Gallery, London.
220: Frederick II and his son, with Kronborg Slot in the background. Detail of a tapestry, commissioned 1581. Nationalmuseet, Copenhagen. **225**: A detail of the Trojan War murals by Giulio Romano. Palazzo del Te, Mantua, *c.*1536–40. **225 below**: *Io and Jupiter* (detail). Oil painting by Antonio Correggio, early 16th century. Kunsthistorisches Museum, Vienna. **229**: Chart after Thomas Mendenhall, 'A Mechanical Solution to a Literary Problem', *The Popular Science Monthly*, December 1901.
233: Putative portrait of Christopher Marlowe. Oil painting by an unknown artist, 1585, before restoration, **left**, and after restoration, **right**. The Master and Fellows of Corpus Christi, Cambridge. **239**: Signature of Christopher Marlowe on a will, November 1585. Courtesy of Kent Record Office, Maidstone. **244**: Elizabeth I going in procession to Blackfriars in 1600. Oil painting attributed to Robert Peake, *c.*1601. Private Collection. **245**: Chart after A. J. Evans, *Shakespeare's Magic Circle*, London, 1956.
248: Detail of the 'Long View' of London from Bankside. Engraving by Wenceslaus Hollar, 1647. **261**: Detail of the Ashbourne portrait of Shakespeare. Oil painting by an unknown artist, 1612. The Folger Shakespeare Library, Washington, DC.

INDEX

Page numbers in italics refer to illustrations